GEMS REVEALING THE MESSIAH

Genesis to Revelation

DEDICATION

    I dedicate this book to my late husband who desired so much to see the publication of "Gems Revealing the Messiah." He was called home to be with the Lord before its completion. One day we will be together again.

    I also dedicate this book to my son and daughter, Barry and Paulette, and my two grandchildren, Jeffrey and Ashley. May this book be a testimony to them of the "Priceless Gem" in my life. He is to be treasured above all earthly treasures.

INDEX

CHAPTER 1 – The Promised Seed..................15

CHAPTER 2 – Apple or Pomegranate...........29

CHAPTER 3 – Five Books of Moses................43

CHAPTER 4 – The Exodus.............................55

CHAPTER 5 – Tabernacling with God 65

CHAPTER 6 – Cutting a Blood Covenant.......79

CHAPTER 7 – Golgotha................................. 85

CHAPTER 8 – Tabernacle Shabbaths... 101

CHAPTER 9 – God's Appointed Feasts.........115

CHAPTER 10 – God's Cycles & Numbers......145

CHAPTER 11 – Prophetic Messengers..........160

CHAPTER 12 – The Twelve Messengers........191

CHAPTER 13 – Catching Away.......... 233

CHAPTER 14 – Why Study Prophecy.............253

CHAPTER 15 – Feast of Tabernacles.............289

CHAPTER 16 – Season of Great Joy...............305

CHAPTER 17 – Seed of King David.................317

CONCLUSION 329

INTRODUCTION

This book was written to bring awareness to the importance of looking into the Word of God from a Hebraic perspective. As a Gentile believer, for years I didn't understand much about the Old Testament, especially the old ceremonies and God's Holy Days (including the seven annual "Feasts of the Lord". I thought they were "Jewish" festivals. In studying their *prophetic* and *symbolic* significance in revealing the Messiah, my desire to share those revelations **("Gems")** resulted in the writing of this book.

The author likens the Word of God to a huge rock mine full of "gems" just waiting to be discovered. Like mining for gems, one has to look deeper beyond the surface to discover the gems. The importance of linking the Old Testament and New Testament is emphasized by the author as well and cannot be underestimated. The New Testament is the fulfillment of the Old and one cannot be understood without the other. From Genesis to Revelation (one Book), many spiritual gems are found in God's unique language spoken through symbols, colors, numbers, metaphors and allegorical stories. Others are discovered in the messages, dreams and visions of the prophets who still have a word for us today, as you will see in this book.

Another purpose for my writing this book is to be part of a move of the Holy Spirit in bringing Jews and Gentiles together as one in the Body of Yeshua. It is so beautiful to see Gentiles, like myself, celebrating the Feasts of the Lord with our Jewish brothers and sisters, as in the early church. The **Holy Spirit** is doing this work, and I believe it is an end-time outpouring that will increase and usher in the return of Yeshua. Many churches today are being moved by the Spirit to embrace the Jewish roots of their faith and are celebrating the Feasts of the Lord.

The Central Figure whose Hebraic name is *Yeshua* (also known as *Jesus* in English) arises in *awesome* ways in the **Lord's Feasts**. The Feasts are for **all** of God's people. Since this book is written with the Jewish roots of our faith in mind, throughout this book, I use the Messiah's Hebraic name, Yeshua, which means "Salvation" or "God saves". When using biblical quotations from different sources, the names "Lord," "Jesus", and "Jesus Christ" stay the same, especially when quoting from the King James Version.

I believe you, the reader, will enjoy and be blessed by the Jewish flavor in this book, as well as my own flavor. It is my prayer that you might have a deeper desire to search for other "Gems Revealing the Messiah", and may THEIR MESSAGE be revealed to you! Shalom!

> Lucinda Harris, Author
> P. O. Box 653
> Hampstead, N.C. 28443

ACKNOWLEDGMENTS

First of all, I give all glory, honor and praise to my Heavenly Father, to Yeshua, my Lord and Savior, and to His Holy Spirit. I am so grateful for the Father's love and the great price my Redeemer paid for my Salvation.

To my Jewish brother in the Lord: Yosef, you have been such a blessing! Most of the contents of this book have been made possible by your generosity in providing me with a Laptop for months. Your words of encouragement, advice and review of the manuscript have meant so much. You have patiently answered many questions, as has Valerie. My love and thanks to you both.

To Mabel, my dear friend and sister in the Lord: Thank you so very much for the many hours you spent replacing spaces between thousands of words that were removed by a computer error. Also, I appreciate your opening up your house for many hours and months which we spent completing this manuscript. I thank Doug too who never complained about the hours his wife spent helping me. God bless. I love you both.

To Marie, another dear friend and sister in the Lord: You have been there to encourage and pray for me from the beginning. You have been with me every step of the way in completing this book. You are a true blessing, and I love you.

To my good friend, Betsy: You have been so faithful in caring for my little dog during the many hours and days that I was away from home working on this manuscript. It meant so much to me. You have also encouraged me along the way. I appreciate you and love you.

To my friend and sister in the Lord, Ms. Mary: Thank you for your encouragement all along the way. Thank you for the many prayers you sent up as I struggled at times to complete this work. God bless you for your prayers and moral support, Ms. Mary. Love you.

To another good friend, Linda: You have been a great encourager! Your enthusiasm and excitement in seeing this book completed has been such an inspiration to me. God bless you, my friend and sister in the Lord. Thank you for the use of your computer in the last hours of completing this manuscript. Had it not been for you, this book would probably still not be in the final phase of publication. You have been such a great blessing! I love you!

To Joyce, a sister in the Lord: I thank you for your meticulous reading of the early drafts of the manuscripts of this work. I know, some of the sentences are still too long. Bless you for your time and prayers, Joyce.

To Calvin: I am grateful for having sat under your teaching of the Torah and the Word of God from a Hebraic perspective. Don't freak out, Cal, if I don't have it all right. I'm a *Goyim* still in boot camp! May Adonai bless you, Donna and family. Love "Lucy".

To Philip and Christy: My special thanks to you both for your interest, suggestions, sketches and information in relation to my manuscript. Your love and prayers have been felt along the way. May Adonai bless you and your family abundantly.

To Sandy: I appreciate your taking time while you were out of town to review the Feasts of the Lord in my manuscript and your input. Thank you again, and bless you Sandy.

To Ramona: Thank you for the many hours you spent checking the theology and historical facts in several chapters, especially the chapters on the prophets. It is appreciated, and may God bless you.

To John and Kathleen: I would like to thank you for your helpful information and work in setting up this book in the beginning, including the font, the first draft of a cover and editing. The book and cover have been changed quite a bit since then, but your help in the beginning was crucial. Thank you so much, and God bless you both for your kindness and generosity.

To Ms. Billie and Stephanie at Carolina Printing Solutions, Burgaw, NC: God bless you both for your hard work and time creating the final cover for this book. It is beautiful and a job well done! May the Lord greatly bless you and your business.

To Pastor Curtis at Broken Bread Fellowship, Burgaw, NC: I am so grateful for your financial support in accomplishing the publication of this book. Thank you for being such a blessing! God bless you, Laurie and your church.

To my sisters and brothers in the Lord at Beth Simcha Messianic Congregation, Wilmington, NC: Many thanks to all of you for your moral support and prayers for me and the book's completion. My love to Rabbi Marty and Karen. God bless you. To Nancy, Joan, Scarlette, Ellen and others who prayed for me, bless you!

I would like to thank other friends for their moral support and prayers as well: Ms. Lottie and Joe, Larry and Sherry, Debbie and Willis and Ironia. Special thanks to Debbie who was instrumental in helping me with last minute computer tasks, including my e-mail account.

Thanks to all of you again for your prayers and support!

ENDORSEMENT

The following is an endorsement by a Jewish brother in the Lord:

Shalom, Margaret:

Your theology as it pertains to the quotations of scripture is "right on". You have done well.

Most Christians reading this work will gain a new insight on what our Creator wanted the people to learn and carry out. If they miss the mark of the Torah, they will not receive the abundant life that Messiah said He brought to Yisrael.

The order of your chapters leads the reader to understanding of events that brought "true salvation" as Adonai had intended thru the Torah and Yeshua.

Your coverage in Chapter 12 of the Church's definition of the "so called rapture" will definitely challenge their thinking as it pertains to Revelation 14. If they have an open mind, they will see the real truth of Messiah's return and what will happen to the saints.

Chapter 11 is excellent. I dare say that most Christians know very little of the prophets. Your detail coverage of each prophet will give great insight to the work Adonai had called them to do. This chapter captures all the essence of the prophets and all in one place. Now the reader won't have to spend a lifetime searching for Messiah through the prophets, they will have it all in this chapter.

The coverage of Chapter 3 (The Five Books of Moses) was great. I could not explain it any better. You opened the mind of the reader to search for themselves the truth. They will be blessed by this chapter in opening up their eyes to truth our G*d gave to the children of Yisrael, not the miss-truth of the Roman Church.

A work well worth the author!!! Congratulations on your research; the simplicity of your explanations and the excellent joining of theology and the scripture to bring out the "real truth".

As Rabbi Sha'ul said, "well done faithful servant"!

In Messiah Yeshua, your servant,

Yosef

CHAPTER 1

THE PROMISED SEED

As we begin our journey in search of **"spiritual gems"**, you, the reader, will see the word **"gem"** along the way throughout this Book. Whenever a spiritual revelation is revealed beyond the natural content of a subject, you will have discovered a **"gem"**!

Let's begin our journey in the book of Genesis to find our first "gem". "Genesis" in Hebrew (*B'resheet*) means "beginnings" where we find the creation of heaven and earth and man in the Garden of Eden. The beautiful Garden of Eden was planted by God. It was for the delight and pleasure of Adam and Eve. Did you know that the word "Eden" means "delight" or "pleasure"?

One of the garden's themes was to "be fruitful and multiply." God (Adonai) planted the garden with many trees and plants; trees with seed-bearing fruits and seed-bearing plants "good for food." It was a beautiful garden with all sorts of fragrant flowers, trees and herbs.

The *tree of life* in the midst of the Garden had special fruit. It was a literal tree and kept Adam and Eve in perfect health and everlasting life. However, one tree was forbidden!

> Genesis 2:9: *"And out of the ground made the Lord God to grow every tree that is pleasant to the sight, and good for food; the tree of life also in the midst of the garden and the tree of knowledge of good and evil."*

> Genesis 2:16-17: *"And the Lord God commanded the man saying, of every tree of the garden thou mayest*

freely eat; but of the tree of the knowledge of good and evil, thou shalt not eat of it; for in the day that thou eatest there of thou shalt surely die . . . ."

We know that the forbidden tree was a "*delight to the eye,*" but its fruit was not to be eaten. According to the lie of the ol' serpent (Satan) lurking in the garden, the tree was a source of great wisdom. He deceived Eve by telling her she would have the ability to become like God! Satan (*HaSatan,* Hebrew) also assured Eve that she would not die from eating the forbidden fruit.

This was a test of obedience for Adam and Eve. They had a *choice* to choose between life and death. We know by Eve spending time to talk with Satan, that she, along with Adam, failed the test. Of course, we have the same choice today and should find it very important **not** to give time nor place for the ol' crafty, evil one to "talk" to us! It usually starts with a thought that the evil one puts in the mind. We must reject it immediately and refuse to think on it.

What was that ol' serpent doing in the garden in the first place? He was roaming about seeking whom he might devour, of course!

We know that Adam and Eve didn't physically die **at the time** for their disobedience, but it did bring a spiritual death and a physical death at the end of their earthly lives. Sin brings separation from God, and the "wages of sin is death". Their previous way of life and communion with God was destroyed. Adam and Eve had never tasted of **sin** until they disobeyed God.

Adam and Eve lost their privileges to eat of the tree of life and to stay in the beautiful paradise God had prepared for them. Their expulsion from the garden was caused by believing the lie of "ol' sleuth foot" and choosing to *disobey God*. Lies and deception are such destructive tools of Satan. He **is** the "father of lies," you know! Of course, yielding to temptation was also a great part of the fall.

> *"And the Lord God said, Behold, the man is become as one of us, to know good and evil; and now lest he put forth his hand, and take also of the tree of life and eat, and live forever . . . .Therefore, the Lord God sent him forth from the Garden of Eden, to till the ground from whence he was taken. So, He drove out the man; and He placed at the east of the Garden of Eden Cherubims, and a flaming sword which turned every way to keep the way of the Tree of Life."* (Gen. 3:22,23)

Satan's plan is always to deceive and destroy our lives and separate us from God. The good news is that God had a back-up plan! Choosing to obey God's Commandments is the way to overcome the evil one!

> *"Blessed are they that do His commandments that they may have right to the tree of life . . . ."* (Rev. 22:14)

Sometimes trees and their fruit are *figurative* in the Word of God. The *Tree of Life* is also *figurative* of Yeshua in the Word of God. He possesses the *fruits* of the Holy Spirit (Ruach HaKodesh, Hebrew) that *yield everlasting life*.

> *"In the beginning was the Word, and the Word was with God, and the Word was God...In him was* **life** *[everlasting] and the life was the light of men."* (John 1:1,4) Emphasis added.

Spiritually, the *righteous* partake of the *Tree of Life*, possess the *fruit* of the Holy Spirit, and have *eternal life!* Did you know that the spiritual fruits of the righteous are also called "*trees of life*"? **"Gem"**!

"The fruit of the righteous is a tree of life…" (Prov. 11:30)

In the Garden of Eden, when God asked Adam and Eve if they had eaten of the fruit, the old blame game began. Adam blamed Eve, and Eve blamed the serpent. Haven't we all at times been guilty of blaming others for our own bad choices?

The "devil made me do it" doesn't work with God. The devil, however, did receive the first and worst curse for deceiving Eve and is yet to receive his final due!

After their disobedience, Adam and Eve stood before God crushed and without hope of redemption. They stood naked and ashamed and tried to cover their nakedness with fig leaves. God, being the *loving Father* that He is, showed them *grace and mercy*. He showed Adam and Eve that He still loved them and covered their nakedness with animal skins. Because of their sin, an innocent animal had to die and shed its blood that day.

However, its blood could not cleanse them from sin or redeem them from the curse of death. The shedding of its blood foreshadowed the shedding of blood by the innocent Lamb of God for mankind's sins. Only His blood can cleanse and redeem man from sin.

So, God revealed the plan of redemption to Adam and Eve as He covered their sin and nakedness. He gave them a revelation of the Sacrificial Lamb to come. What joy they must have felt to know they were not doomed to death; that there was a Way of Salvation and eternal life again through Yeshua!

God, in revealing His redemptive plan, said to the serpent:

> *"Because you have done this, you are cursed more than all livestock and wild animals. You will crawl on your belly and eat dust as long as you live. And I will put enmity between thee and the woman, and between thy seed and **her seed; it [He] shall bruise thy head**, and thou shalt bruise His heel."*(Gen. 3:14-15) Emphasis added.

Do you realize that this was the first and oldest prophecy proclaimed by God Himself of the coming of His Son (the "Seed") through a woman? What a fitting place, in the beginning, in the garden, to have found our first **"Gem" of** great price, **YESHUA,** the "**Promised Seed"**!

> The following scripture records the fulfillment: *"But when the fullness of the time was come, God sent forth His Son, made of a woman, made under law, to redeem them that were slaves to the law that we might receive the adoption of sons."*
>
> I like this definition of "seed" connecting it to life: *"A seed is a source or origin of matter that transmits life."* How true of this *Divine Seed, Yeshua!*

In Genesis 3:14-15, God speaks of enmity between the offspring of the serpent and the offspring of Eve. What did God mean by the *seed of* woman "bruising the serpent's head," and by the serpent "bruising the heel of her Seed"?

We might picture from this scripture someone stomping the head of a snake in attempting to kill it, and at the same time getting a bruise or a bite to the heel. However, looking deeper with spiritual eyes into God's message, we find much more than that.

"Bruising the serpent's head" foretold of a bruising blow to Satan's head (him and his kingdom). Yeshua accomplished that at Golgotha by His death and resurrection. Yeshua took the keys of death and hell from Satan and redeemed man from the curse that began in the Garden of Eden.

Satan tempted Yeshua in the wilderness to hinder His walk and cause Him to fall, as Satan did in the Garden with Adam and Eve. He still tempts us today, but we have the victory in Yeshua if we choose to obey God!

By the death and resurrection of Yeshua, Satan was defeated. The *"bruising to the heel of the Seed"* by the ol' serpent came back to *"BITE"* the ol' serpent himself! Because Yeshua defeated the enemy, we too who live and have our being in Him shall not be defeated by the enemy!

"Nay, in all these things we are more than conquerors through Him that loved us . . . (Romans 8:37).**Amen!**

Satan also attempted to stop the fulfillment of the Father's plan of redemption as Yeshua knelt in the Garden of Gethsemane to pray. Such a bitter cup He drank that night, like the "bite" of a serpent. At Calvary the pain and suffering continued, even to the "bruising" of the nails in Yeshua's hands, feet and torn side.

The dead body of the *"bruised Seed"* was buried in the garden tomb near Golgotha. Then, because the grave couldn't hold Him, He arose to claim His victory over Satan! It was Satan's biggest nightmare!

> *"Now in the place where He was crucified there was a garden; and in the garden a new sepulcher, wherein was never man layed."* (John 19:41)

> *"And they entered in, and found not the body of the Lord Jesus . . . .He is not here, but is risen!"* (Luke 24:3,6)

Satan's plan to destroy man's relationship with the Father began in a **garden** and the victory was won in a **garden!** **"Gem"!**

In the story of David and Goliath, David wielded the first blow to Goliath's head with a stone. However, the last and final blow came when David took Goliath's own sword and cut off Goliath's head. In ancient days, *final victory* meant cutting off the head of the enemy and taking it back to the victor's camp. We know that the best way to kill a snake is to cut his head off, right?

Note David's words before he slew the giant:

> *"You come to me with a sword and a spear, but I come to you in the name of the Lord of armies of heaven and of Israel—the very God whom you have defied. Today the Lord will conquer you, and I will kill you and cut off your head . . . ."* (I Samuel 17:45-46)

Yeshua dealt the first blow to Satan through His victory at Golgotha and His resurrection. Satan will receive the final "bruising" (blow) when Yeshua cuts him and his Kingdom off forever! **"Gem"**!

> *"The adversary who had deceived them was hurled into the lake of fire and sulfur, where the beast and the false prophet were; and they will be tormented day and night forever." (Rev. 20:10)*

Yeshua is also called **"The Seed"** in relation to His ancestors, Abraham and his son Isaac, and to Isaac's son Jacob.

"SEED OF ABRAHAM":

As God calls Abraham out from his country, He promises him that the whole world will be blessed of his Seed [Yeshua]. *"...and in thee shall all the families of the earth be blessed."(Gen. 12:3)*

Gal. 3:16: *"Now to Abraham and his Seed were the promises made. He saith not, 'and to seeds' as of many, but as of One, 'and to thy Seed,' which is Christ."*

Acts 3:25: *". . . saying unto Abraham, and in thy Seed shall all the kindred's of the earth be blessed."*

Not only would the physical descendants of Abraham be blessed by the prophesied Seed, but spiritual descendants as well. There would be spiritual descendants/children (seeds) who would also be blessed through *faith* in "The Seed," Yeshua. I remember singing a song in Sunday School as a young girl called "Father Abraham".

> *"Know ye therefore that they which are of faith, the same are the children of Abraham. So then they which be of faith are blessed with faithful Abraham. Now then, if you are Christ's, then you are Abraham's seed, and heirs according to the promise."(Gal. 3:7,9,29)*

I believe that God spoke *figuratively* of the innumerable *physical descendants of Abraham*—the Nation of Israel— like unto sand upon the seashore (from the earth.) The Jewish nation is of great number and scattered throughout the world in many nations. However, in speaking figuratively of the innumerable *spiritual descendants* (believers) of Abraham, we look up to the heavens (the heavenly realm). One starry night, God told Abraham to gaze up into the heavens, and God said:

> *"Look now toward heaven, and count the stars, if thou be able to count them; and He said unto Abraham: So shall thy seed be. And Abraham believed the Lord, and the Lord counted it to Abraham for righteousness."*(Gen. 15:5-6) Abraham saw God's plan of redemption and believed. What a man of faith!

When was the last time you gazed up into the starry sky and saw the shining stars figurative of the innumerable spiritual seeds of Abraham? I'm one, are you?

"SEED OF ISAAC":

Isaac was the firstborn physical seed promised to Abraham by God. It was through Isaac that the promise of the Messiah would be fulfilled. As spiritual seeds, believers become entitled to the same promises made to Abraham as heirs of the Kingdom of God through the Messiah:

> "Now we, brethren, like Isaac are the children of promise." (Gal. 4:28)

Isaac became the forefather of the twelve tribes of the Nation of Israel who came through his son, Jacob. One of Jacob's sons, Judah, became the head of the Tribe of Judah, from which Yeshua came. God said to Abraham:

> ". . . do as Sarah says, for Isaac is the son through whom my promise of the Seed will be fulfilled." (Genesis 21:12)

After Isaac's birth, God tested Abraham's faith in offering up Isaac, his firstborn son:

> "By faith, Abraham, when he was tried, offered up Isaac; and he that had received the promises offered up his only begotten son of whom it is said, 'That in Isaac shall thy Seed be called.'" (Hebrews 11:17-19)

What a test for Abraham, but he passed it! We know from the Word that God provided a substitute ram for the sacrifice in Isaac's place on Mount Moriah. Did you know that "*Moriah*" means "foreseen of Yah" (God)? God showed Abraham the *prophetic* significance of offering up his firstborn son, Isaac. God's Firstborn Son was sacrificed many years later on the same mountain. God's Firstborn Son also became the Substitute Ram offered up to God. "**Gem**"!

Abraham was a prototype of our heavenly Father who was willing to sacrifice his Son. Isaac was a prototype of Yeshua who willingly submitted to the Father's will. Do you realize that this was also a test for Isaac? He was a young man when

Abraham offered him up to God. He didn't have to submit and allow Abraham to tie him to the altar. Yeshua didn't have to stay nailed to the wooden tree either. He could have called ten thousand angels!

The wood that Isaac carried up the mountain foreshadowed the wooden beam that Yeshua would carry. Unlike Isaac, who did not die by his father's hand, Yeshua **did** die willingly in obedience to His Father's will.

We know that Abraham received the revelation of the Redeemer, for he rejoiced to see the day of Messiah's coming. Listen to Yeshua's own words to His disciples about that revelation to Abraham:

> *"Your father Abraham rejoiced to see my day; and he saw it, and was glad."*(John 8:56)

"SEED OF JACOB," Isaac's son:

Yeshua is called the "Mighty One of Jacob" and "Star out of Jacob," meaning *out of Israel*. Remember when Jacob wrestled with the angel and his name was changed to "Israel"? That foreshadowed the Nation of Israel coming forth from Jacob's son, Judah. It also foreshadowed the Jewish nation struggling with God, but enduring to the end to accept their Messiah and proclaim the blessings and promises of God. Jacob's name was changed from "Jacob" (deceiver) to "Israel" (A Prince)! **"Gem"!**

> *" . . . and thou shalt know that I the Lord am thy Savior and thy Redeemer, the Mighty One of Jacob."*(Isa. 61:16)

Listen as Jacob blesses and prophesies over his son, Judah who became head of the Tribe of Judah, in reference to Yeshua's coming:

> "The scepter shall not depart from Judah, nor a lawgiver from between His feet until Shiloh [Yeshua] comes; and unto Him shall the gathering of the people be."(Gen. 49:10)

Balaam, a prophet of the Old Testament, prophesied of the One to come who would be ruler over Israel and have dominion and destroy its enemies. Balaam saw the coming Messiah, but knew His coming would not be for many years from the time of his vision. He prophesied that the Messiah would come out of the seed of Jacob—of Israel—as a "Star" and a "Scepter." The "Star" denotes His brightness and glory as the "Bright and Morning Star". The "Scepter" denotes His power, authority and dominion as Lawgiver, King and Ruler of the Universe! **"Gem"!**

> "I see Him, but not now: I shall behold Him, but not nigh: there shall come a Star out of Jacob, and a Scepter shall rise out of Israel, and shall smite the corners of Moab, and destroy all the children of Sheth [enemies of Israel]. . . "(Num. 24:17)

This prophecy by Balaam was made about 1,500 years before Yeshua (Shiloh) came. David refers to Yeshua from the Tribe of Judah as his lawgiver in Psalms 60:6-7: *"God hath spoken in His holiness . . . Judah [Yeshua] is my Lawgiver."*

"SEED OF DAVID":

King David was a prototype of Yeshua (Descendant of King David) and *born in* **Bethlehem**. At **thirty years** *of age* he began to rule and reign as ***King of Israel*** from old Jerusalem called the City of David. His earthly rule over Israel was **temporary.**

Yeshua was a descendant of King David and also *born in* **Bethlehem**. At **about thirty years** *of age*, Yeshua also began His ministry and was called the ***"King of the Jews"***. Yeshua's rule is **everlasting! "Gem"**!

Yeshua was sent to the Jews, but many rejected Him as their Messiah and King. Yeshua will sit upon the Davidic throne on earth in Jerusalem and reign as King over all the earth in His *everlas*ting Kingdom!

> *"These are the ancestors of Yeshua, a descendant of King David and of Abraham. Abraham was the father of Isaac; Isaac was the father of Jacob; Jacob was the father of Judah and his brothers . . . ." (*Matthew, Chapter 1*)*
>
> *"Hath not the scripture said that Yeshua cometh of the Seed of David, and out of the town of Bethlehem where David was?"*(John 7:42*)*
>
> *"Remember that Yeshua of the Seed of David was raised from the dead according to the gospel."*(2 Tim. 2:8)

Yeshua Himself declares that He is the Descendant, the "Root and Offspring" of King David and "The Star" (Bright and Morning Star) in the following scripture:

> *"I Yeshua have sent my angel to testify unto you these things in the congregations, I am the Root and Offspring of David, and the Bright and Morning Star."* (Rev. 22:16)

The "Promised Seed" (Gen. 3:15) has come to fulfill the promises of God for our salvation and glorious spiritual inheritance. In the *heavenly paradise* awaiting the redeemed of the Lord there will be **no** *forbidden tree or fruit*. There will be nothing evil in that paradise to bring a curse, especially that ol' serpent, the *"evil seed"*. Yeshua has prevailed in "bruising the head" of the evil one. The final blow will soon come to Satan and his Kingdom! **Hallelujah!**

> *"And there shall in no wise entereth into it anything that defileth, neither whatsoever worketh abomination or maketh a lie, but that which are written in the Lamb's book of life."* (Rev. 21:27)

CHAPTER 2

APPLE OR POMEGRANATE

Before we leave the Garden of Eden where the Promised Seed was first proclaimed, let's look again at the *forbidden fruit tree*. God gave Adam and Eve many fruit-bearing trees and herbs for food in the garden, but remember, there was one tree that God commanded them **not** to eat of, the *"tree of knowledge of good and evil."*

> *"And the Lord God commanded the man saying, of every tree of the garden thou mayest freely eat; but of the tree of the knowledge of good and evil, thou shalt not eat of it; for in the day that thou eatest there of thou shalt surely die..."* (Gen. 2:16-17)

Both the apple and the pomegranate have many seeds and are very productive fruit trees. Surely, these two trees were two of the many *fruit-bearing trees* in the Garden.

Remember, *trees and fruit* in the Word of God are sometimes *figurative* and reveal a deeper significance or picture. One must sometimes look beyond the natural to see a spiritual revelation.

The following are a few examples: The Tree of Life (Yeshua); the Olive Tree with its natural and grafted-in branches (Jew and Gentile believers), the Root (Yeshua), and the Oil of its fruit (the Holy Spirit); the Fig Tree (Nation of Israel); and the Grapevine (Yeshua) and its branches (believers) of whom Yeshua expects much good spiritual fruit!

For centuries, people have believed that the apple was the fruit of the *forbidden tree*. The Word doesn't tell us what kind of tree or fruit it was, but let's **consider** the Pomegranate Tree and its fruit for our next "gem".

In this Chapter, I will give some reasons why I believe one should consider the "pomegranate" as well as the "apple". Keep reading!

Do you know where the concept came from that the forbidden fruit in the garden was an apple? No one knows for sure, only that it has always been assumed by many to have been the apple. However, did you know that the Latin name of the pomegranate contains the word "apple"?

In Latin, the word *"pomegranate"* means "apple with grains" ("grains" meaning multiple seeds) which describes its fertility and productivity. Did you know that pomegranate bushes and trees grow wild in Northern Iraq and Turkey around the old Mesopotamian area which is the possible site of the Garden of Eden?

Another definition of "pomegranate" is "apple-like fruit." In Britain, it is called a "Chinese apple." Even in the U.S., some people call it the "Chinese apple." Could the above be a reason for the assumption that the fruit was an "apple"?

I was surprised one day when I was visiting the library to gather information on the pomegranate and asked the librarian to help me. She said, "Oh, you mean the "Chinese apple"? Many scholars after much research, now also suggest that it **may** have been a pomegranate that Adam and Eve ate of rather than an apple!

The Word states that the forbidden fruit in the garden was "pleasing to the eye." Both the apple and the pomegranate are pleasing to the eye, but which is *more* pleasing? I would say the larger fruit with its deep red jacket, the pomegranate. I know of no other fruit more beautiful than the pomegranate. Its beauty would certainly have caught one's attention and aroused curiosity when told not to take a bite out of it! The temptation to partake of the beautiful, mysterious fruit would have certainly been there!

So, do you think Adam and Eve might have eaten of the "apple-like fruit" ("apple with grains", Latin) or the "Chinese Apple", both names for the pomegranate, rather than the apple? As stated before the scripture doesn't really tell us, but this is surely something to consider.

It is said by Jewish Rabbis that there are 613 laws in the Torah (first five books of the Bible) and 613 seeds in an average full-grown pomegranate. **If** the fruit of the tree of the knowledge of good and evil was a pomegranate, is it possible that the pomegranate tree was associated with the 613 laws of the Torah? Where do we find blessings (good) for obedience to God's Law and curses (evil) for disobedience? In the **Torah**! **"Gem"**!

Why did Satan say that Adam and Eve would become like God? He knew that by partaking of the forbidden tree, Adam and Eve's eyes would be opened to **"sin"** which they had never known, and face its consequences by disobeying God. He knew it would cause them to transgress God's Word. Being the trickster that he is, he also knew if they ate from the forbidden tree, they would fall from their perfect, glorified state and eternal life.

In the future, Adam and Eve would have to **choose** between good and evil, life and death. No longer would they have access to the tree of life that gave them eternal life before the fall and before the knowledge of sin or its consequences by their disobedience.

Did that tree also contain Atonement for Adam and Eve's sin of disobedience? Yes! Yeshua, the *Living Torah*, shed His blood to cleanse us from sin when we break God's Law. Only by Yeshua's atoning blood can we escape the penalty of death that comes with sin. Because it wasn't Yeshua's *appointed time* to come and shed *His own blood* when Adam and Eve sinned, an innocent animal had to die.

When considering the pomegranate as the forbidden fruit, think about this: **If** the fruit was the pomegranate, have you ever thought about its red juice staining Adam and Eve's hands like blood as they ate of it? A **crimson stain** from their sin would have been visible! **"Gem"!**

There does still exist, however, the possibility that the **"apple"** was the fruit of the forbidden tree. So, even though the Word doesn't tell us, shouldn't we at least consider the pomegranate?

Since the pomegranate is found so often in the Word of God, it is worth searching out some other "gems" in relation to it.

There is an interesting *historical fact* about the pomegranate. It was a very popular fruit and a symbol of *fertility* and *fruitfulness* in Israel from 600 to 400 B.C. The pomegranate was a popular motif and adorned many things. There was even a shekel coin circulated in Jerusalem with three pomegranates on it during that period.

In the Song of Solomon, pomegranates are mentioned several times in a garden belonging to King Solomon and his bride. Many see the Song of Solomon as an *allegorical love story* of Yeshua and His Bride. From a *spiritual* viewpoint, the budding grapevine and pomegranates represent spiritual *fruitfulness.*

Yeshua is seen as the King-Bridegroom in the story. The young Bride of Yeshua desires communion with Him, the Lover of her soul. She is devoted to Him and desires to please Him. She invites Him into the garden (representative of her soul) to see if it flourishes and bears good fruit (*spiritual fruit*).

> [Bride:] *"I am my beloved's and I am the one He desires. Come, my Beloved, let us go out into the fields and stay in the villages. Let us get up early and go out to the vineyards and see whether the vines (grapevines) have budded and whether the blossoms have opened and whether the pomegranates are in flower [maturity]."* (Song. 7:10-12)

The Bridegroom comes with *expectancy* of fruit from the budding grapevine and the flowering pomegranates.

> [Bridegroom:] *"I went down into the garden of nuts to see the fruits of the valley, and to see whether the vine flourished, and the pomegranates budded."* (Song. 6:11)

The Song of Solomon reveals an intimate relationship between the King and His bride as they walk and talk in the garden. Yeshua desires that same fellowship and quiet time alone with us as His bride in baring our soul to Him. I am reminded of the words in an old song that my grandmother used to sing, "In the Garden":

> "... I come to the garden alone while the dew is still on the roses ...
> and the voice I hear is so sweet that the birds stop their singing ...
> and He walks with me and He talks with me, and He tells me I am His own.
> And the joys we share as we tarry there, none other has even known."

Spiritually, are we experiencing that *garden* paradise as our soul tarries with Him? Are we allowing the Bridegroom to examine and prune our souls of anything displeasing to Him? Do our lives send forth a sweet fragrance?

Spiritual fruitfulness comes from our relationship with Yeshua, the Lover of our soul. The more we love Him and the more time we spend with Him, the more beautiful and fruitful we become. Amen?

I got off on a little rabbit trail there! I have a habit of doing that sometimes.

Pomegranates also served *as ornaments of beauty* adorning the Temple of King Solomon. They were decorative work made of the finest brass atop two columns of the Temple. The pomegranates glistened in the sun atop the columns, reflecting the sun's (Son's) light.

Two hundred pomegranates of the finest brass crowned the top of two huge columns of Solomon's Temple. Solomon had sent for a man named Hiram to construct them. He was a brass-worker filled with wisdom, understanding and skill for all kinds of brass craftsmanship. He made each column thirty-one and a half feet high and twenty-one feet in circumference at the entrance of the Temple. Wow! Can you imagine what a beautiful and outstanding part of the Temple the two hundred glistening pomegranates were on top of the columns?

> *"As for the capitals on the two columns, there were 200 pomegranates in rows around each capital near the molding by the netting. He erected the columns in the hall of the temple; on erecting the right column, he gave it the name of 'Yakhin' and in erecting the left column, he named it 'Boaz.'"* (I Kgs. 7:20-21)

> *"He erected the columns in front of the temple, one on the right and one on the left. He called the one on the right 'Yakhin' and the one on the left 'Boaz.'"* (2 Chron. 3:17)

One of the columns was named "*Yahkin*," meaning "He shall establish," and the other column named "*Bo'az*," meaning "in Him is strength." Both names are related to the "building of God's temple or house." I wonder if they could be figurative of Yeshua and His Bride? Only in Him and His strength can the bride be part of establishing the temple of God. To me, it just seems to fit the picture. There goes my inquisitive mind!

Now, let's look at the high priest's garment in Exodus with the golden bells and **pomegranates**. The pomegranates were embroidered around the hem of the garment, each with its own golden bell. They moved in sequence together and the bells made a tinkling sound. If the embroidered pomegranates had not been in between the bells, the bells would have made a clanging sound. Could these pomegranates and golden bells be a pro*phetic* picture of the New Covenant (Testament) church seen in one of the seven Feasts of the Lord and fulfilled when Yeshua sent the Holy Spirit? Keep reading!

> *"And at the bottom edge of the robe shall be embroidered pomegranates of blue, and of purple, and of scarlet, round about the hem thereof; and bells of gold between them round about; a golden bell and a pomegranate, a golden bell and a pomegranate, upon the hem of the robe round about. Aaron shall wear the robe whenever he goes in to minister to the Lord; the bells will tinkle as he goes in and out of the presence of the Lord in the Holy Place, so that he will not die.* (Exo. 28:33-34)

Notice the colors in the pomegranates. **Colors** in the Word are part of God's unique language. Symbols are also a part of God's language, especially in the Book of Revelation.

Blue represents the "heavenly" or "of heavenly origin"; **purple** represents "Kingly" or "royal"; and **scarlet** represents "blood," usually the blood of Yeshua in scripture. **Gold** represents "divinity". All of these colors were found on the *High Priest* garment. Who might these colors reveal *figuratively* in the embroidered pomegranate? Yeshua! As you will see later, the golden bells are *figurative* too!

When the high priest went before God to minister in the Holy Place, the people could hear the tinkling sound of the bells on the hem of his garment as he moved about. When the people heard the bells they knew that God had accepted their high priest and his offerings. They knew that the high priest was alive and "all was well". The golden bells made of pure gold tried by fire are figurative of "consecration" and "holiness".

At Yeshua's ascension, He told His followers to tarry in Jerusalem. He would send proof that the Offering of Himself and His blood to God as High Priest had been accepted. The Comforter (Holy Spirit) would come and endow them with power from on High!

In the upper room the Holy Spirit arrived just as Yeshua said. The Spirit came like the sound of a roaring, mighty rushing wind with "tongues like as of fire"! The tongues of fire (an individual "rhema" word by the fire of the Holy Spirit) sat upon each of the Jewish congregation's heads as they were filled with the Holy Spirit (*Ruach HaKodesh,* Hebrew)! As He gave them utterance, they began to speak in many different languages of the world and bore much fruit!

By the way, have you ever noticed the flower-like blood of a pomegranate before it bears fruit? It is shaped like a bell with a many-tongues center!

Can you hear the golden bells of the New Covenant church (including Gentiles who were later converted) with the fiery tongues of the Holy Spirit still ringing out the joyful gospel message that Yeshua is still "alive and well forevermore"? **"Gem"!**

The feast day this happened on was the **Feast of Pentecost** (*Shavuot,* Hebrew) that began in the upper room in Acts 2!

> *"Suddenly there was a sound like the roaring of a mighty wind, and it filled the house where they were*

sitting. And there appeared what looked like flames or tongues of fire and settled upon their heads, and they were all filled with the Holy Spirit and began speaking in other tongues, as the Spirit gave them utterance."(Acts 2:3-4)

Remember, each one of the golden bells moved in sequence with the Pomegranate. Apart from the Pomegranate, the bells would have clanged together and been as sounding brass. Apart from Him, we can do nothing! **"Gem"!**

God's law was engraved by His fire on tablets of *stone* at Mt. Sinai, but now they are engraved by the fire of the Holy Spirit on many (Jew and Gentile) *hearts* of flesh! What a **"Gem"**!

I believe pomegranates and golden bells on the hem of the high priest's garment were not only *prophetic* of Pentecost, but of a *new priesthood.*

The *old Levitical Priesthood* was temporary and represented on the High Priest's *breastplate*. It contained twelve (12) beautiful gemstones with each one representing the Twelve Tribes of Israel under the old priesthood. On the same garment of the High Priest at the *hem*, we see the *new Melchizedek Priesthood* under Yeshua, the **eternal** Priesthood! **"Gem"!**

In discovering the last few "gems" in relation to the **pomegranate**, let's look at the outside and the inside of this fruit.

On the outside, it has a tough jacket *protecting the seeds* inside which wards off damaging worms and insects. It is a large fruit with a beautiful *red blood-colored* jacket. This fruit has a short neck on its *body* with a *crown-like top*. What do you think of when you see a *crown*? A **King**! Where there is a King, there is a Kingdom! **"Gem"!**

> *"God has rescued us from the domain of darkness and transferred us into the Kingdom of His dear Son in whom we have redemption through His blood, even the forgiveness of sins."* (Col. 1:13-14)

Looking at the *inside* with its multiple seeds, notice that the seeds are covered with a translucent skin and reddish juice. Each seed inside is individually clothed or covered with a reddish (blood-colored) translucent skin covering. Another single translucent covering surrounds the seeds holding all of them together as *ONE*. Does this remind you of the body of Yeshua? **"Gem"!**

Could there be a spiritual relationship seen with the spiritual eye between Yeshua and His Body in the "seeds" of the pomegranate? Could the many seeds in the pomegranate be *symbolic* of the *spiritual seeds of Abraham* who are covered by the blood? **"Gem"!**

> *"For as many of you as have been baptized into Yeshua have put on Yeshua. There is neither Jew nor Greek, there is neither bond nor free, there is neither male nor female; for ye are all one in Yeshua. And if ye be Yeshua's, then ye are Abraham's seed, and heirs according to the promise."* (Galatians 3:26-29)

Paul speaks of the children of God who possess the Holy Spirit as being **spiritual children (seeds)** who were promised to Abraham other than the physical children:

> *"In other words, it is not the natural children who are God's children, but it is the children of the promise who are regarded as Abraham's offspring [children]."*(Romans 9:8)

> *"Know ye therefore that they which are of faith, the same are the children [seeds] of Abraham."* (Gal. 3:7)

Now, what do you see when a knife pierces through the side of the pomegranate into its heart? *Red, blood-colored juice and water flow out from its side!* It leaves a *crimson stain* on everything it touches. Though your sins be as scarlet, they shall be washed as white as snow. What an awesome picture and **"Gem"** of Yeshua's blood sacrifice!

Just as the first bride was taken from Adam's side, Yeshua's Bride came forth at Golgotha as blood and water flowed (as in birth) from His side. *Spiritually,* the Bride of Yeshua continues to produce many children (spiritual seeds) for His everlasting Kingdom! **"Gem"!**

When I see the pomegranate, I am reminded of my *Redemption* purchased by Yeshua's blood. By its many seeds inside, I am reminded that I am one of the spiritual "seeds of Abraham" and an heir in the Kingdom of God. To me, there is no other fruit like the ***pomegranate*** that *symbolizes* or is *figurative* **of** my Redeemer, High Priest-King and His kingdom. That is the way **I** see the pomegranate!

The Pomegranate

Upon a large tree, tall and sturdy,
The pomegranate grows,

On the outside the skin is red,
The color of blood,
Within its covering are numerous seeds,
A productive fruit, bringing forth much fruit,
When pieced through the heart, Red juice and water flow;

Crowning two pillars of the temple,
Established and strong,
One named Jahkin, the other named Boaz,
Made of finest brass, reflecting the Son,
Many come to worship with hearts of praise
And joyful songs;

Ornaments adorned the High Priest's robe,
Pomegranates sown around the hem,
Each with its own golden bell,
The tongues ring out a joyful sound,
The High Priest lives and "all is well";

Oh, Pomegranate, so beautiful to the eye,
Within your natural beauty a revelation lies,
With spiritual eyes, a symbol you will see,
Yeshua's sacrifice for His bride at Calvary.

Whether the forbidden fruit was an apple or a pomegranate, most importantly, let us be fruitful and multiply all you spiritual "seeds of Abraham"!

Give thanks to the Father which hath made us fit to be partakers of the inheritance of the Kingdom. Paul, in writing to the Congregation in Colossae refers to "fruitfulness" and living worthy and pleasing to Yeshua, our Redeemer and King:

"We have not stopped praying for you, asking God to fill you with the knowledge of His will in all the wisdom and

understanding which the Spirit gives; so that you may live lives worthy of the Lord and entirely pleasing to Him, being fruitful in every good work and multiplying in the full knowledge of God." (Col. 1:9-10) **Shalom!**

CHAPTER 3

THE FIVE BOOKS OF MOSES

Did you know that the **"Torah"** is actually the first five books of the Bible? Did you know that the first five books—the Torah—are called "The Five Books of Moses" or the "Law of Moses" and that it was a Covenant between God and Israel called the "Book of the Covenant"?

As a Gentile, I **didn't know** for years. I don't recall hearing the word *"Torah"* or *"Pentateuch"* (Greek) except that it was the "old law" which we were no longer under. Teachings from Genesis, Exodus, Leviticus, Numbers and Deuteronomy were referred to by the title of each Book, but never referred to as books of the Torah. That is a sad thing since the Torah is a **"Gem"** in itself and holds a wealth of information to be treasured!

The Torah translated into English means "law," but the Hebrew word actually means "instructions" or "teachings." Moses was given the Torah, which contained God's teachings and instructions to His people on how to live a life pleasing to Him. The Torah should be seen as the revealing of God and His ways and the revealing of the coming Messiah. It should not be viewed so much as "do's" and "don'ts" under the "old law". It is so much more than that, as you will see in this Chapter.

The Torah might be considered a "code of conduct". The Torah was given to teach and instruct the Israelites concerning sin and the transgressions of sin. In the Word, Adam and Eve were the first to have the knowledge of sin. Without the knowledge of sin, and its consequences, the people *would not have known what God considered sin*. God reveals Himself in the Torah as the One True God. He is seen as a merciful, long-suffering God when dealing with the sins of the people. There would also not have been any rule of law for Israel to follow as a Nation without the Torah. It would have been like a Nation without a Constitution.

At Mt. Sinai, the people had stood at the foot of the mountain and were terrified at the loud, long blasting of the shofar, fire, lightenings and thunderings as God spoke the Ten Commandments. As the Ten Commandments were spoken from the mouth of God with fire, the people became terrified! They asked Moses to receive the rest of the Law atop the mountain. They feared they would die at God's presence. So, Moses ascended up to the top of the mountain for forty days and forty nights to receive the rest of the Law.

Moses recorded the rest of the Torah (not including the Ten Commandments) in his *own handwriting* as God dictated it to him atop the mountain. That is why the Torah is also called the **"Law of Moses."** The Torah was written in Moses' handwriting on a parchment scroll and contained civil, moral and ceremonial laws. **God engraved** the *Ten Commandments* onto the tablets of stone with His ***fiery words.***

The "Law of Moses" is also called the **"Book of the Covenant"**. A covenant (agreement) between God and the people of Israel was made at Mount Sinai. It was considered a marriage proposal between God and Israel. It was to be a *spiritual relationship* likened unto a relationship between husband and wife. Each was to love the other and be faithful to one another. The Israelites said, "I do" to God's proposal. Have you ever wondered where the vow "I do" between husband and wife originated? At salvation, believers are saying "I do" or "I will" to our Bridegroom, Yeshua! **"Gem"!**

> *"And Moses came and told the people all the words of the Lord, and all the judgments; and all the people answered with one voice, and said, All the words which the Lord hath said, will we do."* (Exodus 24:3)

> *"And Moses took the blood and sprinkled it on the people, and said, Behold the blood of the Covenant, which the Lord hath made with you concerning all of these words."* (Exodus 24:8)

The Covenant between God and Israel had barely been made when Israel broke her vows to God. She turned almost immediately from Him to build a molten calf made of silver and gold. She made sacrifices unto it and worshipped it.

> *"They have turned aside quickly out of the way which I commanded them; they have made them a molten calf, and have worshipped it, and have sacrificed there unto, and said, These be thy gods, O Israel, which have brought thee out of the land of Egypt."* (Exodus 32:8)

> *"And it came to pass as soon as he [Moses] came nigh unto the camp, that he saw the calf, and the dancing; and Moses' anger waxed hot, and he cast the tables out of his hands, and broke them beneath the mount."* (Exo. 32:19)

Moses was so angry that he broke the *first set* of the Ten Commandments. He ascended back up the mountain for 40 more days and nights to receive the second set. **God engraved** the second set of Commandments with His ***fiery finger*** onto the tablets of stone instead of with His *fiery words,* but both **with the Spirit of the Living God!** "**Gem**"!

At Pentecost in the New Testament, "God's law" was *engraved* onto the hearts of the Jewish congregation by tongues of fire *(fiery words)* of God's Holy Spirit! Apostle Paul in the New Testament spoke these words:

> *"...written not with ink, but with the Spirit of the Living God; not in tables of stone, but in fleshly tables of the heart."* *(2 Cor. 3:3)* "***Gem***"!

The **"Ten Commandments"** are *part* of the Torah and embraced as the *heart* of the Torah. As stated before, they were the only part of the Torah not written in Moses' handwriting.

The **Ten Commandments** are called the "moral laws" of the Torah and the **"Law of God"**, *not* "Moses' Law".

God's Law is *engraved* in every believer's heart and is established by *faith* in Yeshua. The giving of the Law of God at Mt. Sinai foreshadowed the giving of the Law at Pentecost under the New Covenant and prophesied by Jeremiah.

> *"I will put My laws [Ten Commandments] in their mind and write them on their hearts; and I will be their God, and they shall be my people."* (Jeremiah 31:33)

Before the indwelling of the Holy Spirit, the Israelites could not keep the written law and its external regulations. Neither could the written law confer righteousness or the perfect remedy for their sins. God knew that they couldn't keep His law, being flesh, so He sent His Son and the Holy Spirit in

due time. It had always been in His plan. Only by **faith** in Yeshua by way of His blood can one be declared righteous, cleansed from sin and obey God's law (in the Spirit).

The **written** Law (Torah) under the Old Covenant pointed to the *spiritual* Law of God through Yeshua (Incarnate Living Law). It did not eliminate the Torah and its instructions and lessons for daily living in pleasing God. The *fuller fulfillment* is seen in Yeshua, **Spirit**, *the Living Torah,* the *Living Word* that dwells in us through the Holy Spirit! **Praise Him!**

In the New Testament, the Apostle Paul refers to the "Law through faith".

> *"Do we then make void the Law through faith? Certainly not! On the contrary, we establish the law . . ."* (Rom. 3:31)

Yeshua treasures the Torah, and its words are one with Him. Yeshua Himself said that He did not come to change or abolish the Torah by any means. He demonstrated how to walk in the freedom and grace of the Torah by the *Holy Spirit*, **not** by the *letter of the law* (fleshly). He did not eliminate His Father's teachings and instructions in the Torah, but brought them to *life in the Spirit*, from flesh to Spirit and revealed them in His daily walk.

> *"Do not think that I came to abolish the Law* [Torah] *or the Prophets; I did not come to abolish, but to fulfill."*
>
> *"But if you believe not his* [Moses] *writings* [Torah]*, how shall ye believe my words?"* (John 5:47)

Apostle Paul spoke these words in the New Testament:

> *"For what the law could not do, in that it was weak through the flesh, God sending His Son in the likeness of sinful flesh, and for sin, condemned sin in the flesh. That the righteousness of the law might be fulfilled in us, who walk not after the flesh, but after the Spirit."* (Romans 8:2-4)

> *"For as many as are of the **works** of the law [Moses Law] are under the curse...No one is justified by the law...the law is not of faith...Yeshua has redeemed us from the curse of the Law."* (Gal. 3:10-13)

Remember, Jewish Rabbis say that there are 613 laws (603 plus the 10 Commandments) in the Torah. How could anyone abide by 613 laws? By obeying the *Ten Commandments* upon which all of the laws hang. How do we know that? Keep reading!

A Torah teacher in the New Testament asked Yeshua this question: "Which is the most important law of them all?" The question was in reference to the 613 laws.

First, Yeshua answered by quoting the *Sh'ma* ("hear") from the Torah. Secondly, Yeshua said to "love your neighbor as yourself."

> *"Yeshua answered, 'The most important is, Hear, O Israel, the Lord your God, the Lord is one, and you are to love God your God with all your heart, with all your soul, with all your understanding and with all your strength.' The second is this: 'You are to love your neighbor as yourself.'"*(Mark 12:28-31)

In quoting the Sh'ma, Yeshua was expanding on the first five of the Ten Commandments relating to loving God as the only God with all of our heart and honoring our father and mother. Secondly, Yeshua referred to the last five commandments relating to loving our neighbor as ourselves. **That's everyone!**

Yeshua actually articulated **"God's Law"**, the **Ten Commandments,** into *two* laws, the way to abide by **all** (613 laws) of the Torah, in the *love of God* through the Holy Spirit! **"Gem"!**

> *"If you love me, keep my commandments. If you keep my commandments, you will abide in my love, just as I have kept my Father's commandments and abide in His love."* (John 14:15;15:10)

> *"Love worketh no ill to his neighbor, therefore* **love** *is the fulfilling of the Law."* (Romans 13:10)

Remember when two of the disciples of Yeshua were walking to the village of Emmaus, about seven miles from Jerusalem? They were walking, talking and reasoning about the recent events in relation to Yeshua's crucifixion and resurrection. Yeshua drew near and went with them, but they didn't recognize Him. Yeshua asked them why they were sad. Then, the disciples proceeded to tell of the events of Yeshua's crucifixion, and said they had trusted Him to redeem them from the Romans. (Luke 24:13-32)

Yeshua reminded them of all that the prophets had prophesied about the Messiah, *beginning* with **Moses in the Torah**. Yeshua expounded on the scriptures from the Torah and the words of the prophets pertaining to Himself. It must have been like a teacher telling a wonderful story to his students. This Teacher, however, told His personal story by opening up and explaining the old scriptures to the two disciples. As they listened to His story, they began to see and understand the real purpose for the Messiah's coming, but had not yet recognized that He was that Messiah.

When they all reached Emmaus, the disciples constrained Him saying, "Abide with us". They wanted to spend more time with Him and hear more of His teaching. We have the Word of God that contains His teachings now, but a future time is coming when we will sit at His feet and hear the scriptures taught from the Teacher that causes one's *heart to burn within*!

> *"But they constrained Him saying, abide with us . . . And it came to pass, as He sat at meat with them, He took bread and blessed it, and brake it, and gave to them. And their eyes were opened, and they knew Him; and He vanished out of sight. And they said one to another, Did not our hearts burn within us by the way, and while He opened to us the scriptures?"* (Luke 24:29,30-32)

Yeshua stayed and shared the evening meal with them. Then, at the meal as Yeshua broke the bread and blessed it, the two disciples' eyes were opened. They knew Him, that He was the Messiah in the midst of the story!

As Yeshua broke the bread He revealed to them that it represented His body. What else could have convinced them at the breaking of the bread that He was their Messiah? As He broke the bread, they would have seen the **nail prints** in His hands! How is that for an awesome **"Gem"**?

Yeshua is the greatest Torah Teacher of all teachers. He and His followers in the New Testament taught the wise instructions and teachings of God in the Torah.

People of many nations and tribes will go up to Jerusalem to hear Yeshua read and teach the Torah during the Millennium. Our *hearts will burn within us* as we abide with Him and hear Him expand on the Torah. What sweet spiritual meat that will be!

The following is one of the greatest prophetic truths concerning the teaching of the Torah in that Age:

> *"And it shall come to pass in the last days, that the mountain of the Lord's house shall be established in top of the mountains, and shall be exalted above the hills; and all nations will flow unto it. And many people shall say, Come, let us go up to the house of the God of Jacob; and He [Yeshua]will teach us of His ways, and we walk in His paths; for out of Zion [God's Kingdom] shall go forth the law [Torah]; and the Word of the Lord from Jerusalem."*(Isaiah 2:2-3)

There were many **ceremonial laws** of "Moses' Law" in the Torah. One of the laws required blood for the remission of sin which carried a penalty of death without remission. Remission of sin could only be accomplished by applying the blood of sacrificial animals under the old "Law of Moses". However, it was only a *temporary remedy* since the law could not justify sin with the blood of animals.

The sacrificing of animals for the remission of sin was a *prophetic* picture pointing to fulfillment by Yeshua, the Sacrificial Lamb of God. Only Yeshua by His own blood could justify and cleanse from sin and remove the curse and penalty of death under the old law. Without the shedding of blood, there is no remission for sin.

> In the Book of Matthew, Yeshua said: *"For this is my blood of the New Testament, which is shed for many for the remission of sins."* (Mt. 26:28)

Some other important parts of the Torah include the following:

Lessons of blessings for *obedience* and consequences for *disobedience* are learned from valuable stories and events surrounding Biblical patriarchs and matriarchs in the Torah. There is a purpose and a lesson to be learned in each story. Can you imagine the Word of God without them? So much knowledge and insight into their lives is gained in the Torah.

The birth of the Nation of Israel and its history is told in the Torah, and what a history lesson it is! The **Torah** is the very *foundation* of the Word of God! Without it, none of the scripture would make any sense.

Instructions were given to Moses in the Torah for building an earthly **Tabernacle** after the people left Egypt, which is found in the Book of Exodus. It is called "Moses' Tabernacle". It was a place where God would come down and meet with His people during their wilderness journey. In its structure and furnishings, we see a *prophetic* picture/story revealing God's plan of redemption through Yeshua. It is filled with *spiritual gems* revealing Yeshua **and** the Redeemed of the Lord. The instructions for the earthly tabernacle was a copy of the *heavenly* tabernacle. One day the saints of God will abide in that heavenly tabernacle in the presence of God forever!

Instructions for the keeping of the Sabbaths, including the *"Feasts of the Lord"* were given to Moses in the book of Leviticus, Chapter 23. They are a *prophetic* picture revealing the first *and* second coming of the Messiah and our Atonement. The feasts celebrate Yeshua's coming as Redeemer, High Priest and King. The Feasts of the Lord are loaded with many "spiritual gems". In the New Testament, Paul invites *all* of the redeemed (Jew and Gentile) to celebrate the Feasts, *memorials* to Yeshua.

There are many **moral** and **sexual morality laws** (teachings) in the Torah that are still beneficial and could surely benefit America today. There are also **dietary laws** (instructions) that could be beneficial as well, especially with the problem of obesity, diabetes and heart attacks in our country.

The following is an example of words of *wisdom* and *instruction* from the heavenly Father in the Torah:

> *"... for the Lord your God proveth you, to know whether you love the Lord your God with all your heart and with all your soul. Ye shall walk after the Lord your God, and fear Him, and keep His commandments, and obey His voice, and ye shall serve Him, and cleave unto Him."(Deut. 13:4)*

Have you ever thought that the wisdom to be treasured, spoken of in Proverbs 4, could be the Torah (the Father's instruction/teaching)?

> *"Listen, my sons, to a Father's instruction; pay attention and gain understanding. I give you sound learning, so do not forsake my teaching."(Proverbs 4:1,2)*

The **Torah**, the first Five Books of the Bible, is a **"Gem"** to be embraced and cherished. God Himself came down upon Mount Sinai and *personally* gave the Torah to Moses and the people. It is a gift to us containing God's personal words of wisdom, instructions, teachings and much more for our benefit. The Torah *reveals God* and His plan of redemption for mankind. It *reveals* the role of *Yeshua* in the fulfillment of God's redemptive plan!

King David loved the Torah and he expressed it many times in Psalm 119. The following is one of those verses:

> *"How happy are those whose way of life is blameless, who live by the Torah of God! How happy are those who observe His instruction, who seek Him wholeheartedly!"*(Ps. 119:1-2) **Amen!**

CHAPTER 4

THE EXODUS

Most are familiar with the story of the Israelites' exodus out of Egypt on the night of the Passover feast. God had pronounced plagues upon Pharaoh and the Egyptians because of Pharaoh's refusal to let the Israelites give their sacrifices unto God in the wilderness.

On the night of the exodus, a lamb was killed by each household. Instructions were given to Moses by God that night to apply the blood of the lamb to the doorposts of the Israelites' houses. A branch of hyssop was dipped into the blood of a lamb, then mingled with water and sprinkled onto the doorposts of the houses. The blood on the doorpost would protect the people from the tenth plague of death to every firstborn son, man and animal.

Moses and the children of Israel had asked Pharaoh for permission to go into the wilderness so they could offer up their sacrifices and worship God. Moses requested a three-day (about 60 miles) journey. That was the only reason for Moses' request. It was not to leave out of Egypt permanently or to escape. The Torah instructed the people of Israel not to worship God with their offerings and sacrifices with the pagans or with idols as the Egyptians did in the City.

> "We will go three days journey into the wilderness, and sacrifice to the Lord our God, as He shall command us. And Pharaoh said, I will let you go, that ye may sacrifice to the Lord your God in the wilderness; only ye shall not go very far away: intreat (pray) for me."(Exo. 8:27-28)

The Israelites knew that animal sacrifices were the only acceptable offerings to God for cleansing and purification. The Israelites' sacrifices and offerings involved a blood covenant with God and were taken very seriously. The blood covenant required the blood of an innocent animal dying in the place of the guilty person(s).

> *"For the life of a creature is in the blood, and I have given it to you to make atonement for yourselves on the altar; it is the blood that makes atonement for one's life."*(Lev. 17:11)

We know that it was Yeshua's blood that made atonement for our sins: *"For this is my blood of the New Testament which is shed for many for the remission of sins."* (Mt. 26:28)

Now, since only Yeshua's blood can atone for our sins, the question has been raised as to the salvation of those who were sprinkled with the blood of animals before Yeshua came. Were they saved? Of course! If they believed by faith that their Messiah was forthcoming to shed His blood for their sins, and they repented with a sincere heart for their sins, they were saved.

Hebrews 11 is filled with those old patriarchs and matriarchs saved by *faith*. What is faith? It is the confident assurance that something we believe is going to happen, even though we cannot see it at the time. Noah, Abraham, Isaac, Jacob, Joseph, Moses and many saints of old were saved by faith even though they didn't see all that God had promised them, especially the coming of Yeshua. We too have to repent of our sins and receive Yeshua by faith, looking forward to His second coming and holding fast to all that He has promised. Amen?

After agreeing to let the Israelites go into the wilderness to worship their God with animal sacrifices, Pharaoh failed to honor his promise. Pharaoh refused several times to let Moses and the people go. God kept warning Pharaoh through Moses of plagues that would come as a consequence. Pharaoh, in defiance and contempt of God's warnings, failed to honor Moses' demands, so the plagues fell.

> *"The Lord commanded Moses, 'and tell them, Jehovah, the God of the Hebrews, demands that you let His people go to sacrifice to Him. If you refuse, the power of God will send a deadly plague' . . . ."* (Exo. 9:1-4)

> *". . . so I will crush Egypt with a final major disaster and then lead my people out. The Egyptians will find that I am indeed God when I show them my power and force them to let my people go."* (Exodus 7:4-5)

The ten plagues actually proved to the Egyptians that their gods of the earth and sky had no power. God showed who was Creator of all creation and that He was greater than any of their false gods!

Speaking of their gods, I have included their names, what they represented and God's demonstration of His power over them:

> (1) "Hapi," god of the Nile: God turned the Nile River to blood. All the fish died and stank, so the Egyptians would loathe drinking its bloody, stinking waters!(Exo. :19-21)

(2) "Heka," toad goddess of the land: The Egyptians saw frogs as symbols of inspiration, and they were so sacred to the people that death came to anyone who killed a frog, so the tale goes. They may have had a different view after being invaded by them! (Exo. 8:1-7)

(3) "Geb," god of earth and vegetation. Egyptian priests had rituals of shaving their heads to prevent lice. God's plague of lice stopped the rituals, making them of no effect against the millions of invading lice. How many times a day can you shave your head?(Exo. 8:16-17)

(4) "Khepfi," god of insects. The plague of flies had to have been disgusting. Can you see hoards of nasty flies landing on everything, especially your food?(Exo. 8:21-24)

(5) "Apis," god of livestock, a bull god, and "Hathor," the cow goddess. God sent the deadly plague that killed all of the Egyptians' cattle and sheep, yet not one of the Israelites' cattle died! (Exo. 9:3-6)

(6) "Thoth," god of medicine. The Egyptians sacrificed humans and scattered their ashes as medical blessings upon people. Moses threw the ashes from the furnace up toward heaven to God. The ashes fell back down to the ground as dust causing ugly boils upon the animals and the people of Egypt. How gross that must have been! (Exo. 9:8-10)

(7) "Nut," the sky goddess and "Isis," goddess of life, and "Seth," protector of crops. God sent a plague of hail (actually a hailstorm) from the sky because these gods originated in the sky during the time of

the flax and barley crops. It was the people's source of food, so God destroyed the crops with the hailstorm. Besides the hail with the plague, there was thunder and lightning with the fire of the lightning running along the ground. The fire from the lightning killed both man and beasts in the fields. Never was there a hailstorm like that one! The hail smote every herb of the field, and broke every tree of the field. This plague was like killing three gods with one stone.(Exo. 9:22-25)

(8) "Anubis," god of the fields. The latter crops of wheat and rye left from the hail were destroyed by the locusts that God sent in swarms to devour this crop of food. Not only did they devour the crop of food, they devoured every herb and all the fruit on the trees left from the hailstorm. There were so many locusts that they darkened the light of day and one could not even see the ground! (Exo. 10:12-15)

I wonder if they were the same type of locusts that John the Baptist ate with wild honey?

(9) "Ra" or "Amon-Re," sun god. God sent darkness over the land for three days. There was no light, just total darkness all around the Egyptians, but no darkness was found around the Israelites. The Israelites had light in their dwellings.(Exo. 10:21-23)

(10) "Pharaoh," the King of the gods (god-King). Not only was Pharaoh considered a god over all, but his son as well, who would succeed him. Pharaoh was considered an incarnation of "Ra," the sun god, and "Osiris," the giver of life. So, God

showed Pharaoh by the plague of death to every firstborn that He is the giver of life. God gives life, and He can take it away. We know that Pharaoh's son died the night the death angel passed over his palace. (Exo. 11:4-6)

Let's look further at the tenth plague in relation to the Israelites on the night of Passover. Moses was given specific instructions by God to protect the Israelites from the plague.

Moses called for the Elders of Israel and told them to select lambs for their families on the *tenth day* of the month of *Nisan*. Then, they were to slaughter the Passover lamb on the *fourteenth day* of the month. There was to be a lamb for each household. The blood of the sacrificed lamb was to be applied by sprinkling it upon the doorposts of each house with a branch of hyssop. The blood of the lamb would serve as a sign, marking the houses where the firstborn was to be spared. When the death angel saw the blood on the doorposts he would *pass over*, and death would not strike that house. On the night of the fourteenth of Nisan, the Egyptians' firstborn died, human and beasts alike, while the Israelites were spared.

The **Passover** (called *"Pesach"* in Hebrew) is one of the feasts that God commanded Moses and the Israelites to celebrate perpetually. It is the *first* of the seven annual "Feasts of the Lord", and is in the spring. Death had "passed over" because of the blood of the sacrificed lamb. Every believer should understand the significance of this Feast of the Lord. It foreshadowed the future fulfillment by the Sacrificial Lamb of God, our Passover Lamb, Yeshua!

Yeshua always observed Passover and all of the feasts of His Father in accordance with the Torah. The Jewish people have always kept the Passover celebration in memory of their exodus out of Egypt and slavery. However, the Passover supper or *Seder* (Hebrew) in the New Testament brought a new meaning to the old celebration of Passover for Yeshua's followers. Yeshua revealed Himself to them as the Passover Lamb. He introduced them to the two new *symbols* representing His Body and blood.

The Passover foreshadowed the coming Lamb of God who would bring many out of bondage and slavery to sin through His body and His blood as the Sacrificial Lamb. Passover celebrates "freedom"; freedom from the bondage of sin and its curse. All of the redeemed should celebrate the Passover feast with great joy as a *memorial* to their Passover Lamb each year.

The application of blood of the sacrificial lamb upon the doorposts of the Israelites' houses kept the death angel from their houses. Yeshua lives and has applied His blood to the doorpost of every believer's heart and eternal death has passed over. The redeemed have everlasting life. They shall live and not die because of the blood of the Lamb. **Gem!**

> *"Neither by the blood of goats and calves, but by His own blood He entered in once into the Holy of Holies, having obtained eternal redemption for us."*(Hebrews 9:12)

Do you realize that there was an eleventh event of final judgment (Number 11 represents "judgment") for Pharaoh? A major disaster befell Pharaoh and his army. It was his death and that of his whole army when they drowned in the Red Sea. Some call it the Reed Sea. God opened up a path through the Red Sea wide enough for over 2 million people to pass through during the night. Some scholars say it would have been about a mile wide.

Once the Israelites were safe on the other side, the Lord released the walls of water. The chariots' wheels of Pharaoh's army fell off by sticking in the mud, and all of Pharaoh's army drowned. Defying and tempting God brought about Pharaoh and his army's fate. (Exodus 14:24-28)

> As Moses and the people stood safely on the other side, they sang a song of triumph: *"Who is like unto thee, O Lord, among the gods; Who is like thee, glorious in holiness, fearful in praises, doing wonders..."* (Exo. 15:11)
>
> Yes, Who is like unto Thee, O Lord?! No one and certainly no other god! Amen!
>
> The women, along with Miriam, took timbrels in hand and danced before the Lord:
>
> *Then Miriam the prophetess, the sister of Aaron, took a timbrel in her hand, and all the women went out after her with timbrels and with dances. And Miriam answered them, Sing unto the Lord, for He hath triumphed gloriously, the horse and his rider hath He thrown into the sea."*(Exodus 15:20-21)

Also, as the Israelites stood safely on the other side of the Red Sea, they shouted, *"The Lord shall reign forever and ever."* (Exo. 15:18)

Do you realize that the parting of the Red Sea for the translation of the Israelites to the other side may have foreshadowed a future translation? At the appearing of Messiah the clouds will roll back and the saints will be translated from earth to the other side! **"Gem"!**

In the last days, once we are safely on the other side, the end time "vials of the wrath of God" will be poured out again upon the earth. The story of the first exodus out of Egypt is a **key** to understanding the last days and the book of Revelation. There is a great parallel between the two. The antichrist will be like a Pharaoh with a great army. They will defy God, and meet the same fate of total destruction.

The army of Pharaoh was swallowed up by *water.* The armies of the last-day antichrist will be swallowed up by *fire!* **"Gem"!**

By the way, the place of this miraculous demonstration of God's power in parting the Red Sea has been discovered. I saw pictures taken by scuba divers of parts of chariot wheels at the bottom of the sea. So many things are being discovered and uncovered in these last days to prove the truth and accuracy of God's Word!

Plagues will also fall upon the people of the earth in rapid succession and with increased severity during the last days (Rev. 16-18). I believe the faithful remnant will escape the plagues as the Israelites did in their exodus out of Egypt.

Also, the good news is that the end of this age brings total restoration of heaven and earth as the Millennial Age begins. What a glorious day of celebration when we stand safely on the other side and shout, ***"The Lord shall reign forever and forever!"*** **"Gem"!**

CHAPTER 5

TABERNACLING WITH GOD

After the Exodus, God gave Moses instructions for a tabernacle. The purpose of Moses' Tabernacle was to provide an earthly tabernacle (temporary dwelling place) in which God would meet and commune **("tabernacle")** with His people. The Tabernacle was made after the pattern of the *heavenly tabernacle*. It was transported from place to place as the Israelites journeyed. The people were reminded always that God was with them and would meet with them (tabernacle with them).

> God said to Moses: *"And let them make me a sanctuary that I may dwell among them, according to all that I show thee after the pattern of the heavenly, shall you make it."* (Exo. 25:8)

It has always been at the heart of God to commune with His people as He did in the Garden with Adam and Eve. He walked and talked with them until sin broke their communion. That's why the scriptures say that the Lamb of God was slain from the foundation of the earth. Salvation for mankind was just as sure as if it had already been accomplished.

God gave Moses very specific instructions for preparing a place (an earthly tabernacle) in which to **tabernacle** (dwell) amongst His people. Those instructions were not only for its construction, but for certain temple services and ordinances. The beautiful picture-story of redemption is revealed throughout the tabernacle. Studying the Tabernacle of Moses has been one of the greatest blessings in my walk with the Lord.

Yeshua is revealed in the whole structure and every article in the Tabernacle. Not only is Yeshua revealed throughout, but also *the redeemed* of the Lord. In fact, God's whole *plan of redemption*, from the Door and Foundation to the Ark of the Covenant in the Holy of Holies, including the offerings and sacrifices, is revealed in the Tabernacle which is loaded with "gems", but there is not enough space in this book to include them!

Moses' earthly tabernacle "made with hands" was only a prototype of the holy, heavenly tabernacle (temple). Yeshua after His resurrection entered into the heavenly tabernacle on our behalf with His blood. Everything in the man-made tabernacle had to be purified with the blood.

However, the heavenly tabernacle had to be purified with the perfect, ultimate sacrificial blood of Yeshua. He entered the Holy of Holies and sprinkled His blood on the Mercy Seat of the Ark of the Covenant once and for all as High Priest for all of God's people.

> *"It was therefore necessary that the patterns of things in the heavens should be purified with these* [blood of sacrificed animals]; *but the heavenly things themselves with better sacrifices than these. For Christ is not entered into the holy places made with hands, which are the figures* [copies] *of the true tabernacle; but into heaven itself, now to appear in the presence of God for us."* (Hebrews 9:23-24)

Several ceremonies were performed as part of the ordinances of the Tabernacle. They required "sprinkling of blood" with hyssop and blood mingled with blood. Specific instructions were given to Moses concerning these ceremonies. One of them was for the cleansing of leprosy. Numerous blood sacrifices of animals and birds are seen throughout the Old Testament for various cleansings. Two birds were required in this particular ceremony for the cleansing of leprosy (spiritually symbolic of sin) which pointed to Yeshua's sacrifice.

> *"Then shall the priest command to take for him that is to be cleansed two birds alive and clean, and cedar wood, and scarlet, and hyssop; and the priest shall command that one of the birds be killed in the earthen vessel over running water: As for the living bird, he shall take it, and the cedar wood and the scarlet, and the hyssop, and shall dip them and the living bird in the blood of the dead bird: And he shall sprinkle upon him that is to be cleansed from the leprosy seven times, and shall pronounce him clean, and shall let the living bird loose into the open field."*
> (Lev. 14:4-7)

In this ceremony, one bird was killed in an *earthen vessel*. Water was poured over the dead bird so that its *blood was mingled with the water*, becoming a blood and water preparation in which to dip the living bird before using it to sprinkle the leper or unclean person. This is a *prophetic* picture revealing Yeshua, the Earthen Vessel and His sacrifice! **"Gem"**!

Yeshua had to first die and shed His blood to cleanse the sinner. Blood mingled with water was seen flowing from Yeshua's side at His death. He became the *prophetic fulfillment* of the dead bird in this ceremony **and** the living bird dipped in

His own blood mingled with water. He arose from the dead and ever lives to sprinkle the lepers (unclean ones)! The leper was sprinkled seven times intimating a complete cleansing. Yeshua sprinkles the sinner with His blood and cleanses him by the washing of His Word. It is a complete cleansing, and the unclean one is pronounced clean! Another awesome **"Gem"**!

Next, let's look at the *cedar wood* upon which the *living bird* was bound. Cedar wood comes from an evergreen tree (long-living tree) that grows to great heights and its wood is very durable and not apt to putrefy. Many of the trees grew abundantly upon a hill in Lebanon, and were called the Cedars of Lebanon. Their wood was used to build houses, temples and palaces. Many cedars of Lebanon were furnished to King Solomon for the building of the temple, his palace and a house for his bride.

Cedar wood *figuratively* signifies strength, durability and stability, some *characteristics* of Yeshua, the Builder of a house (mansion) for His Bride after His resurrection.

> *"Let not your hearts be troubled; ye believe in God, believe also in me. In my Father's house are many mansions: If it were not so, I would have told you so. I go to prepare a place for you."* (John 14:1,2)

King Solomon even made a chariot of the cedar wood of the Trees of Lebanon in which to ride with his bride. The chariot had pillars of silver, the bottom was of gold, and the overhead covering was purple. King Solomon's chariot was made because of his *love* for his bride. The very midst of the chariot was paved with love. Swing down sweet chariot and let me ride! I just couldn't resist that one!

> "King Solomon made himself a chariot of the wood of Lebanon. He made the pillars thereof with silver, the bottom thereof of gold, the covering of it with purple, the midst thereof being paved with love . . . " (Sol. 3:9,10)

The bride's *description* of her beloved bridegroom (King Solomon) speaks of his countenance symbolically in relation to the cedar trees". . . *His countenance is as Lebanon, excellent as the cedars,"* meaning His port and mien as Lebanon, that stately hill of cedar trees, and its aspect beautiful and charming. (Sol.5:15)

> Ps. 104:16 and Ps. 92:12,13 refer symbolically to the palm tree and cedars of Lebanon in relation to the righteous: *"The trees of the Lord are full of sap; the cedars of Lebanon which He planted."*
>
> *"The righteous shall flourish like the palm tree; he shall grow like a cedar in Lebanon. Those that be planted in the house of the Lord shall flourish in the courts of our God."*

I keep getting off onto those rabbit trails!

Getting back to the ceremonial cleansing for leprosy, remember the living bird in this ceremony was bound to a piece of *cedar wood*. After looking at the above scriptures, could it have been the wood of one of the great cedars of Lebanon upon which Yeshua hung? What more appropriate wood for Yeshua's cross than the wood of a tall, stately and majestic cedar of Lebanon? The Word of God doesn't tell us, but to me, it just seems to fit the picture. However, legend states that the tree was a dogwood tree upon which He was crucified.

Now, let's look at the *scarlet thread stained with blood* that secured the living bird to the cedar wood. The thread was of wool from a lamb. *Spiritually*, the Scarlet Thread is *figurative* of Yeshua's blood-stained Body, the Lamb of God bound to the tree. **"Gem"**!

Our blood-stained Savior also stayed securely fixed upon the tree of His own free will, and not by the nails. They did not hold Him there. It was the **agape love** of God beyond human comprehension. Yeshua could have come down at any time, but we know that His love held Him there for a leprous (sinful) people. Our cleansing from sin and the securing of our soul from Sheol depended upon His staying until our salvation was secure and complete, as He cried **"It is finished"**. Awesome love!

In looking at the *hyssop branch* used for sprinkling the leper or unclean one, we will discover another "gem". The hyssop branch was the bushy green herb also tied to the cedar wood and dipped in the blood and water preparation of the dead bird. Hyssop was used in purification ceremonies intimating a cleansing and healing of the leper from the scars of his disease. The hyssop also took away the stench associated with a leper or the unclean one.

Hyssop can also be used medicinally for many purposes. When crushed and mixed with liquid to make a paste-like substance, it can be used to heal bruises, black eyes and superficial wounds. It can even be rubbed on the chest to clear up lung congestion. Isn't it ironic that the purposes for which it is used describe physical conditions related to Yeshua's body on the tree? Could there be a connection? Keep reading!

What do you suppose the Hebrew root word for "hyssop" is? Get ready for a shocker! It is **"esob"** meaning **"Holy Herb,"** metaphor for **Yeshua**! At salvation, by His blood He cleanses us from sin, heals us of our diseases, takes away the stench of sin and washes us clean by His Word, all the things intimated by the use of hyssop associated with the leper or unclean one in this prophetic ceremony. What a **"Gem"** of revelation in this ceremony revealing Yeshua's death and resurrection, our Salvation and cleansing!

The hyssop branch was literally seen at Golgotha, identifying it with Yeshua, the Fulfillment of this ceremony. It was dipped in sour wine mixed with water and offered up to Yeshua, who had become as the leprous one.

> *"And one ran and filled a sponge full of vinegar, and put it on a reed* [hyssop branch], *and gave Him to drink, saying, Let Him alone; let us see whether Elias will come to take him down."*
> (Mark 15:36)

The old ceremony could only cleanse **outwardly**, but it pointed to a **future inwardly cleansing** by Yeshua. Only by Yeshua's blood and the washing of Water by His Word can sinners (unclean ones like lepers) be cleansed *inwardly* to the very soul.

> *"Let us draw near with a true heart in full assurance of faith, having our hearts sprinkled from an evil conscience, and our bodies washed with pure water."*(Hebrews 10:22)

> "... *Yeshua also loved His Body of Believers and gave Himself for them; that He might sanctify and cleanse them with the washing of Water by the Word.* (Ephesians 5:26)

After a leper or unclean person had completed his ceremonial cleansing outside the camp (place of disgrace), he was discharged from his pollution and restored to his original state. He was then declared clean and could return to his house and family. Sinners receive cleansing and restoration at salvation and are discharged from the pollutions of the past! **"Gem"! Hallelujah!**

Yeshua, after the application of His own blood mingled with water, died for sinners (spiritual lepers). He died outside the gates of the City (north side of Jerusalem, place of disgrace). After He arose and ascended to the Father, He was discharged from the pollution and conditions laid upon Him as our Substitute. He has returned to His heavenly origin and sits at the right hand of His Father enjoying the privileges of His origin. Fantastic **"Gem"!**

> *"Looking unto Yeshua the author and finisher of our faith; who for the joy set before Him endured the cross, despising the shame, and is set down at the right hand of the throne of God."*(Hebrews 12:2)

King David, after his sin with Bathsheba and the murder of her husband, cried: "Purge me with hyssop." He was very familiar with the ceremonial cleansing of sin by the sprinkling of blood and water with hyssop. King David also knew that the ceremony foreshadowed the Messiah's blood, which could cleanse inwardly. His cry went deep from the very depth of his heart as he asked for a purging of his conscience from the guilt of his sin. David was crying out to the Sprinkler of the Blood, for forgiveness and cleansing inwardly of his conscience where conviction had seized him.

David was very grieved that his sin had broken his relationship and communion with the Father. Adam and Eve must surely have had the same feeling. David desired the restoration of that relationship as he cried:

> "Purge me with hyssop, and I shall be clean;
> wash me, and I shall be whiter than snow.
> Create in me a clean heart, O God; and renew a
> right spirit within me."(Psalm 51:7)Yes, Lord,
> purge us!

Cleansing of the Tabernacle

In another type of "sprinkling of blood" ceremony, all of the articles of Moses' tabernacle were sprinkled with blood and water. Moses was commanded by God to sprinkle blood with hyssop on all the articles and furnishings in the tabernacle for purification in the worship of God. It typified the things in the heavenly temple being purified by the blood of the Sacrificial Lamb when He ascended to heaven at His resurrection.

> "For when Moses had spoken every precept to all the
> people according to the law, he took the blood of calves
> and of goats, with water, and scarlet wool, and hyssop,
> and sprinkled both the book [scroll], and all the people.
> Morever he sprinkled with blood both the tabernacle,
> and all the vessels of the ministry. And almost all things
> are by the law purged with blood; and without shedding
> of blood is no remission." (Heb. 9:19,21-22)

> *"It was necessary then for the copies of the heavenly things to be purified with those sacrifices, but the heavenly things themselves with better sacrifice."* (Hebrews 9:23)

The most important "sprinkling of blood" was upon the Mercy Seat (Covering) of the Ark of the Covenant by the High Priest once a year on the Day of Atonement. He applied the blood for himself and his family and for the Nation of Israel.

Yeshua, our High Priest, has entered the Holy of Holies in the heavenly tabernacle with His own blood for the sins of *all* mankind *once* and *for all*. By His blood, every believer has received a Blood Covering because of God's love and mercy!

> *"But this man, after he had offered one sacrifice for sins forever, sat down on the right hand of God."*
> (Heb.10:12)

> *"For I will be merciful and gracious toward their sins, and I will remember their deeds of unrighteousness no more."* (Hebrews 8:12)

Thank you, Lord!

Spiritually, it is also relevant to our earthly temples (tabernacles) as well. Believers' hearts have been sprinkled and purified by His blood as the temple of the Holy Spirit (Ruach HaKodesh). This temple (our body) is a holy place of worship unto the Lord.

Yeshua came as the first true Living Tabernacle in the flesh at His birth. Yeshua is the WORD which became flesh and dwelt (tabernacled) among us. He still tabernacles among us through the Holy Spirit (*Ruach HaKodesh*). We are living tabernacles (dwelling places) for God through the Holy Spirit. How marvelous!

God also gave Moses specific instructions, including materials and certain colors for the garments of the high priest and the priests who ministered with him. Their attire was a prophetic picture of Yeshua, High Priest, and His priests. One day the redeemed of the Lord will serve their High Priest who intercedes for them in the *Heavenly* Tabernacle.

> *"We have such a priest who is set on the right hand of the throne of the majesty in the heavens; a minister of the sanctuary*, and of the *true tabernacle, which the Lord made, and not by human hands."* (Heb. 8:2)

God not only communed with His people in the Tabernacle on appointed holy days (Sabbaths), but He refreshed, strengthened and provided for His people in the difficult times of their journey. He was always there with them. God is always there for us as well through the Holy Spirit (*Ruach HaKodesh*, Hebrew). He desires our fellowship and will refresh, strengthen and provide for us through difficult times in our journey here on earth. One day soon our journey on earth will be ended, and we will abide in the Heavenly Tabernacle on earth in Jerusalem in His presence forever!

Moses Tabernacle

Interwoven in a tabernacle,
A coming Messiah is foretold,
From the structure to the articles within,
A divine revelation from heaven did unfold,
A plan of Redemption for mankind's sins,

In offerings and sacrifices, the Messiah is seen.

Curtains of fine white linen hung throughout,
A veil into the Holy of Holies now torn away,
Embroidered with Cherubim,
Furniture and items of gold,
Silver and bronze too were all about.

Fine details for the high priest's garment,
From headdress to the hem with golden bells,
And woven pomegranates by God designed,
Specific colors designated with a message within,
Heavenly hues of white, scarlet, purple and blue.

One must look with the spiritual eye to see,
From the entrance door to the throne room,
One from heaven looms therein,
White spoke of His righteousness and purity,
Scarlet stood for His blood shed at Golgotha,
Purple denoted royalty, the King of Kings,
Blue represented His heavenly origin,

Gold depicted His divine nature and deity,
Silver represented those redeemed by His blood,
Bronze altar, place of sacrifice for judgment of sin.

Son of God, Son of Man, fulfilled the Father's plan,
The Word, the True Living Tabernacle,
Not made with hands,
High Priest and soon-coming King revealed therein,
Emmanuel, dwelling in living earthly tabernacles,
Oh my soul, with my Redeemer living within,
Rejoice and sing!

"In the beginning was the Word, and the Word was with God and the Word was God . . . and

the Word became flesh and dwelt among us." (John 1:1-14)

"And in Him you too are being built together to become a dwelling in which God lives by His Spirit." (Ephesians 2:22) **Amen!**

CHAPTER 6

CUTTING A BLOOD COVENANT

For years as a Christian, I never saw the broader picture of what took place at Golgotha. I knew Yeshua died and shed His blood to cleanse one from sin, but never heard **"covenant"** emphasized or the significance of the New Blood Covenant.

Since the time of Adam, making and cutting covenants between tribes and friends was a way of life in almost every culture of the ancient world. Every believer needs to understand the love and significance of God's Blood Covenant that secured our redemption by the blood of His Son, Yeshua.

First of all, let's look at a definition of "blood covenant": A solemn, binding agreement or promise(s) made under the seal of blood between two or more parties for the performance of some action(s); to bind together as "one" in establishing a personal relationship or friendship of unwaivering loyalty to each other. David and Jonathan are a very good example.

We know that the old covenants cut between God and man were not perfect and were breakable by man, being human. Therefore, a new and unbreakable covenant was made between God and His sinless, perfect Son, an everlasting covenant with better promises to those enjoined to it.

> *"But now hath he obtained a more excellent ministry, by how much also he is the mediator of a better covenant which was established upon better promises; for if that first covenant had been faultless, then no place would have been sought for the second."* (Heb. 8:6,7)

The above scripture, "the first" is referring to the Abrahamic Covenant. Abraham was human and capable of breaking the blood covenant made between himself and God which foreshadowed the New Blood Covenant.

To understand more of the Old Covenant (Testament) **"cutting of a blood covenant"** and how it foreshadowed the New Blood Covenant, let's look at some of the **rites** in "cutting" or the "hewing" in Hebrew, of a blood covenant:

(1) ***"Terms"*** were made and agreed upon for the blood covenant between the parties.
God and Yeshua made and agreed upon the terms before the world was formed! **"Gem"!**

(2) ***"A representative"*** of good upstanding and character was chosen to represent each party.

God who swore by Himself represented the Kingdom of God, and Yeshua was chosen by God to represent the household (family) of His kingdom. **"Gem"!**

(3) ***"A site"*** was chosen for the cutting of the covenant where all could witness the killing of the sacrificial animal and the shedding of its blood. The shedding of blood was required in the old covenants for the remission of sin(s).

Golgotha was the chosen "site" for the Lamb of God! **"Gem"!**

(4) ***"A coat/robe and weapons were exchanged"*** as seen with David and Jonathan *symbolizing* exchange

of authority: "All that I have, and all of my authority I give to you."

Yeshua has given us His authority and power through the Holy Spirit who has empowered us to walk in the ways of God through the blood of Yeshua.

Also, what garments did we exchange for our salvation? FILTHY RAGS!

"I will greatly rejoice in the Lord, my soul shall be joyful in my God. For He hath clothed me with the garment of salvation, He has covered me with the robe of righteousness, as a Bridegroom decketh Himself with ornaments, and as a bride adorneth herself with her jewels." (Isa. 61:10)

"But we all as an unclean thing, and all our righteousness are as FILTHY RAGS…." (Isa. 64:6) **"Gem"!**

"Exchanging weapons" *symbolized* each one fighting the other's battles. We are not alone in our battles, God fights our battles too! **"Gem"!**

(5) **The "walk of blood"** took place after the animal was killed and cut into pieces and laid opposite each other. The parties then walked up and down through the blood agreeing to the terms of the covenant.

Yeshua's back was laid open, and His organs were exposed as He carried that wooden beam up the hill to Golgotha. His blood-soaked body caused a path up to Calvary as He performed the "walk of blood" in His own blood! **"Gem"**!

(6) ***"Way of the of Blood"*** took place when the blood from the animal flowed like an alley down onto the earth between the pieces of the animal that had been cut into pieces and laid opposite each other. It was called the "way of the blood".

At Golgotha, as Yeshua's blood-soaked body hung there, the stream of blood that flowed down that tree onto the earth must have looked like the alley of blood. Yeshua became the "Way of the blood" at Golgotha! **"Gem"**!

(7) A *"permanent scar"* was made between the parties of a blood covenant.

Yeshua still carries the **scars** of the crucifixion on His body, as the New Blood Covenant was cut between Father and Son that *"whosoever will"* might be **one** in covenant with the Father and Son! **"Amazing Gem"**!

(8) *"The Final Rite"* was the partaking of a **covenant meal** with **bread** and **wine**. This meal *symbolized* the parties' giving of themselves to the other even unto the point of death. They ate the meal in **"remembrance"** of the covenant rites, and what they had witnessed in the "cutting of the blood covenant". They were to **"remember"** (that being a **key word**) when cutting covenant; the sight, the ceremony, and the terms of the covenant cut and

sealed in blood. It was also a "fellowship" and "friendship" meal binding them together forever as **"one"**.

Let us **never forget** the price paid for our covenant of **love** with the Father and Son!

At the Last (final) Supper (meal), Yeshua said: "Take eat, this is my body which is broken for you; this do in **remembrance** of me." Then, He took the cup of wine and said: "This cup is the **New Covenant [cut]** in my blood; this do ye as oft as ye drink it in **remembrance** of me." Emphasis added. **"Amazing gem"!**

Can you understand and see more clearly now the whole picture of "Blood Covenant" and Yeshua's words, "This is the New Covenant in my blood"?

In John 17, we see the very heart of Yeshua as He faced death before cutting the New Blood Covenant as the Sacrificial Lamb of God. He prayed that the "love" and "oneness" (as in covenant) between Him and His Father be also in His disciples.

> *Neither pray I for these [disciples] only, but for them also which believe on me through their word, that they all be one...and that they also may be one in us, that the world may believe that thou has sent me. And the glory which thou givest me, I have given them, that they may be "one" even as we are "one." And I have declared unto them thy name and will declare it; that the love wherewith thou hast loved me may be in them, and I in them."* **Amen and praise the Lord!**

CHAPTER 7

GOLGOTHA

Many Jewish people watching Yeshua's crucifixion should have been reminded of the "sprinkling of blood with hyssop" in the old covenant ceremonies. As they witnessed Yeshua's crucifixion, they saw the literal hyssop branch being offered to Yeshua after being dipped in sour wine (figurative of blood) and water. They saw blood and water running from His side, yet many failed to see the **Fulfillment** of the old covenant rites and ceremonies that revealed their Messiah on that Passover day.

> *"Later, knowing that all was now completed, and so that the scripture would be fulfilled, Yeshua said, I am thirsty. A jar of wine vinegar was there, so they soaked a sponge in it, put the sponge on a stalk of the hyssop plant, and lifted it to Yeshua's lips. When He had received the drink, Yeshua said, 'It is finished.'"(John 19:29-30)*

The Jewish people also saw the crown of thorns placed upon His head identifying Him with the accursed and unclean. Jews had associated thorns with a curse ever since the ground was cursed with thorns and thistles in the Garden of Eden.

> *"...cursed is the ground for thy sake; in sorrow thou shalt eat of it all the days of thy life; thorns and thistles shall it bring forth to thee...(Gen. 3:17,18)*

In the *prophetic picture* of Yeshua's sacrifice seen in the substitute ram provided by God to Abraham in place of Isaac, there is another revelation in relation to Yeshua.

When Isaac asked his father where the sacrifice was and Abraham said that God would provide it, where was it found? It was caught in a nearby *thorny thicket* with its head surrounded by *thorns like a crown*! Awesome prophetic picture! **"Gem"**!

There is one other little "gem" in this story. When God said He would provide the Sacrifice, there is a deeper Hebrew meaning of God's words in providing the Sacrifice. God's words should actually be interpreted as "it is done" or "it has already been provided". **Before** Isaac asked, it was provided! Do you see the parallel to God's Son in this revelation? **"Gem"**!

Yeshua's blood was poured out for all peoples' sins on that Passover day as He became the Passover Lamb wearing the mocking, thorny crown as our Sacrifice and Substitute Ram!

> *"So Yeshua was once offered to bear the sins of many..."*
> (Heb. 9:28)

Caiaphas, the High Priest, along with many other unbelieving priests, was killing sacrificial lambs for the Passover Feast on that day in the Temple. Their Messiah, the Passover Lamb was being killed and hanging on the tree just outside the Temple walls.

> *"And every priest standeth daily ministering and offering often times the same sacrifices [of animals] which can never take away sins; but this Man, after He had offered one sacrifice for sins for ever sat down at the right hand of God;...For by one offering He hath*

> *perfected forever them that are sanctified [by His blood]."* (Heb. 10:14) Praise the Lord!

Did you know that Caiaphas and the religious leaders didn't want the plaque to read "King of the Jews"? They went to Pilate and asked him not to allow the plaque to read "King of the Jews", but rather that **"Yeshua said** He was the King of the Jews".

> *"Then said the chief priest of the Jews to Pilate, write not, "the King of the Jews, but that He said, I am King of the Jews."* (John 19:21)

The plaque directly and correctly identified Yeshua as the "King of the Jews" who was sent to the Jewish people. Still, many Jews failed to see that their prophesied King had come. They failed to see that He was their *suffering Messiah* of Isaiah 53. No wonder Yeshua wept with a broken heart as He cried:

> *"Jerusalem, Jerusalem! The one killing the prophets, and stoning the ones having been sent to her; how often I desired to gather your children, in the way that a hen gathers her chicks under her wings; and you did not desire it. Behold, your house is left unto you desolate. And truly, I say unto you, you shall not at all see me again until you say, "Blessed is He who comes in the name of the Lord."* (Luke 13, 34,35)

Zechariah prophesied of a future day when the Jewish remnant in Jerusalem will look upon their Messiah and mourn:

> *"And they shall look on me, whom they have pierced, and they shall mourn for an only Son,*

> *and shall be bitter for Him, like the bitterness over the firstborn."*(Zech. 12:9,10)

The main reason that many Jews missed their Messiah's first coming was because they were looking for the Messiah as the King who would deliver them from the tyranny of the Roman government. They had gone through hundreds of years of suppression and captivity. Even the Apostles were looking for the government to be returned to Israel.

> *"When they had therefore come together they asked of Him, Master wilt thou at this time restore again the Kingdom of Israel?"*(Acts 1:6)

In the Old Testament, a King couldn't *officially* be a King without a *crowning* declaring Him King. The Roman soldiers, even though it was a scornful, mocking *crowning*, made a declaration declaring Yeshua "King of the Jews." They placed the crown upon His head and the plaque over His head. Did you ever think about that part of Yeshua's crucifixion? **"Gem"**!

A King in the Old Testament also had an *"appointed time"* to be crowned and declared King. Many times it would be at Passover. At Golgotha, three and one-half years after Yeshua's ministry, He was crowned and declared "King of the Jews" at *Passover*. It was Yeshua's *"appointed time"* to die and be crowned as the "King of the Jews". Another **"Gem"**!

There is another *"appointed time"* when Yeshua will be crowned and declared King. He will not be mocked and crowned in a shameful way, but crowned at a glorious coronation. He will be crowned and declared "King of Kings" and "Lord of Lords" over all peoples and nations. As it was customary to shout,

"Long Live the King," so we too shall shout it at His heavenly coronation. **"Long Live the King"!**

> "And He has on His vesture and on His thigh a name written, King of Kings and Lord of Lords."(Rev. 19:16)

Did you know that King David was crowned *twice*? It was *prophetic* of Yeshua's *two crownings*; one crowning at Golgotha, His earthly crowning as "King of the Jews"; and the other heavenly crowning as "King of Kings." What a joyous coronation that will be! **"Gem"!**

David's first appointment and crowning was as "King of Judah" (over the southern part of Israel) at Hebron (2 Samuel 2:1-7). Then, he was later crowned King over the northern part of Israel (2 Sam. 5:1-5) making him King over *"all Israel"*. David reigned from the old City of Jerusalem (called the "City of David"). Soon our King will reign on earth from Jerusalem over *"all"* Israel, including grafted-in Gentiles, and over *"all"* nations in the Millennium. **"Gem"!**

Another *prophetic picture* of Golgotha is found in an incident that took place during the wilderness journey of Moses and the Israelites. It revealed a "Gem" about Yeshua as He hung upon the stake (tree) at Golgotha.

Remember when the Israelites were being bitten by poisonous snakes? It was to punish them for their murmuring against God and complaining about Moses. Many died and the people began to repent and ask Moses to pray unto God to take away the serpents.

God told Moses to make a serpent of bronze (represents "judgment") and place it upon a pole (stake). Then, if a serpent bit one of the people, they could look upon the serpent of bronze on the stake and not die. Look at this scripture in the New Testament revealing the fulfillment by Yeshua:

> *"And as Moses lifted up the serpent in the wilderness, even so must the Son of Man be lifted up on a stake, so that anyone who believes in Him should not perish, but have eternal life."*(John 3:14-15) **"Gem"**!

Yeshua bore the full weight of God's wrath and judgment for sin in our place on that stake. Because He suffered the penalty for our sins, we are no longer under the curse of death for sin. What an awesome prophetic picture of Yeshua's crucifixion and our deliverance from the curse of the law for sin.

> *"Yeshua hath redeemed us from the curse of the law, being made a curse for us; for it is written, cursed is everyone that hangeth on a tree."*(Gal. 3:13)

> *"For God hath made Him to be sin for us, who knew no sin; that we might be made the righteousness of God in Him."* (2 Cor. 5:21)

After Yeshua's body was removed from the tree, He was wrapped in a linen cloth for burial.

> *"Then took they the body of Yeshua and wound it in linen clothes with the spices, as the manner of the Jews is to bury."* (John 19:40)

Did you know that Nicodemus brought a mixture of myrrh and aloes weighing about a *hundred pounds* for Yeshua's burial cloth? The spices were very costly.

> *"And there came also Nicodemus...and brought a mixture of myrrh and aloes, about one hundred pounds."* (John 19:39)

Myrrh was one of the spices brought to Yeshua by the Magi, and *prophetic* of His suffering, crucifixion and burial. It was applied to Yeshua's burial cloth. Have you ever bought an incense stick of myrrh and smelled the aroma as it burned after lighting it? It has the most wonderful fragrance. Try it!

Did you know that the resin of a myrrh bush is bitter to taste and oozes out in *red drops* like blood when crushed, but emits a sweet fragrance? In the Garden of Gethsemane, Yeshua prayed: *"Not my will, but Thine be done"* as He drank the bitter cup. Drops of blood oozed out of the pores of His body! With a crushed, broken heart, He surrendered to His Father's will, sending forth a sweet fragrance like Myrrh. **"Gem"**!

The **Word** states that Yeshua was in the grave three full days and three full nights. How can anyone count three complete twelve-hour days and three complete twelve-hour nights from Friday (called "Good Friday") until Sunday morning, according to our present-day tradition? We can't, because it is erroneous.

The truth is He was not crucified on a Friday. I know some say that it referred to three twelve-hour periods, but that is not a complete day by the Word. God's day is a 24-hour day, from sundown one day to sundown the following day. Genesis, Chapter One, *"evening to evening* [24 hours]" is a "day."

Yeshua's crucifixion was on a Wednesday evening, the fourteenth (14th) of Nisan. Counting from sundown on Wednesday afternoon until Saturday at sundown is three days and three nights by God's time (three twenty-four hour periods). Yeshua died at 3 p.m. in the afternoon (evening) and was placed in the tomb just before sundown, immediately before the Feast of Unleavened Bread, that began after sundown on the fifteenth (15th).

Joseph of Arimathea had sought Pilate for Yeshua's body so he could get Yeshua's body buried before the High Holy Sabbath (Unleavened Bread Feast) which began at sundown. Pilate's soldiers went to break Yeshua's legs to hasten His death so Joseph could take His body. However, Yeshua was already dead, so His legs were not broken, in fulfillment of the prophecy that not one bone of His body would be broken.

> *"He keepeth all His bones: not one of them is broken."*(Psalm 34:20)

The Jews also sought Pilate to get the bodies of Yeshua and the two criminals off the cross, but for a different reason that bodies not remain on the cross on a Sabbath:

> *"The Jews therefore, because it was preparation* [Passover day] *that the bodies should not remain upon the cross on the Sabbath day* [for that Sabbath day was a high Sabbath day], *besought Pilate that their legs* [Yeshua and the criminals] *be broken, and they might be taken away . . . But when they came to Yeshua, and saw that He was dead already, they brake not His legs."*(John 19:31,33).

Yeshua was bound to the tree on the fourteenth (14th) of Nisan (Wednesday) at 9 a.m., died at 3 p.m. and was placed in the tomb by sundown before the Feast of Unleavened Bread (a High Holy Sabbath) that began at sundown on the 15th of Nisan.

There is a prophecy in Daniel of the Messiah's ministry being "cutoff" in the "midst" of a prophetic week. A "prophetic week" equals seven years, one year for each day of a week. Yeshua's ministry lasted three and a half years, which is midway through a prophetic week of seven years.

I believe Daniel's prophecy concerning Yeshua's ministry is possibly a dual prophecy. First of all, Yeshua was crucified (cutoff) after three and a half years of ministry. Secondly, I believe Yeshua was "cutoff" in the middle of a literal week, Wednesday.

In relation to the resurrection of Yeshua on the 3rd day, the Word states that the women arrived at the tomb "early the first day of the week". So, many assume that it was Sunday *morning*, and that He had just arisen early that *morning*. However, let's look more closely at the scriptures from a Jewish perspective.

In the original Greek, "early on the first day of the week" refers actually to the "early part of the *evening* (not early morning). On God's calendar that would have been around 6 p.m. or at sundown, the beginning of a Jewish day. So "early part of the first day of the week," Sunday, would have begun *Saturday evening at sundown*. Remember that God's day as recorded in the book of Genesis is from evening to evening.

Also, remember that Paul was writing from a Jewish perspective with the Jewish calendar in mind. One other important consideration should be the original Hebrew text which reads: *"As it began to draw on towards the first day of the week"*.

A violent earthquake occurred almost simultaneously on that day as the two women approached the grave. So, is it likely that Yeshua had just arisen, maybe just seconds or minutes before the women arrived? If an earthquake happened at Yeshua's death, it seems logical to me that a second *earthquake* happened at the moment of His resurrection. Have you ever thought of that? Both were violent earthquakes! Yeshua's passing through the atmosphere and heavens must have really given Satan and his demons a violent shaking too! A final earthquake will take place when Yeshua's feet touch the Mount of Olives. It will give Satan another great shaking *and* binding! **Hallelujah!**

I believe Yeshua's resurrection occurred almost simultaneously with the earthquake.

Also, since Thursday was a High Sabbath (first day of Unleavened Bread), Friday was most likely the first day that the women had a chance to prepare the spices for Yeshua's body. Friday was known as the "day of preparation" for the weekly Sabbath. Saturday, the weekly Sabbath, was a rest day. So, Saturday after sundown was the first opportunity they had to take the spices. There is a possibility, I suppose, that the women waited until the morning, but Yeshua had already arisen according to the angel.

There is another interesting thing in reference to the dates of "Passovers" on an ancient calendar that has been kept for centuries.

Most bible scholars agree that Yeshua began His ministry in the fall of A.D. 27 at His baptism near His thirtieth birthday. After three and a half years' ministry, Yeshua's crucifixion would have been in the spring at Passover in A.D. 31. The following calculations are said to be the most accurate calculations according to computations preserved from the days of Moses!

Dates: A.D. 27 Wednesday, April 9

A.D. 28 Monday, April 26

A.D. 29 Saturday, April 16

A.D. 30 Wednesday, April 5

A.D. 31 Wednesday, April 25

A.D. 32 Monday, April 14

The year A.D. 30-31 had 13 months and places Passover 30 days later in April rather than some erroneous calculations on another day of the week in March calculated on 12 months. However, both years (A.D. 30 and A.D. 31) have Passover falling on a Wednesday (mid-week). Very interesting!

What advantages have the Jews in knowing the dates and special days of God? Much! God committed His oracles (scriptures) to them, and this included the knowledge of the days, weeks and months of the sacred calendar of God.

I even discovered in my research that June 17, A.D. 31 is believed by some scholars to be the date of the first New Testament Feast of Pentecost.

By the way, "sunrise services" on Sunday morning is a tradition started by man and is not Biblical. In fact, did you know that the Babylonian pagans worshipped their sun god/goddess by facing east as the sun came up? Sunrise service has its roots in pagan Babylon.

Yeshua arose victoriously over (1) death, (2) hell and (3) the grave on the **third day** after His crucifixion, the seventeenth (17th) of Nisan called "The Feast of Firstfruits."

When Yeshua appeared to Mary Magdalene in the garden after His resurrection, she mistook Him for the gardener. As soon as He called her name she knew His voice and cried, "*Rabboni*" (Master.)

> "... *She, supposing Him to be the gardener, saith unto Him, Sir, if thou hath borne Him hence, tell me where thou hast layed Him, and I will take Him away. Jesus said to her, Mary. She turned herself and saith unto Him, Rabboni; which is to say, Master.*"(John 20:15-16)

Why didn't Mary recognize Yeshua? Were there physical signs that altered His appearance? Was He still carrying the marks of His crucifixion upon His face and His body? We do know that Yeshua showed the nail prints in His hands and His torn side to doubting Thomas.

There is one other interesting thing about the myrrh bush. It has thorns 6 to 8 inches long, certainly not a rose bush type of thorn. Thorns from the myrrh bush could have easily made a crown shaped like a wreath with pointed ends for Yeshua's crown. Can you imagine thorns that size being pressed onto His head? I believe part of Yeshua's suffering was directly related to the *myrrh bush* as His thorny crown that left deep scars on His face.

The prophet, Isaiah, describes Yeshua's response to His Father's will, and Yeshua's sufferings:

> *"The Lord God hath opened mine ear, and I was not rebellious, neither turned away back. I gave my back to the smiters, and my cheeks to them that plucked off the hair: I hid not my face from shame and spitting."* (Isa. 50:5,6)

> *"As many were astonished at thee; his visage [face] was so marred more than any man, and his form more than the sons of men."* (Isa. 52:14)

> *"Surely, he hath borne our griefs, and carried our sorrows; yet we did esteem him stricken, smitten of God and afflicted. But he was wounded for our transgressions, he was bruised for our iniquities...and with his stripes we are healed."* (Isa. 53:4,5)

Some interesting derivatives for *myrrh* are "liberty", "bitter-sweet/suffering" and "sweet smelling." Yeshua came to set the captives free, His suffering was bitter, but of a sweet fragrance to His Father.

A derivative for *frankincense*, another spice brought by the wise men to Yeshua, is "purity" and is associated with fire. It was placed in a golden censer by the priests and burned at the Altar of Incense. It sent up a white smoke representing the ascending intercessory prayers to God. It was also placed upon the Shewbread at the Table of Shewbread, a place of communion and fellowship for the priests. Frankicense was bitter to taste, but sent forth a sweet fragrance when baked in the fire.

Yeshua's life and words, pure and holy, tried by fire are seen in the *frankincense*. As His prayers ascended up to the Father, they became a sweet fragrance. Did you know that *frankincense* grows on rocks and its sap flows from a tree pierced in darkness (during the night)?

Yeshua, Mediator and Intercessor, is seen in the Frankincense. He still lives to make intercession for us at the right hand of God. **Gem!**

> *"Who is he that condemneth? It is Christ that died, yea rather, that is risen again, who is even at the right hand of God, who also maketh intercession for us."* (Rom. 8:34)

Other spice derivatives are: cinnamon is "holiness of heart." Sweet calamus is "uprightness" and also translated "rod" or "branch". Olive oil is "anointing" and "joy." Aloe, another spice, is translated "intimacy".

In the Song of Solomon, the following spices are mentioned: *"Spikenard and saffron, calamus and cinnamon, with all trees of frankincense, myrrh and aloes, with all the chief spices."* (Sol. 4:14)

A few other spices and herbs are: *henna*, which yields a red stain and means, "ransom"; *saffron*, "faith"; *nard*, "light"; and *spikenard*, "costly, precious."

"Spikenard" was the ointment in the alabaster box brought by the woman who poured it out on Yeshua's head. It was as though she was identifying Him as the Anointed One. Her most costly and precious ointment meant nothing to her in comparison with her Lord who was about to give His life for her. **"Gem!**

> *"And being in Bethany in the house of Simon, the leper, as he sat at meat, there came a woman having an alabaster box of ointment of spikenard very precious, and she brake the box and poured it on His head."(Mark 14:1,3,)*
>
> Yeshua replied: *"She hath done what she could. She is come aforehand to anoint my body for burying."* (Mark 14:8)

Another woman, Mary of Bethany who was the sister of Lazarus, also anointed Yeshua's feet with a *pound* of the precious ointment of spikenard. Mary's great love for her Lord is expressed in the following scripture:

> *"There [at Bethany] they made him a supper; and Martha served...Then took Mary a pound of ointment of spikenard, very costly, and anointed the feet of Jesus, and wiped his feet with her hair; and the house was filled with the odour of the ointment."* (John 12:1-3)
>
> *"It was that Mary which anointed the Lord with ointment, and wiped his feet with her hair, whose brother Lazarus was sick."* (John 11:2)

At Golgotha, Yeshua the Passover Lamb is the Anointed One who came and offered the ultimate and perfect blood sacrifice for sin unto salvation. He is coming again, not as the Lamb to be sacrificed for sin, but as the Lion of Judah and as King to deliver those who know Him and who are eagerly awaiting His return! **Hallelujah and Selah!**

> *"So, Yeshua was once offered to bear the sins of many; and unto them that look for Him shall He appear the second time not to deal with sin unto salvation, but to deliver those who are eagerly waiting for Him."* (Hebrews 9:28) Don't miss him!

CHAPTER 8

TABERNACLE SABBATHS

As part of the Tabernacle's ordinances, God appointed certain days called **"Sabbaths"** at which time the people were commanded to assemble and meet with God. There were *"high holy days"* and *"high Sabbaths"* within the **Sabbaths.**

One of the *Sabbaths* was the *"weekly Sabbath"* which is called "Shabbat" in Hebrew. It **preceded** the list of "Sabbaths", which included the annual "Feasts of the Lord". The *weekly Sabbath* will be the focus of this Chapter.

> *"The Lord said unto Moses, announce to the people of Israel that they are to celebrate several annual festivals (feasts), appointed times when all Israel will assemble and worship me. These are in addition to your weekly Sabbaths, the seventh day of the week. Six days shall work be done; but the seventh day is the Sabbath of rest, and holy convocation; ye shall do no work therein; it is the Sabbath of the Lord in all your dwellings."*
> (Leviticus 23:2,3)

Jewish people begin celebrating Shabbat on Friday evening with a special meal and candles. It is a family time of relaxation. Reading the Word and singing songs can also be a part of the evening.

I know that the Sabbath is seen by many Gentiles as a "Jewish" thing, and that Sunday is the day of rest and worship for Gentiles. I know that God honors the praise and worship on Sunday because He sees the heart of man. However, after praying about the change and searching the scriptures, I found no Biblical evidence to prove that the Sabbath had ever been changed to Sunday by God.

Yes, I know that we should worship God every day, but Gentiles do acknowledge one *literal day* a week for rest and worship. So, why not keep Saturday instead of Sunday?

Most Christians will tell you that it is because Yeshua arose on Sunday, and it celebrates His resurrection. Did you realize, however, that *God set* a special time to celebrate Yeshua's resurrection annually on the *anniversary* of His resurrection? It is one of the seven (7) Feasts of the Lord, the Feast of Firstfruits. By keeping this Feast, one will be celebrating the actual *anniversary* of Yeshua's resurrection. We will discuss this Feast later in another Chapter and who changed the Sabbath.

The following scripture caught my attention during my search for the truth about the Sabbath:

> *"Remember the Sabbath day by keeping it holy. Six days you shall labor and do all your work, but the seventh day is a Sabbath to the Lord your God. On it you shall not do any work, neither you nor your son or daughter, nor your manservant nor maidservant, nor your animals, nor the foreigner [Gentile] within your gates."* (Exo. 20:8-10)

Before we go on, I would like to share my testimony of how God revealed some biblical and historical truths to me regarding the weekly Sabbath. As I was earnestly seeking the Lord for answers in relation to the weekly Sabbath, unexpected things began to happen. Truths were revealed to me that I had never been taught as a Gentile.

First, I was invited to attend a Saturday service held at a private home. It was the home of a nurse (Gentile) that I worked with at the time. She and her husband kept the Sabbath at home. Her husband taught the biblical and historical view of the weekly Sabbath. That was the first source of teaching I had received in relation to the Sabbath. I learned that Roman Emperor Constantine by Decree (Law) changed the weekly Sabbath to Sunday.

Then, there was the day that my husband brought a book home to me that contained much information about the Old Testament and the Sabbath.

My husband had been browsing around in a store and the owner asked him if he wanted a free book. The owner had found an old box of books and was giving them away. The owner stated they were "religious" books. My husband stated that his wife might be interested, and he took one.

That book being placed directly into my hands was a *supernatural* act of God. That book confirmed so many of the same scriptural and historical facts that I had previously learned in the home of the nurse and her husband.

Shortly after that, I found a Messianic Congregation where I could honor the Sabbath, keep the Feasts of the Lord and learn more of the Word from a Hebraic perspective. I had ridden past that congregation for years and never noticed the sign "Messianic Congregation." I know it was in God's timing and at the right season of my spiritual life that I saw the sign and began to attend the Congregation.

We have seasons in our spiritual life that change from time to time. I have gone from my season of salvation in a little Baptist church, to a deeper walk in *the Holy Spirit* at Pentecostal churches and on to learning more of the Word from a *Hebraic perspective.* I treasure each one that has contributed to my walk with the Lord. Each one had something I needed at that particular time in my walk, and still does. I still feel free to attend church on Sunday.

The Messianic Congregation brought me a step further in my understanding and knowledge of the Torah and the Old Testament, much of which I have shared in this book. The word of God is a Jewish Book by Jewish Authors and reveals the Jewish Messiah.

Now, let's look *biblically* at the weekly Sabbath. It is the **Fourth Commandment**. Most every believer agrees that the Ten Commandments (God's Law) are still to be observed, so why has the Fourth Commandment been omitted in many faiths?

The Fourth Commandment reads: *"Remember the Sabbath Day to keep it holy."* Why does this Commandment begin with **"Remember"**? Is it because God is reminding all mankind of the Sabbath's establishment in the Garden of Eden? It was established at the ***beginning of creation*** before Israel became a nation.

Yeshua also said: *"If you love me, keep my commandments".*

Could the word, **"remember"** also be for future generations because God knew that man would change His day to Sunday? Yeshua Himself said the weekly Sabbath was made for the benefit of man.

> *"And He said unto them, the Sabbath was made for man, and not man for the Sabbath. therefore the Son of Man is Lord also of the Sabbath."* (Mark 2:27-28)

Yeshua is "Lord of the Sabbath". I believe it means He has *all authority* to decide its observances which were not in accordance with the Pharisees' rules. Yeshua healed the sick and ministered on the Sabbath, something the Pharisees would never have done. Yeshua kept the weekly Sabbath by performing the works of the Father, not by performing rituals to look holy.

The Sabbath is a good time to do the works of the Lord as Yeshua did, all to the glory of the Father.

> *"What man shall there be among you, that shall have one sheep, and if it fall into a pit on the sabbath day, will he not lay hold on it, and lift it out? How much then is a man better than a sheep? Wherefore it is lawful to do well on the sabbath days."* (Mt. 12:11,12)

Spiritually, Yeshua is every believer's eternal "Sabbath Rest" every day. However, I could not find biblical evidence to prove that Yeshua had ever changed or eliminated His Father's *literal day* of rest established at the beginning of creation. Yeshua and His followers never deviated from keeping the weekly Sabbath.

Did you know that we will be keeping it during the Millennium? It has been said that keeping the weekly Sabbath and the Feasts of the Lord now are rehearsals for the real thing later!

> *"And it shall come to pass, that from one new moon to another, and from one Sabbath to another, shall all flesh come to worship before me, saith the Lord." (Isaiah 66:23)*

The *weekly Sabbath* begins at sundown on Friday evening and ends at sundown Saturday evening. It is important to understand the Jewish Biblical day. The time of day in "hours" and "parts of the day" are mentioned often in the Word of God. I have included the following in explaining the Biblical Day:

Biblical Day: Begins at sundown (evening), from 6 p.m. one day to 6 p.m. of the following evening (not like ours, midnight to midnight). (See Genesis 1:5,8,13,19,23,31)

The 24-hour day divided into two twelve-hour periods: (1) from 6 p.m. to 6 a.m. called "evening" (our "night") and (2) 6 a.m. to 6 p.m. called "morning" (our day).

Broken down further, the biblical "morning" is divided into two smaller periods: (1) 6 a.m. to noon called "morning part" of the biblical day, and (2) noon to 6 p.m. called "evening part" of the biblical day.

In calculating the time of the "morning part" of the **day** by "hour", one must **count from 6 a.m**. An example is found in Matt. 20:3 where we see the "third hour" of the day, which was 9 a.m., also the time Yeshua was bound to the tree.

In Matt. 20:5, in speaking of the "sixth" and "ninth" hour of the day, it was at noon and at 3 p.m. The "ninth hour" of the day was the hour Yeshua died in the "evening part" of the "day," which was at 3 p.m.

In Matt. 20:6, Peter and John go up to the temple to pray at the "eleventh hour" of the day, which was 5 p.m.

The "midnight hour" stays the same. Here are a few scriptures of happenings at midnight:

In Exodus 12:29, it was at the *midnight hour* that death of the firstborn took place in Egypt.

It was at the *midnight hour* when the Holy Spirit (Comforter) came at Pentecost (Shavuot)! (Acts 16:2)

In Mark 13:35, it was at *midnight* that Peter heard the cock crowing.

It was at *midnight* that Boaz awoke, startled to find Ruth lying at his feet, and her words to him: *"It is I, Ruth. Make me your wife according to God's law for you are my close relative."*

Is it possible that Yeshua will come for His Bride at the *midnight hour* and she will say, *"It is I. Make me your wife"*? **Glory!**

The following is an interesting scripture in relation to the hour of the Bridegroom's return:

> *"And at midnight there was a cry made, Behold, the Bridegroom cometh, go ye out to meet Him."* (Matt. 25:6)

I know, I took a little side-track there, but the Jewish weeks and times of the day are very important in understanding God's calendar and His time-table in the Word of God.

Getting back to the weekly Sabbath (Saturday), did you know that it is the *only day* that God *blessed* and *sanctified*? It is *commemorative* of creation.

> *" And God blessed the seventh day, and sanctified it; because that in it He had rested from all His work which He had created and made."* (Gen. 2:2-3)

> *"Remember the Sabbath day, to keep it holy...For in six days the Lord made heaven and earth, the sea, and all that in them is, and rested the seventh day: wherefore the Lord blessed the Sabbath day, and hallowed it."* (Exo. 20:8,11)

To the Jewish people, the weekly Sabbath (*Shabbat*) is about worship and worshipping the one true Creator of things in heaven and earth. His name is even placed upon it. The Hebrew root word for "Sabbath" is "*Shabbath.*" "*Sha*" means Eternal One. "*Ab,*" the root word of "*Abba,*" means Father. "*Bath*" or "*Beth*" means house of or sign of. The Hebrew root word means "Eternal Father's sign" or "sign of the Eternal Father." This day *honors Father God.*

The Israelites were commanded to keep the Sabbath throughout their generations as a *perpetual covenant* with God. Keeping the Sabbath was a *mark* or *sign* identifying the children of Israel with God. It left no doubt as to Who the Israelites served; the One True God and no other gods.

> *"Speak thou also unto the children of Israel, saying: Verily my Sabbaths [includes the weekly Sabbath]; are a sign between me and you throughout your generations; that ye may know that I am the Lord that doth sanctify you...Wherefore the children of Israel shall keep the sabbath throughout their generations for a perpetual covenant. It is a sign between me and the children of Israel for ever; for in six days the Lord made heaven and earth, and on the seventh day he rested, and was refreshed."* (Exo. 31:13,16,17)

Now, let's look at some *historical facts* about the weekly Sabbath:

It is a historical fact that Roman Emperor Constantine, together with the Roman Church, changed the Sabbath day of worship to Sunday. Sunday (Sun-Day) was Constantine's day of worship to honor the pagan sun goddess Mithras. Sunday was called "The venerable day of the sun". Constantine was *not* a Christian and continued to worship his many gods and goddesses. The mingling of Christians with pagan worship grew and increased under Constantine's rule.

At the Council of Laodicea, A.D. 364, a law (Canon XXIX) decreed: "Christians shall not judaize and be idle on Saturday but shall work on that day; but the "Lord's day" [Sunday] they shall especially honor . . . ."

The law applied to everyone, Jew and Gentile alike. Before the Decree, Jew and Gentile believers kept the weekly Sabbath. More than three hundred years after Yeshua's death and resurrection, the Sabbath was still being observed until **man** changed God's Law. The penalty for disobeying Canon XXIX was death. Roman Emperor Constantine by the Decree (law) established Sunday. I could find nowhere in scripture where God changed the day. Did Yeshua tell His followers to change it? No.

After the law, many believers fled to other countries to avoid death. The true remnant continued to keep the Jewish ordinances and held to the truths of God's Word. They might have remained a "little flock," but they never died. Many Jewish descendants throughout the centuries in many countries continued to keep God's ordinances, especially the Sabbath.

In A.D. 325, at the Council of Nicea, it was decreed that "Easter Sunday" (pagan holiday) worshipping the goddess, "Ishtar" was the *only day* to observe Yeshua's resurrection.

Did you know that the Roman Catholic Church takes the most credit for changing the Sabbath day of worship to Sunday? They knew that Saturday had always been the day of worship for those of faith for centuries, but changed the day to Sunday anyway.

Roman Emperor Constantine gave Papal Rome a great seat of authority in Rome during his reign. Together they formed a church-state coalition. A coalition like the one in those days could exist again during the end-time tribulation period. The one-world political system and a one-world religious system are described in the book of Revelation.

Papal Rome went along with much of Constantine's agenda, including the killing of Jews and Christians. It is a historical fact that Papal Rome considered the change of the day of worship to Sunday to be an act of "her power and authority over religious matters."

Because the Roman Catholic Church does not accept the Word of God as the only rule of faith, they look to the church's leaders to guide them, especially the "apostolic fathers". That includes changing and making their own laws, such as celibacy of priests and nuns, regulation of Catholic marriages, purgatory, priests as mediators (instead of Yeshua) between man and God, using "Holy Father" as a title for the Pope, and calling Mary, "Mother of the Church".

One Pope, Leo XIII, stated: "We hold the place of God Almighty." I do not mean to offend any Catholic, but does man have such authority over God? No!

I love the Catholics and know that many of them love and serve the Lord. I mean no offense by any means. Catholics are responsible for a lot of charitable work, but I am merely stating historical facts. Many of the Roman Catholic Church's laws such as the above are **not scriptural**, but **man-made.** God **never forbid** priests or nuns to marry. That is **not** Biblical. Zacharias, John the Baptist's father, was only one of many. In the New Testament, Paul taught that it was *better to marry* than to *burn with lusts*. In Genesis 1:27-28, the Word states that God made **male and female**, blessed them and told them to be **fruitful and multiply**. Could this be one of the reasons for the shameful acts now being exposed in the Catholic Church?

In early records (1800's), it is recorded that the Roman Church also changed Wednesday, called "crucifixion day," to Friday. The records show that "Ash Wednesday" was first observed for decades as the day of Yeshua's crucifixion until the Church later changed it to Friday. It was the "apostolic fathers" that began to make the changes. The old **Papacy knew** the holy days and laws of God better than anyone. Yet, **they** made the changes for the church and recorded them anyway.

If I am not mistaken, references in the "Didascalia" and "Epiphanius" support the Tuesday night Seder, the arrest of Yeshua in the morning hours of Wednesday and His crucifixion on that day.

Emperor Constantine also changed and renamed *religious holidays* after his gods. "Christmas" was instituted by Constantine and celebrated on the twenty-fifth day of December. The pagans celebrated "Saturnalia" at the same time. Constantine encouraged the Christians to celebrate their holidays at the same times and dates as the pagans. By doing so, Christians slowly began to mingle and merge with the pagans and adopt pagan customs, many of which still exist today.

So, Jews and Gentiles who continued to keep the weekly Sabbath and the Feasts of the Lord after the Decrees were easily distinguished from the pagans. In fact, keeping the Sabbath and the Feasts of the Lord were the ***main mark*** of God that believers carried. It was also the main sign that they served God, and no other god(s).

Could that be why God commanded His people to keep His Holy Days, including the Sabbath, as a ***sign*** of who they served, God or man? Believers will also be required to take the "mark" of the antichrist in the last days and will have to choose between God and man. May we be like Shadrach, Meshach and Abednego when we are tried:

> *". . . Blessed be the God of Shadrach, Meshach and Abednego who hath sent His angel, and delivered His servants that trusted in Him and have disobeyed the King's word, and yielded their bodies, that they might nor serve nor worship any god, except their own God."* (Dan. 3:28)What a word for us today!

The mark of the antichrist's followers and the mark of Yeshua's followers will be seen by their actions. Many believers will be deceived by the antichrist and bow down to the world system and his image. Their hands will perform evil works, and they will be slaves to his evil plans. There will also be those who have the mind of Yeshua who worship God and refuse to bow to the antichrist. Their hands will perform the works of their Heavenly Father!

It is all about worship and supremacy with Satan (*HaSatan*, Hebrew). He has always desired to be exalted and worshipped above God and to reign supreme. Of course, it will never happen. That doesn't keep him from still trying. Listen to his end declared by God:

> *"For thou hast said in thine heart, I will ascend into heaven, I will exalt my throne above the stars of God; I will sit also upon the mount of the congregation, in the sides of the north: I will*

ascend above the heights of the clouds; I will be like the most High."(Isaiah 16:13-14)

"Yet thou shalt be brought down to hell, down to its lowest depth. They that see thee shall look narrowly upon thee, and consider thee, saying. Is this the man that made the earth to tremble; that did shake Kingdoms . . . ?"(Isaiah 16:15-16)

Have you ever thought about history repeating itself in relation to the days of Emperor Constantine? The coming antichrist will be watching to see who worships him and who worships Almighty God. Will he also legalize Sunday as **his** day? Would Christians continue to worship on that day? It might be something to consider. Either way, the antichrist will require *his mark* and *worship*.

In closing, I leave the following scripture:

"If you keep the Sabbath holy, not doing thy own pleasure on my holy day; and call the Sabbath a delight, the holy of the Lord, honorable; and shalt honor Him, not doing thine own ways, nor finding thine own pleasures, nor speaking thine own words: Thou shalt delight

thyself in the Lord; and I will cause thee to ride upon the high places of the earth, and feed thee with the heritage of Jacob thy father; for the mouth of the Lord hath spoken it."(Isaiah 58:13-14)

CHAPTER 9

GOD'S APPOINTED FEASTS

Other than the weekly Sabbath, God had other appointed Sabbaths (holy days) on which to tabernacle with His people, including the **"Feasts of the Lord"**. The Hebrew word for "feast" is ***"mo'ed"***. It means an ***"appointed time"*** or ***"set time"*** to meet with God. Another Hebrew word, ***"mikrah"*** means ***"sacred assembly"*** (holy convocations) and applicable to the Feasts. It is important to remember that all of the Feasts point to Yeshua. One must look for Him in the midst of the *symbolic* and *figurative language* of God seen throughout the Word of God.

We will cover the first four (4) of the seven (7) annual "Feasts of the Lord" in this Chapter. The remaining three (3) that take place in the fall are, you might say, interwoven throughout remaining Chapters. It may take some searching to find those Gems!

> *"Speak unto the children of Israel, and say unto them, concerning the feasts [mo'ed] of the Lord, these are the feasts of the Lord, even holy convocations [mikrah], which ye shall proclaim in their seasons."* (Lev. 23:2,4)

The feasts were also to be observed at God's appointed **"place"**. His redemptive plan is accomplished in **Jerusalem**. It is the place where important events surrounding the plan of God are fulfilled.

The "Feasts of the Lord" consisted of seven (7) major annual feasts. Within these seven feasts, God's plan for the redemption of man and Yeshua's role in fulfilling them is revealed. Each feast reveals a *phase* of God's plan of salvation through Yeshua. They reveal Yeshua's *first* and *second* coming and much more! The feasts have **never** been done away with and the fall feasts foreshadow the *ultimate* and complete fulfillment by Yeshua.

These annual feasts are appointed days by God for **"all"** of His people to fellowship with Him. They are **not** just "Jewish" festivals. They are designed to release increased blessings into our lives and to keep us reminded each year of our Salvation, Yeshua. They are very important to us today as they reveal Yeshua's *second coming and beyond!*

Although the feasts can be made legalistic, it is **not** what God intended. Many *secular* "memorials" take place annually and are faithfully celebrated. The Feasts of the Lord are "memorials" to Yeshua, the Central Figure in all of the Feasts.

The "appointed days" for the seven annual Feasts of the Lord have *symbolic* and *prophetic* significance pointing to Yeshua. They are also historical and agricultural in context. They are celebrated in specific seasons and on specific days on the Jewish calendar (I call it God's calendar).

Did you know it is believed that God comes very near during His feasts because they are **His** *appointed days*? He rejoices over us and with us in these special times of communion and celebration. They are *"annual memorials"* to Yeshua, our Redeemer, and times of thanksgiving to the Father for His Son.

Prophetically speaking, of the seven appointed feasts, four (4) have been literally fulfilled by Yeshua. The spring feasts are as follows: **Passover** (*Pesach*, Hebrew), **Unleavened Bread** (*Hag HaMatzah*, Hebrew) and **Firstfruits** (*Bikkurim*, Hebrew). These feasts were fulfilled by Yeshua's *death, burial and resurrection*. The early summer feast of **Pentecost** (*Shavuot*, Hebrew) was fulfilled by Yeshua's sending of the *Holy Spirit* (*Ruach HaKodesh*, Hebrew).

The three fall feasts are the **Feast of Trumpets** *(Rosh HaShanah,* Hebrew*)*, **Day of Atonement** *(Yom Kippur,* Hebrew*)* and **Feast of Tabernacles** *(Sukkot,* Hebrew*).* These feasts have **not** been **ultimately** fulfilled, but will be competed at Yeshua's *return* exactly as prophesied, just as the Spring and Summer feasts were at His *first coming.*

By the way, Zechariah the prophet prophesied that God's people, along with many nations, would still be celebrating the **Feast of Tabernacles** in the thousand-year Millennium.

> *"In the end, everyone that is left of the nations that came against Jerusalem shall even go up from year to year to worship the King, the Lord of Hosts, and to keep the Feast of Tabernacles."* (Zech. 14:14)

As a Gentile believer, I had no idea for years that the Seven Feasts were *prophetic* of Yeshua's *first* and *second coming.*

For years, I had always celebrated two days during the spring holiday called "Easter". One of those days was "Good

Friday" (believed to be the day of Yeshua's crucifixion) which was totally in error. Yeshua was not crucified on Friday. I also learned that "Easter Sunday" was not God's name for that day. It was actually named after a goddess named "Ishtar".

Since the Gregorian calendar used by most of the world is of Babylonian and Assyrian origin, it is no wonder that many of the weekdays and months carry the names of pagan gods and goddesses. Let's begin with Sunday, the first day of the week on the Gregorian calendar and following:

Sun-day was named after the sun god, Mithras; *Monday* after the goddess of the moon, Artemisor Asherah ("queen of heaven"); *Tues-day* after the god Tiu, a Druid-Celtic idol; *Wednes-day* after the Teutonic god Woden; *Thurs-day* after the god Thor; *Fri-day* after the goddess Frigga (wife of Woden); and *Satur-day* after the Romans' deity of agriculture, Saturnus.

A big party was also dedicated to the god Satyr at the end of the Roman year at the solstice celebration called "Saturnalia" in December. Satyr was a goat-legged half-man with horns and pointed ears. What a sight he must have been!

Let's also look at the *months* of the Gregorian calendar and their pagan names while we are on the subject:

January is named after the god Janus; *February* after female idol Februa; *March* after the god Mars; *April* after Greek god Aphrodite; *May* after fertility deity Maia; *June* dedicated to a Roman female deity Juno; *July* dedicated to Julius Caesar (honored as son of the sun); and *August* honored Augustus Caesar in honor of himself, as did Julius Caesar before him.

September, October, November and *December* are named from Latin words for numbers rather than gods.

So, what are God's names for the days of the week? "First Day," "Second Day," "Third Day" . . . "Seventh Day (called *"Shabbat,"* the weekly Sabbath).

Many times *God's months* are referenced as "First Month," "Second Month," "Third Month," etc. The Fall Festivals fall in the "seventh month" of the *religious calendar*. God's months have specific names as well and are seen on the Jewish calendar.

There are two Biblical Calendars. The first is called the "Civil Calendar". This calendar did not exist during Yeshua's time. The first month is Tishrei (mid-Sept.to mid-Oct.). Rosh HaShanah (Jewish New Year) is the first day in the Civil Calendar and the beginning of the **Jewish New Year.**

The second calendar is the "religious" calendar. **God established** the Religious Calendar with its first month being Abib (ancient name), now called "Nisan" (mid-March to mid-April). This calendar sets the religious holy days and the Feasts of the Lord which were observed by Yeshua and His followers.

> *"This month shall be unto you the beginning of months: it shall be the first month of the year to you."*(Exo. 12:2)

It is also the month that the Israelites left Egypt:

"This day came ye out in the month of Abib."(Exo. 13:4)

After *Nisan*, the first of God's months on the religious calendar, the following months are:

L*yar* (mid-April to mid-May); *Sivan* (mid-May to mid-June); *Tammuz* (mid-June to mid-July); *Av* (mid-July to mid-August); *Elul* (mid-August to mid-September); *Tishrei* (mid-September to mid-October); *Cheshvan* (mid-October to mid-November); *Kislev* (mid-November to mid-December); *Tevet* (mid-December to mid-January); *Shevat* (mid-January to mid-February); and *Adar*, the last month (twelfth month) (mid-February to mid-March). There is also a thirteenth month about every three years named Adar II.

The pagan holidays, including Easter, were never celebrated by the faithful followers of Yeshua. They were considered *abominations* to God. I would encourage every believer to read up on the history of pagan Easter with its Easter bunny, dyed eggs and sunrise service.

Personally, I can no longer call Yeshua's resurrection day "Easter Sunday." Many believers knowing the truth about pagan "Easter" call it "Resurrection Day" instead. That is far better than calling it by a pagan name. However, **"Firstfruits"** is actually the correct Biblical name of this Holy Day.

Since Constantine's decree, "Easter" has always been celebrated near the time of "Passover" ("*Pesach*"). **In no way** is "Passover" connected to this pagan celebration!

In questioning whether or not Gentiles should celebrate Passover and the Feasts, I found **my** answer in the New Testament.

The Apostle Paul, in speaking to the Gentiles, explained that at one time they were separate from the Messiah. For a long time the Gentiles were excluded from citizenship in Israel and were foreigners to the covenant promises to Abraham. Paul continues to say that the Gentiles who were once far away have been brought near through the blood of Yeshua. Gentile believers are part of the Body of the Jewish Messiah and Israel. *Spiritually*, as part of Yeshua's Body, I am intimately connected to Him and His Jewish roots and to Israel.

Over and over again, God spoke of "all of Israel" in the Old Testament, and it extended to include "all of spiritual Israel," Jews and grafted-in Gentile believers.

Do I celebrate the feasts? Yes, but not as bondage or as being "under the old law". Do I have to keep them? No! However, they keep me in *remembrance* each year of my Salvation, His sacrifice and His soon return to earth. I see the Feasts as an opportunity to rejoice in my Salvation and give praise and glory to the Father for my Redemption and soon-coming King!

Yeshua kept the feasts, His disciples kept them, and the early Gentile believers joined in with the Jewish people to celebrate them. The feasts are all about God's redemptive plan for Jew and Gentile. At least, that is the way I see it.

In the New Testament, Paul along with the Jews and Gentiles observed the feasts because they were *"appointed times"* to meet with the Father.

> "But God, who is rich in mercy, for His great love where with He loved us, even when we were

> *dead in sins, hath quickened us together with Yeshua (by grace are you saved); and hath raised us up together, and made us sit together in heavenly places in Yeshua."* (Ephesians 2:6)

> *"That the Gentiles should be fellow heirs and of the same body, and partakers of His promise in Yeshua by the gospel."* (Ephesians 3:6)

I like this definition of the feasts: "A periodic religious observance commemorating an important moment from the past and the future." **Amen!**

Passover Feast (called **"*Pesach*"** in Hebrew) is a Spring feast. The appointed time for Passover is on the fourteenth (14th) day of *Nisan* (mid-March to mid-April) beginning at sundown, around 6 p.m.

> *"In the fourteenth day of the first month [Nisan/Abib] at even is the Lord's Passover."* (Lev. 23:5)

A young lamb for each household was actually chosen and brought into the house on the *tenth day* of the month of Nisan. The lamb was examined for any sickness or flaws until its death on the fourteenth, at 3:00 p.m. This was *prophetic* of Yeshua the Passover Lamb who was spotless and without defect. Yeshua rode into Jerusalem on the tenth of Nisan and was examined by the people and religious leaders for four days as He taught in the temple. He was the innocent, pure Lamb of God found to be without blemish. Pontius Pilate himself declared, "I find no fault in this man."

> "... In the tenth day of this month they shall take to them every man a lamb ... a lamb for an house ... Your lamb shall be without blemish, a male of the first year; ye shall take it out from the sheep or the goats. And ye shall keep it until the fourteenth day of the same month: and the whole congregation of Israel shall kill it in the evening."(Exodus 12:3-6)

Let's look at the last several days of Yeshua's life before His crucifixion. He fulfilled the prophecies of the scriptures as the Passover Lamb to the exact month, date and time.

Yeshua had supper at Lazarus's house six days prior to the Passover after He had raised Lazarus from the dead. On the seventh day, He entered Jerusalem for the first day of Passover.

> "Then Yeshua six days before the Passover came to Bethany, where Lazarus was which had been dead, who He raised from the dead. There they made Him a supper; and Martha served, but Lazarus was one of them that sat at the table with Him."(John 12:1-2)

> "On the next day many people that were come to the feast, when they heard that Yeshua was coming to Jerusalem, took branches of palm trees, and went forth to meet him, and cried, Hosanna: Blessed is the King of Israel that cometh in the name of the Lord. And Yeshua when He had found a young ass, sat thereon; as it is written [in Zech. 9:9.]"(John 12:12-14)

This would have been on the tenth day of Nisan, the day the lambs were to be taken into the household to be examined for defect or disease until the fourteenth day of Nisan.

Yeshua was the Lamb brought before the household of God and before the priests, scribes and Pharisees. They observed Him until the fourteenth day of Nisan when He would be crucified. Instead of them recognizing Him and being joyful, they sought to kill Him. Luke refers to this in Luke 19:

> "If only thou hadst known, even thou, at least in this thy day, the things which belong unto thy peace. But now they are hid from thine eyes . . . And He went into the temple, and began to cast out them that sold therein, and them that bought . . . And He taught daily in the temple. But the chief priests and the scribes and the chief of the people sought to destroy Him." (Luke 19:29,41,42,45,47)

> "And they (the chief priests and scribes) watched Him, and sent forth spies which should pretend themselves just ordinary men . . . so they might deliver Him unto the power and authority of the governor."(Luke 20:19-20)

After Yeshua entered Jerusalem on the tenth (10th) day of Nisan, He went to the temple and taught daily for four days. The tenth day was also the day that Yeshua ran the money changers from the Temple in Jerusalem.

Yeshua taught on Nisan the tenth (Saturday) in the synagogue, on the eleventh (Sunday), the twelfth (Monday), and thirteenth (Tuesday). On Tuesday evening, shortly after sundown, which began the fourteenth (14th) day of Nisan (beginning of Wednesday), Yeshua shared His last supper with His disciples that evening. Remember that God's day begins in the evening at sundown of one day and ends at sundown the next day. Did you know that Yeshua and His disciples sang a prayer from the book of Psalms at the last supper?

> *"And when they had sung a prayer, they went out into the Mount of Olives."* (Matt. 26:30)

Yeshua was arrested later in the night in the Garden of Gethsemane and tried illegally (night trials not legal) by the religious leaders during the night of the fourteenth (14th).

Still being the fourteenth day of Nisan, a Wednesday morning at 9:00 a.m., Yeshua was nailed to the tree. He died in the "evening part" of the day (at 3 p.m.) at the same time the literal lambs were being slain for the Passover meal.

As the high priest in the temple slit the throat of the last lamb for Passover, he would always literally say, "It is finished." Outside the temple the Lamb of God cried, "It is finished". Yeshua's last words even fulfilled the prophetic utterance that had always been spoken by the high priest on Passover. **"Gem"!**

Do you know the only time in the Word that Yeshua did not refer to His heavenly Father as "Father?" Remember when Yeshua cried out, *"Eloi, Eloi, la-masabachthani"* meaning, "My God, My God, why hast thou forsaken me?" That is the English translation. However, the Hebrew word *"Eloi"* means " Almighty One".

Why was it the only time that Yeshua didn't call God "Father"? He was crying out from His fleshly (human) body born of Mary. He was also as One who had never known sin as

He took the judgment of God and penalty for all mankind's sins. His holy and sinless Divine relationship with His Father was broken as His Father became **Judge** and placed His wrath on sin upon His Son. The Father-Son relationship had never been broken and Yeshua had never been separated from that Divine, sinless relationship until that moment. As any human being would, He **felt** rejected, forsaken and alone and cried out in despair.

As He cried, "it is finished", He bowed His head and gave up the ghost. The slain Lamb of God had become the Sacrificial Lamb, our Pass-Over from the penalty of death to eternal life.

"For even Yeshua our Passover is sacrificed for us."(I Cor. 5:7)

Concerning the Feast of Passover (*Pesach*), I once questioned a teaching I had received concerning this feast. I had been taught in some churches that the observance of the Passover had been replaced with Communion. Did Yeshua change the observance, and how?

On the night of the Last Supper, at the end of the meal, Yeshua revealed to His disciples that **unleavened bread and wine** were to represent His Body and Blood. Yeshua revealed to them that He was the Sacrificial Lamb who was about to pour out His own blood for the remission of sin. **No longer** would it take the blood of a *literal lamb* to atone for sin.

The disciples and His followers continued to keep the Feast of Passover once a year on the **anniversary** of the first Passover. The two symbols of Unleavened Bread and Wine representing Yeshua's Body and Blood were partaken of at the **end of the meal** ("Sedar", Hebrew) as commanded by Yeshua in remembrance of His sacrifice.

> *"And He took bread, and gave thanks, and broke it, and gave them saying, This is my body which is given for you: This do in remembrance of me. Likewise also the cup after supper, saying, This cup is the New Testament in my blood, which is shed for you."* (Luke 22:19,20)

> *"And this day shall be unto you for a memorial; and ye shall keep it a feast to the Lord throughout your generations; ye shall keep it a feast by an ordinance forever."* (Exodus 12:14)

Yeshua also washed the disciples' feet on that Passover night. In relation to the "foot washing", some believe the foot washing is not to be taken literally; that it was just an example of Yeshua's humbleness as a Servant. However, have you ever been part of a foot washing at Passover? It is such a humbling experience. As you wash another's feet and pray for that one, *you* will experience such a feeling of humbleness. Both the one who is washing feet and the one receiving the washing are blessed.

Most importantly, as we make foot washing a part of the Passover celebration, we should recall Yeshua, and His willingness to be a Servant. It should remind us that we are also servants directly identified with the Servant. Most of all, we should be reminded that shortly after on that night, Yeshua *humbled Himself* to the point of death at Golgotha."**Gem**"!

> *"If I then, your Lord and Master, have washed your feet; ye also ought to wash one another's feet. For I have given you an example that you should do as I have done to you."* (John 13:14-15)

There were several cups of wine on the Passover table that night. One of the cups of wine on the table at Passover, the third cup, called the "Cup of Redemption" represented Yeshua's blood. That last Passover Supper was also a *betrothal ceremony* as Yeshua lifted up the cup, drank from it and said, "...share this among yourselves", as custom in a Jewish betrothal ceremony! **"Gem"!**

These words are also associated with this cup: *"I will redeem you with a mighty outstretched arm."*

Cup of Redemption

Cup filled with the blood of the Vine
Firstfruit pressed in a winepress in the Garden
Beads of blood came forth as He prayed
Not my will be done Father, but Thine
His yielding set me free, sealed my pardon

Cup of Redemption, offered up to the Father
Filled with the blood of the crucified Lamb
No more blood of bulls and goats
The ultimate one-time Sacrifice was given
Fulfilled in Yeshua, Son of God, Son of Man

Cup of New Wine, shedding of blood foretold
Yeshua's atoning blood for unredeemed man
Given freely as it ran down Golgotha's tree
Wine most costly and more precious than gold
Sealed God's covenant with you and with me

Come, drink in remembrance of the Bridegroom
The purchase price for His bride has been paid
At the wedding we will dance and sing
Share the Cup of Redemption face to face
Forever in the presence of our Redeemer-King!

"Blessed are those who are invited to the marriage supper of the Lamb!"(Rev. 19:9)

Most Gentiles and Messianic Jews celebrate Communion at different times of the year in remembrance of Yeshua, and that's o.k. However, all should certainly celebrate it at the end of the Passover meal (Seder) on the anniversary of Passover according to the Jewish calendar.

Passover is not to be a ritual, and doesn't have to be observed at a Jewish synagogue or Messianic Congregation. You can observe Passover and the other Feasts in a simple way in your home, if you choose. God looks at the heart. I know our Father would be blessed and you as well.

There are many books giving simple instructions on how to observe the feasts of the Lord in your home. Just be sure the material is from a born-again perspective for believers.

Some books even give recipes for different Jewish dishes for the meal that are scrumptious. I make a Passover cake with wine and almonds that always brings compliments. Passover is such a wonderful time to fellowship and share a meal with other believers or with those who need salvation. This feast is for **all**, saints and sinners!

The **Feast of Unleavened Bread** (called "*Hag HaMatzah*," Hebrew) is the *second* annual Feast. This Feast is another appointment with God immediately following the first day of Passover (Nisan 14th).

Unleavened Bread began at sundown after 6 p.m. on the 14th, which was the beginning of the fifteenth of Abib/Nisan. This Feast of Unleavened Bread was so much a part of Passover that the names were used interchangeably or synonymously. This Feast is *prophetic* of Yeshua's **death and burial**.

> *"Now the Feast of Unleavened Bread drew nigh, which is called the Passover."* (Luke 22:1)

> *"Seven days shall you eat unleavened bread; even the first day you shall put away leaven out of your houses; for whosoever eateth leavened bread from the first day until the seventh day that soul shall be cut off from Israel."* (Exo. 12:15) The "First day" referred to was the fourteenth, Passover Day.

> *"And on the fifteenth day of the same month is the feast of unleavened bread unto the Lord: Seven days ye must eat unleavened bread."* (Lev. 23:6)

Historically, Israel remembers and celebrates this Feast in remembrance of their hasty flight out of Egypt. They had no time to prepare the bread they took with yeast. So, they left with unleavened bread.

> *"With the dough they had brought from Egypt, they baked cakes of unleavened bread. The dough was without yeast because they had*

been driven out of Egypt and did not have time to prepare food for themselves." (Exodus 12:39)

The Unleavened Bread is *symbolic* of Yeshua's sinless Body broken for us. *Spiritually*, this Feast represents our divine separation from the bondage of sin and our escape from Egypt (type of the world). We become set apart from the world, and are to begin living a holy, consecrated life unto the Lord. We are to walk in newness of life, so that the anointing of the Holy Spirit (Ruach HaKodesh, Hebrew) will rest upon us.

Did you know that anointing oil was placed upon the unleavened bread before it was baked? At Yeshua's baptism, the Anointing Oil (Holy Spirit) rested upon Him, the Bread of Life? "**Gem**"!

"And Yeshua, when He was baptized, went up straightway out of the water; and lo, the heavens were opened unto Him, and He saw the Spirit of God descending like a dove, and lighting upon Him . . . " (Matt. 3:17)

"I am the living bread which came down from heaven: If any man eat this bread, he shall live forever. The bread that I will give is my flesh, which I will give for the life of the world." (John 6:51)

I have included another poem that you might enjoy:

Unleavened Bread

Bread of Heaven, Bread of Life

Believers' Bread sent from above
Gift of Salvation sent from the Father
Living Bread sent with amazing love

Unleavened Bread of sweet savor
Holy, Acceptable Offering to the Father
Broken and bruised, given in my place
My iniquities forgiven by His Divine Grace

Bread in abundance for "whosoever will"
Salvation to impart, eternal life to give
Burdens He will lift, wounds He will heal
Every need, every void He will fill

Come, partake of this Bread daily
In Him lies strength for each new day
Faith and power to overcome the adversary
And grace to walk in all of His ways

Take, eat in remembrance of the slain Lamb
Worthy is He who bore mans' sins upon His body
Soon He will return to catch His bride away
A banquet table for the marriage supper awaits
What a glorious communion that day!

Literally, before Passover, Jewish people go through their house and remove any and all leavened bread in preparation for the Unleavened Bread feast. No leavened bread is allowed in the house during the week of Passover.

Spiritually, this is *figurative* of searching for any unprofessed sin in our spiritual house after receiving Yeshua. At salvation (Passover from death to life), we become a new creature and the temple (house) of the Holy Spirit. Water baptism symbolizes our death (burying) of the old creature and rising up to newness of life (a new creature) in Yeshua.

Immediately after receiving Yeshua into our lives (house), the cleaning out of leaven (symbolic of sin) should begin. In cleansing the temple (house), it requires us to do a daily searching of sin (leaven) until a completed time of perfection. Seven (seven days of Passover) represents completeness, totality or fullness. We should allow the Holy Spirit (*Ruach HaKodesh*) to reveal sin in our lives and help us change day by day until our perfection is completed at His coming.

> *"Purge out therefore the old leaven* [sin]*, that ye may be a new lump, as ye are unleavened* [cleansed from sin].*For even Yeshua our Passover is sacrificed for us."*(I Cor.5:7)

> *"Therefore we are buried with Him by baptism into death, that like as Yeshua was raised up from the dead by the glory of the Father, even so we should walk in newness of life."* (Romans 6:4)

At the Last Supper, Yeshua spoke of one sitting at the table who had betrayed Him, which we know was Judas. Yeshua dismissed him from the table and told him to go do quickly what he was to do. Judas, whom Satan had entered (Luke 22:3), had sinned and was the leaven (sinful one) removed from the table. How's that for a **"Gem"**?

Yeshua's body without sin and incorruptible never decomposed in the grave like man's corruptible flesh. Matzah, the cracker-like flatbread without yeast used during Passover is an excellent *symbol of* Yeshua's body and is eaten for seven days (throughout the week of Passover).

Matzah (also called "Bread of Affliction") is pierced with many holes and has many rows of striped and burnt areas throughout reminding us of Yeshua's bruised, torn and pierced Body. His Body was pierced for our transgressions, bruised for our iniquities, and He was wounded for our transgressions. His beard was plucked out and a crown of thorns pressed down onto His head. He was beaten with a reed and spit upon.

Not only did Yeshua, the Bread of Life, suffer from physical pain, but from unimaginable and incomprehensible emotional and mental pain. The Father had **not forsaken** Yeshua. His Body would not see decay, and death would not hold Him in the grave. He was resurrected and sits at the right hand of His Father!

Did you know that Peter spoke of death not being able to hold Yeshua?

> Peter states: *"God has raised Him up and freed Him from the suffering of death; it was impossible that death could keep its hold on Him."*(Acts 2:26,27)

Apostle Peter also quoted the following prophecy by David from Psalms 16:9-10:

> *"Therefore my heart is glad and my tongue rejoices; my body also will live in hope because you will not abandon me to the grave, nor will you let your Holy One see decay."*

Did you get that? David spoke of Yeshua's incorruptible body that never saw natural man's decay hundreds of years before Yeshua's burial! Amazing prophecy by David, and a **"Gem"**!

The Body of Believers will also be raised incorruptible and put on immortality at His coming! What a day that will be!

> *"For this corruptible must put on incorruption, and this mortal must put on immortality. So when this corruptible shall have put on incorruption, and this mortal shall have put on immortality, then shall the saying be brought to pass that is written, death is swallowed up in victory."*(I Cor. 15:53-54)

Now, how do we know that believers, including Gentiles were keeping the Feasts after Yeshua's resurrection?

In the book of Corinthians, the brethren (mostly Gentile) were encouraged by Paul to "enter in" to the joyful celebration of Passover and other Feasts of the Lord. This was about twenty-five years after Yeshua's resurrection.

Apostle Paul also taught a *spiritual* aspect in reference to the Feast of Unleavened Bread. Paul taught that a small amount of yeast (leaven) in the bread spreads throughout the whole loaf.

Paul in a rebuke to the sexual immorality found in the Congregation at Corinth, compares the Congregation to a batch of dough *with yeast*. He warns that in allowing a little leaven (symbolic of sin), it would result in the proliferation and spread of sin throughout the whole congregation, as yeast does in a batch of dough.

> *"Don't you know that a little yeast works through the whole batch of dough? Get rid of the old yeast* [sin] *that you may be a new batch without yeast, because in reality you are unleavened, for our Passover Lamb, the Messiah, has been sacrificed. So, let us keep the feast, not with old yeast* [sin before salvation], *nor with yeast of malice and of evil, but with unleavened bread of sincerity and truth."* (I Cor.5:6-8)

How do we know that Paul and the other believers continued to celebrate the other feasts of the Lord? In Acts 20:16, we see Paul hastening to Jerusalem to keep the Feast of Pentecost. Again, in I Cor. 16:8, Paul tarries in Ephesus until Pentecost.

In Acts 12:1-3 during the Feast of Unleavened Bread, Herod the King killed the Apostle James.

Also in Acts 12:4, the Passover is mentioned. King James Version incorrectly translated *"Pesach"* (Hebrew for Passover) with the Greek word *"pascha"* as "Easter." It has been corrected in the New King James Version.

Paul is seen going to Jerusalem for the Feast of Tabernacles in Acts 18:21. In Verse 6 of Chapter 18, the people Paul was addressing were Gentile and Jewish believers.

Paul sailed to Philippi in Greece right after the days of Unleavened Bread in Acts 20:6.

Paul refers to the "fast day" understood to be the Day of Atonement in his hazardous sailing conditions during the time of the feast in Acts 27:9. So it appears that Paul encouraged the keeping of the God-appointed Feasts.

We have seen that the first two feasts, *Passover* and *Unleavened Bread* were fulfilled by Yeshua's *death and burial*.

The next and *third spring* feast, **Feast of Firstfruits**, is celebrated on the third day after Yeshua's crucifixion. After three nights and three days in the grave, He arose on Feast of Firstfruits, the seventeenth (17th) day of the month of Nisan (Abib). This feast reveals **Yeshua's resurrection**!

In Israel, the **Feast of Firstfruits** is at the time of the early spring *barley crop*. The Israelites were not allowed to harvest any of the barley until the "firstfruits offering" (the first portion of the harvest) had been offered up to God for His blessing.

The Nation of Israel was very familiar with the concept of the ***first*** being offered to God. The firstborn of man and beast, and the first fruits from the earth were presented to God. It was to be with thanksgiving and a pleasing offering to God. The people had the assurance of God's blessing upon the offering and an abundant *wheat harvest* in the fall.

> *"You shall bring in the sheaf of the first fruits of your harvest to the priest. And he shall wave the sheaf before the Lord for you to be accepted; on the day after the sabbath the priest shall wave it...You shall count fifty days to the day after the seventh sabbath; then you shall present a new grain offering to the Lord."* (Lev. 23:10,11,16)

On the first day of the week following Passover, the early *barley harvest* began. The first grain to ripen was the *barley*.

The people cut the first ripe sheaf and removed the barley grain, filling a bowl. The first ripe sheaf was then waved before God by the High Priest. The *offering of barley* was called the *"lone sheaf."* The lone sheaf was to be the first, the choicest, the best and pre-eminent of the wheat harvest to follow with God's blessing. The "sheaf" is *figurative* of a **Person**. Watch for "**Gems**".

The Lone Sheaf, the First of the harvest, the Choiciest, the Best and Pre-eminent of the great fall harvest, typified Yeshua, God's Firstborn. As the High Priest on the day of Yeshua's resurrection waved the "sheaf" before God on Firstfruits , the Firstborn Son of God (First of the dead to be resurrected) arose from the grave (from the heart of the earth). He offered Himself to His Father as the Holy, Acceptable Offering for the many resurrected saints who would follow! **"Gem"***!*

Yeshua, the Firstfruit from the dead, paved the way for a great *harvest* of saints (also called "firstfruits") to be resurrected and blessed by the Father!

This firstfruit offering also required a burnt offering, a lamb one year old (in the prime of its life). Yeshua was that Lamb (Burnt Offering) that died in the prime of His life.

Yeshua's resurrection assured the saints' resurrection. Because Yeshua arose victorious over death, we too are victorious over death. Remember, the same Spirit that raised

Yeshua from the dead, lives in us! In a *spiritual sense*, we are already resurrected with Him, but our bodies are not yet incorruptible! Praise the Lord!

Feast of Firstfruits is *prophetic* and was fulfilled by Yeshua's *resurrection* on the third day (seventeenth of Nisan) after His crucifixion. The Feast of Firstfruits is all about **resurrection**!

At Yeshua's return, many saints (also called "firstfruits unto God") will be resurrected with incorruptible bodies.

> *"But now is Yeshua risen from the dead, and become the firstfruits of them that slept. For since by man came death, by man came also the resurrection of the dead. For as in Adam all die, even so in Yeshua shall all be made alive. But every man in his own order; Yeshua the firstfruit; afterward they that are Yeshua's at His coming."* (I Cor. 15:22-23)

The "counting of the omer" also began on the Feast of Firstfruits. Omer is a measure of barley (about a half-gallon of barley). The people were to count up to fifty days with a measure each day. On the *fiftieth day*, the first day of the early *wheat harvest*, the **Feast of Pentecost (Shavuot)** began.

The *counting of the omer* is like a chain linking Passover to Pentecost (Shavuot, Hebrew) with Pentecost (sending of the Holy Spirit) appearing to be the *completion of Passover*. Portions are read each day during the "counting of the omer" from Psalms 119.

The **Feast of Pentecost** (meaning fiftieth in Greek) and called *"Shavuot"* in Hebrew, means "weeks." This Feast is the *fourth* feast and is in early summer, around June or July at the time of the early *wheat harvest*. It is also called "The Feast of Weeks" because seven weeks (forty-nine days) are counted from Firstfruits (counting of the omer).

This Feast is *prophetic* of the sending of the Holy Spirit (Ruach HaKodesh, Hebrew) on the fiftieth day after Yeshua's resurrection.

> *"From the day after the Sabbath, the day you brought the sheaf of the wave offering, count off seven full weeks. Count off fifty days up to the day after the seventh Sabbath, and then present an offering of new grain to the Lord. From wherever you live, bring two loaves made with two-tenths of an ephah of fine flour, baked with yeast, as a wave offering of firstfruits to the Lord . . ."* (Lev. 23:15-17)

Pentecost marked the first day of the early *wheat harvest* with the full harvest to come in the fall. This feast required an offering or first portion from the harvest, as was required in all of the feasts. The offering was to show joy and thanksgiving to the Lord for the *wheat harvest* and to receive God's blessing. The offering made unto God at this feast was made with *two loaves of wheat bread* kneaded with yeast. They were also waved (called "wave offering") before God by the high priest for acceptance and blessing.

After the Holy Spirit fell on the one hundred and twenty Jewish disciples in the upper room at Pentecost (*Shavuot*), many

Gentiles joined themselves to the believing Jews in the First Century. Jew and Gentile became "one new man" in the Body of Yeshua. Paul refers to Jew and Gentile as "one new man" in Ephesians 2:14-16.

> *"But now in Yeshua ye who sometimes were far off* [Gentiles] *are made nigh by the blood of Yeshua. For He is our peace, who hath made both* [Jew and Gentile] *one body, and hath broken down the middle wall of partition between us . . . And that He might reconcile both unto God in one body by the cross . . . ."*

This could only have been made possible by the sending of the Holy Spirit (*Ruach HaKodesh*). It began on the Feast of Pentecost (*Shavuot*) as the Jews, especially Peter, began to preach the Gospel in the power of the Holy Spirit. So, the Jews *first* brought the message of the Messiah's resurrection and the Holy Spirit!

So, what or who do you think the two loaves of leavened bread (symbolic of sin or imperfect man) represented? They represented two imperfect peoples. Most scholars agree that one loaf represented the Jewish nation (Israel). The other loaf represented the Firstfruits (Believers, Jew and Gentile). Sin still existed in both peoples, but both are loved, chosen and blessed by the Father! **"Gem"**!

This Feast also required a "freewill offering" to the poor, the widow and stranger:

> *"And when ye reap the harvest of your land, thou shalt not make clean riddance of the corners of the field when thou reapest, neither shalt thou gather any gleaning of*

thy harvest; thou shalt leave them unto the poor, the widow, the stranger and the foreigner..." (Lev. 23:22)

The Book of Ruth is read at this Feast. In the story of Ruth (non-Jewish) and Naomi (Jew) in the Book of Ruth, did you know that Ruth was gleaning the corners of the fields left for the poor at the time of this Feast?

Ruth was gathering the grain, especially to see that her mother-in-law did not do without proper nourishment. Ruth's kindness to her mother-in-law is an example of the way believers should treat the Jewish people. This is a beautiful story of Ruth's love for Naomi and the Jewish people and how God blessed her.

This is also a story of Naomi's love for Ruth. Naomi taught Ruth the Torah and the ways of God. We should love the Jewish people for giving us the Torah and the Word of God. Boaz (a prototype of Yeshua) loved Ruth and took her to be his wife. Can you see the beautiful, *prophetic* picture here of a non-Jewish woman with a Jewish Bridegroom? **"Gem"**!

Do you realize that there is a great transition and change taking place in the Body of Yeshua in these last days? The Holy Spirit is bringing about this change. He is drawing Jews and Gentiles together again as one in the Messiah, the one new man that Paul spoke about. The two were as one in the early church, and it is already happening again in our day! It is a *crucial element* in the restoration of Israel and the Body of Yeshua in these last days!

The New Testament Pentecost (*Shavuot*) as previously discussed, commemorates the anniversary of the Old

Testament Pentecost and is connected to the giving of the Torah and the Ten Commandments.

Under the New *Blood Covenant* on the Day of Pentecost (*Shavuot*), the Jewish congregation of one hundred twenty were filled with the Holy Spirit (Ruach HaKodesh, Hebrew)! The gifts of the Holy Spirit were manifested gloriously by the fire of God! (Acts 2).

The Jewish followers of Yeshua in the upper room broke forth and started the greatest revival ever known, turning the world upside down. Peter alone preached a sermon that won three thousand souls to the Kingdom. According to the Word of God concerning the Feasts of the Lord, they are to be kept in their seasons.

> *". . . Concerning the feasts of the Lord, which ye shall proclaim to be holy convocations, even these are my feasts which ye shall proclaim in their seasons."*(Lev. 23:2)

CHAPTER 10

GOD'S CYCLES AND NUMBERS

The "Feasts of the Lord" are part of God's **annual cycles**. God is a God of **cycles**. Besides the annual cycle of Feasts, there are many other *cycles*. The "weekly Sabbath" is part of God's **weekly cycle**.

Besides those, there are the sun and moon **cycles,** *monthly* **cycles,** *seedtime* and *harvest* **cycles,** *winter* and *summer* **cycles,** *day* and *night* **cycles,** *life* and *death* **cycles**.

Did you know that God gave Noah a promise concerning His **cycles** at the time He gave the token of the rainbow?

> *"While the earth remaineth , seedtime and harvest, and cold and heat, and summer and winter, and day and night shall not cease."*"**Gem**"! (Gen. 8:22)

Besides cycles, **Numbers** are also a very important part of the Word of God. They open doors of deeper truths and understanding of God's language. There is not room in this book to cover them all, but we will cover a few to show the significance of Numbers in God's Word.

Let's begin with Number One, which represents "UNITY". In the Godhead, Father, Son and Holy Spirit are Three-In-One.

In I John 5:7, Apostle Paul speaks of the Father ,Son (Word) and Holy Spirit being ONE:

> "For there are three that bear record in heaven, the Father, the Word, and the Holy Ghost; and these three are One."

> "Hear, O Israel; the Lord our God is **one** Lord". (Deut. 6:4)

In speaking of UNITY of believers in the Body of Yeshua, Paul writes:

> "There is one body, and one Spirit, and we have all been called to the same hope of our glorious calling; one Lord, one faith, one baptism, for there is only one God and Father of us all, who is above all, and through all, and in you all."(Eph. 4:4-6)

Number 2—Two Witnesses—In the Word of God, the Number "two" usually refers to two witnesses which establishes a truth. *"Out of the mouth of two or three witnesses shall every word be established."*

In Revelation 11:3, there are "two witnesses" and their testimonies in the last days:

> *"And I will give power unto my two witnesses, and they shall prophesy a thousand two hundred and threescore days [1,260 days], clothed in sackcloth. These are the two olive trees, and the two candlesticks standing before the God of the earth."*

Moses and Elijah stand as two witnesses at the ascension of Yeshua after His resurrection; one to the Law and one to the Prophets.

Number 3—Resurrection—Yeshua quoted the prophecy in Jonah in speaking of His resurrection:

> *"For as Jonas was three days and three nights in the fish's belly, so shall the Son of Man be three days and three nights in the heart of the earth."*(Matt. 12:40)

Number 4—Creation/Universal—*"For by Him were all things created, that are in heaven, and that are in earth, visible and invisible, whether they be [1] thrones,[2]dominions, [3]principalities, or [4] powers."*(Col. 1:16)

> *"And the Lord said, I will destroy man whom I have created from the face of the earth, both [1] man, [2] beast, [3] the creeping things and the [4] fowls of the air."*(Gen. 6:7)

When Peter dreamed of the 4-corner sheet, there were four unclean animals in it: (1) four-footed beasts, (2) wild beasts, (3) creeping things; and (4) fowls of the air. God revealed to him that the dream represented sharing the gospel with Gentiles (whom the Jews believed to be unclean and not worthy to receive the gospel).

Peter received the revelation that the gospel was for the whole world; (1) every nation, (2) kindred, (3) tongue and (4) people. God is Creator and rules over the whole world whether it be (1) thrones, (2) dominions, (3) principalities or (4) powers. (Acts 10:12,15,34)

> *"And I saw another angel fly in the midst of heaven, having the everlasting gospel to preach unto them that dwell on the earth, and to every*

nation, and kindred, and tongue, and people, saying with a loud voice, Fear God, and give glory to Him; for the hour of His judgment has come; and worship Him that made heaven, and earth, and the sea, and the fountains of waters. (Rev. 14:6-7) Amen!

Number 5—Grace—Ephesians 1:7: *"In whom we have redemption through His blood, the forgiveness of sin, according to the riches of His grace."* There are five Greek words in the statement: *"My grace is sufficient for thee."*

The fifth time the name of Noah appears in Genesis 6:8 states: *"Noah found grace in the eyes of the Lord."*

Number 6—Man/Flesh—Satan's influence: When the image of Nebuchadnezzar was set up to be worshipped, it was six cubits broad according to Daniel 3:1-5. The people played six kinds of instruments in worshipping the image; gold, silver, brass, iron, wood and stone. (Daniel 5:4)

In the book of Revelation, the number with three sixes or the number 666 represents the name of the beast, with the triple evil influence of Satan. I believe this represents the evilest rule of Satan ever: (1) the dragon (Satan), (2) the antichrist and the (3) false prophet, all forming a wicked triune.

Could this be in stark contrast to God's Holy Triune, Father, Son and Holy Spirit? The wicked triune is composed of Satan (father of lies and murder), the antichrist (Satan's incarnated son) and the false prophet (with the spirit of deceit and blasphemy).

> *"And they worshipped the dragon* [Satan] *who gave power unto the beast* [antichrist], *and they worshipped the beast saying, who is like unto the beast? Who is able to make war with him? And there was given unto him a mouth* [false prophet] *speaking great things and blasphemies; and power was given unto him to continue forty and two months. And he opened his mouth in blasphemy against God to blaspheme His name, and His tabernacle* [temple] *and them that dwell in heaven."(Rev. 13:4-6)*

The Number 66 represents image or idol, which is part of the number 666, the evil triune. We know that the antichrist will set up idols and images to be worshipped which are part of the evil triune.

Number 7 —Completeness, Totality or Bringing to an End—There are too many "sevens" in the Word to include them all, so here are a few:

Seen in the very beginning in the Garden of Eden, the Number Seven is God's number in finishing or completing a thing, a **very specific number** in God's numerical system.

> *"Thus the heaven and the earth were finished, and all of the hosts of them. And on the seventh day, God ended His work which He had made; and He rested on the seventh day from all of His work. Every seventh day of the week is a Sabbath, holy unto the Lord, and the day He blessed."(Gen. 2:1-3)*

At Golgotha, Yeshua made seven statements before He died:

> *"Father forgive them," "Today thou shalt be with Me in paradise," "Woman, behold thy son, and [to the disciple] behold thy mother"," "My God, My God, why has Thou forsaken me?" "I thirst," "it is finished" and "Father, into Thy hands I commend my spirit".* (Luke 23:46)

In the book of Revelation there are seven spirits, seven stars, seven congregations, seven angels, seven seals, seven trumpets and seven vials of wrath in relation to the Lord's appearing to bring to completion the last earthly Kingdom.

In Revelation 1:4 there are seven spirits (representing the Holy Spirit) before the throne of God, a number of completeness or totality. Yeshua possessed the (1) spirit of the Lord, (2) spirit of wisdom, (3) spirit of understanding, (4) spirit of counsel, (5) spirit of might, (6) spirit of knowledge, and the (7) spirit of fear of the Lord. (Isaiah 11:1-2)

Seven angels with the seven last vials of judgment are seen in Revelation 16 being poured out: *"Then the seventh angel poured out his vial into the air; and there came a great voice out of the temple of heaven, from the throne, saying, 'It is done.'"*

There are many "sevens" in the story of Joshua and the city of Jericho. There were seven priests, seven trumpets, seven days of marching, and on the seventh day, they compassed the city seven times, shouted and the walls fell, bringing complete victory on the seventh day. (Joshua 6:15,16)

> *"On the seventh day they rose early at daybreak, and marched around the city as usual, only on that day they compassed the city*

seven times. And the seventh time, when the priests had blown the seven trumpets, Joshua said to the people, Shout! For the Lord has given you the city."

In the days of Noah's flood, God said in Genesis 7: *"Yet seven days, and I will cause it to rain upon the earth forty days and forty nights."*

God gave the people a grace period of seven final days, even after Noah had been preaching and warning the people of the coming flood for over 120 years. The last day of grace (seventh) came as God shut the door to the ark, and the earth was destroyed.

Can you see a parallel in the story of Noah and the flood with the last seven years of the end times spoken of by the prophets? God is a God of mercy, grace and long suffering, but there is coming a day when He will shut the door to salvation.

At the great sound of the seventh trumpet by the seventh angel in the book of Revelation, the kingdoms of the earth become the Kingdoms of Yeshua:

"And the seventh angel sounded [blew the trumpet]; *and there were great voices in heaven saying, the Kingdoms of this world are become the Kingdoms of our Lord, and of the Messiah and He shall reign forever and ever."* (Rev. 11:15)

Number 8—New Birth/New Beginning—Eight is two times four, the number of creation. When we are born again, we become a new creature with a new beginning; putting off the old fleshly nature. We become a new creation transformed by the new spiritual birth in the Holy Spirit.

> *"Knowing this, that our old man is crucified with him, that the body of sin might be destroyed, that hencforth we should not serve sin."* (Romans 6:6)

In Yeshua's conversation with Nicodemus on the subject of the new birth, the word "born" is seen eight times. (John 3:3-8)

There were eight people saved in Noah's ark to start anew and replenish the earth.

> Number 9—Fruits/Gifts of the Spirit—Follows Number 8 (new birth)". *The fruit of the spirit is love, joy, peace, longsuffering, gentleness, goodness, faith, meekness, temperance; against such there is no law."* (Gal. 5:22-23)

There are nine gifts of the Holy Spirit: *word of wisdom, word of knowledge, faith, healing, working of miracles, prophecy, discerning of spirits, divers kinds of tongues, and interpretation of tongues.* (I Cor. 12:8-11)

Number 10—God's Law—(The Ten Commandments) (Exo. 20:3-17) God gave the Ten Commandments to His people at Mt. Sinai as a covenant between Himself and His people. They are called the "Law of God". God also showed that His law prevailed over the idolatrous law and pagan gods and their practices in Egypt by *sending ten plagues* upon the Egyptians. He demonstrated His power as the one and only True God, and that His law prevails over the law of man.

Number 11—Judgment—Dinah was the eleventh child born unto Jacob, and her name means "Judgment."(Gen. 20:32, Gen. 30:21) Isaiah foretold the judgment that would come upon Judah by naming eleven different kinds of men: leaders, armies, judges, prophets, elders, army officers, business men, lawyers, magicians, politicians, and Israel's Kings. (Isa. 3:1-3)

The final catastrophic event (the eleventh) in judgment of Pharaoh's army was their drowning in the Red Sea at the completion of the ten plagues.

Number 12- Divine Authority and Rule of God's **Government** over all of creation.

God's divine rule and authority is seen in the twelve signs of the Zodiac. Listen to this conversation between God and Job about some of the constellations of the Zodiac and God' rule over them:

> God said to Job: *"Canst thou bind the sweet influence of Pleides, or loose the bands of Orion? Canst thou bring forth Mazzaroth in his season? Or canst thou guide Arcturus with his sons? Knowest thou the ordinances of heaven? Canst thou set the rule thereof in the earth?"*

Remember in a previous chapter that one of the stars was Arcturus? The other name in the above scripture, "Mazzaroth," translates to mean "signs of the Zodiac," and we know that there are twelve. Yes, as stated before, the Constellations have their origin with God and not the evil one. God even named the stars.

There is a very interesting story in the Old Testament where God is seen controlling the elements, particularly the stars.

During a battle with Sisera, Captain of Jabin's army (Israel's enemy), the influence of the stars brought down rain at the right time causing a flood in the small River of Kishon. It caused part of Jabin's army to drown and be swept away. Those not swept away were killed with Barak's (Jewish military leader) sword.

According to Judges 4:7, God drew Sisera there with the army, and changed the courses of the stars in order to bring about the flood. Awesome!

Listen to the song of victory that Deborah (prophetess of Israel) sang after the victorious battle over Sisera, Captain of Jabin's army: *"They fought from heaven, the stars in their courses fought against Sisera. The River Kishon swept them away."* (Judges 5:20-21)

Sisera didn't die at that time, but escaped. He was later killed by a Jewish woman as he hid in her tent. Jael drove a peg through his head while he was sleeping in her tent! Can you imagine that? What a tough and brave Jewish woman she was!

Some other examples of God's divine authority involving the number "twelve" are:

God appointed twelve months to the year, twelve hours to the day and twelve hours to the night. (John 11:9) God made two great lights to shine over them; the greater light by day, and the lesser light by night. God gave the sun to rule twelve hours by day, and the moon to rule twelve hours by night.

> In Genesis 1:16, we read: *"And God made two great lights; the greater light to rule the day, and the lesser light to rule the night: he made the stars also."*

In I Kings 18:22-24, Elijah had four barrels of water poured over the altar three times. That made twelve barrels of water used in the contest with the prophets of Baal. As God's fire consumed the water Elijah said, *"Let it be known this day that thou are God in Israel."* The God of Israel displayed His divine power and authority over the gods of Baal.

Remember when Yeshua was feeding the crowd of more than 5,000 with only five barley loaves and two fishes? The disciples gathered up 12 baskets of the fragments of the loaves and fishes. The 12 baskets represented the *divine power and rule* by which the miracle was wrought. It was also prophetic of each of the 12 disciples ruling in the Kingdom of God with divine power and authority. There were 12 disciples and 12 baskets of bread, a basket for each disciple containing the power and authority to rule with the authority of Yeshua. (Matt. 14:17-20)**Gem!**

There were twelve precious stones representing the twelve tribes of Israel on the breastplate (close to God's heart) of the high priest's garment in the Old Testament. Yeshua appointed twelve disciples to follow Him in the New Testament, which totals twenty-four. Before moving on to number twenty-four for "priesthood," I have listed the twelve tribes and the gemstones representing each on the old breastplate. Many of the heads of the Tribes were named by circumstances surrounding their births. (See Genesis 29 and 30)

TRIBE OF:

JUDAH, the first– Sardius stone– A sparkling ruby-red stone - Judah meaning "praise" and representing the redemptive work of Yeshua. His birth was welcomed and praised;

ISAACHAR – The Topaz – Bright yellow stone – Isaachar meaning "the reward";

ZEBULIN – The Carbuncle – Sparkling white stone - Zebulin meaning "dwelling" or "rest";

REUBEN – The Emerald – Ocean green stone - Reuben meaning "see a son" or "behold a son";

SIMEON – The Sapphire – Blue hard stone - Simeon meaning "to hear" or "God heard";

GAD – The Diamond – Sparkling white hard stone - Gad meaning "A troop like unto the Son";

EPHRAIM – The Ligure – Yellow agate stone – Ephraim meaning "double blessing – doubly fruitful";

MANASSEH – The variegated hard Quartz stone – Manasseh meaning "to forget or forgive";

BENJAMIN – The Amethyst – Purple stone - Benjamin meaning "Kingship" or "royalty"; son of my right hand;

DAN – The Beryl – Mostly greenish-blue stone – Dan meaning "judge" or "judgment";

ASHER – The Onyx – Flashing luster stone as fire - Asher meaning "happy and blessed";

NAPHTALI, the last— The Jasper stone – Many-colored crystal clear stone (quartz)- Naphtali meaning "wrestling" and "prevailing"(overcomer).

Notice that the **first** and **last** stones are the Sardius and the Jasper. These are the same two stones in the Book of Revelation that Apostle John saw as *figurative* of Yeshua, the One (Yeshua) sitting on the throne. The Sardius, blood-red, speaks of the redemptive work of Yeshua and the Jasper, many-colored crystalline (quartz), speaks of His brilliance in reflecting the glory of God! Also, Yeshua is the Beginning and the End, the **Alpha** and **Omega**, out of the Nation of Israel! **"Gem"**!

The 12 apostles of the New Testament are represented by *gemstones* in the heavenly city, New Jerusalem. New Jerusalem has twelve gates of pearl, each bearing the names of the twelve Tribes of Israel. Each gate is guarded by an angel.

There are twelve layers of foundation stones inlayed with twelve different gems with the names of the twelve apostles upon each one; the tree of life has twelve kinds of fruits and bears its fruit every month of all twelve months; the City measures twelve thousand furlongs in every direction, and the wall is 144 cubits high (twelve times twelve). We see in this scripture God's divine rule in the Heavenly Kingdom.

> "...and showed me that great city, the holy Jerusalem, descending out of heaven from God...and had a wall great and high, and had **twelve gates**, and at the gates **twelve angels**, and names written thereon, which are the names of the **twelve tribes** of Israel..." (Rev. 21:10,12)

> *"And the building of the wall of it was Jasper; and the city was pure gold like unto clear glass. And the foundations of the wall of the city were garnished with all manner of precious stones...and the wall of the city had **twelve foundations**, and in them the names of the **twelve apostles** of the Lamb."* (Rev. 21:14)

There are "all manner of precious stones". Could this be the many "lively stones"?

The Number Twelve is definitely connected to the *divine authority and rule* of **God's government** over **all** creation and His Heavenly Kingdom. He is the Most High God, Ruler of Heaven and Earth.

Before going on to Number Thirteen, since the Number Twenty-Four ties into the Number Twelve of divine authority and rule times two, we will look at it first. The Number Twenty-Four represents "priesthood." To understand it fully, one needs to read about the Old Testament priesthood in I Chronicles 24:1-9.

Number 24 - Priesthood: There were twenty-four courses (divisions) in the old Levitical Priesthood. There were thousands of priests, so they were divided up and placed under one of twenty-four divisions. Each division had a chief priest, so there were twenty-four head priests over all the other thousands of priests. The twenty-four chief priests represented the whole Levitical Priesthood (from the tribe of Levi).

In the book of Revelation, we see an order similar to the old priesthood:

> *"And round about the throne were four and twenty seats; and upon the seats I saw four and twenty elders sitting, clothed in white raiment; and they had on their heads crowns of gold."* (Rev. 4:4)

It is believed that the twenty-four elders in the book of Revelation are heads (rulers) over thousands of priests who serve under them in Yeshua's heavenly priesthood. Twelve Elders (heads) over the priests of the twelve Tribes of Israel and the twelve Apostles (heads) over the New Testament saints (priests). Look at John's description of the twenty-four Elders and their song:

> *"And when He had taken the scroll, the four beasts and four and twenty elders fell down before the Lamb...And they sang a new song, saying, Thou art worthy to take the scroll, and to open the seals thereof, for thou wast slain, and hast redeemed us to God by thy blood out of every kindred, and tongue, and people, and nation and thou hast made us Kings and priests unto our God..."* (Rev. 5:8-10)

The Levitical priesthood was temporary and imperfect, and under the old blood covenant of animal sacrifices. Yeshua came to bring a superior priesthood which superseded the Levitical priesthood. By His own blood, Yeshua brought in the new, everlasting and unchangeable priesthood, the Melchizedek Priesthood.

"But this man, because he continueth ever, hath an unchangeable priesthood." (Hebrews 7:17,24)

In comparing Yeshua's priesthood with the old Levitical priesthood, let's look at **three** gems in paralleling the two priesthoods:

Under the old Levitical priesthood, it changed at Aaron's death and passed on to his sons; under Yeshua's priesthood, it is unchangeable, everlasting and passed on to no one;

Under the old priesthood, the sacrificial system required the blood of animals for atonement of sin. At the death of the sacrificial Lamb of God, atonement was made by His blood once and for all.

Last, but not least, the high priest of the old priesthood interceded for his sins and the sins of the people (nation). Under Yeshua's new priesthood, no human priest intercedes for God's people; only Yeshua, High Priest, Who liveth to make intercession for His people. How's that for **three** marvelous "**gems**" in one?

The old priesthood was still in effect when the angel appeared to Zacharias, a priest seen in the New Testament and father of John the Baptist. Zacharias was serving his turn in the temple when the angel came and announced the birth of John the Baptist. He was at the Altar of Incense praying when the angel appeared. The Word states that Zacharias was "of the course of Abiah" which was the eighth division of the twenty-four divisions.(Luke 1:5)

Under the ancient Melchizedek priesthood the offices of King and High Priest were merged into one office with only one person (King-Priest) ruling. Yeshua's priesthood is likened unto that priesthood because Yeshua will rule as King-Priest (two offices In One) over His priesthood.

Melchizedek, an ancient King and High Priest, was ruling in Jerusalem during the time of Abraham. He was not only King of Salem (Jerusalem) but also a High Priest unto God. It was a picture and type of Yeshua and His heavenly priesthood proclaimed by God Himself. By the way, Melchizedek means "King of Righteousness", and "King of Salem" means "King of Peace". Yeshua will rule and reign as Righteous King, and King of Peace. There will be no war during His reign. "**Gem**"!

> *"God hath sworn and will not repent; Thou are a Priest for ever after the order of Melchizedek." (Ps. 110:4)*

> *"...first being by interpretation King of Righteousness, and after that also King of Salem, which is, King of Peace." (Heb. 7:1,2)*

The saints of God will serve as kings and priests in a royal priesthood like unto the Melchizedek rule, but much more glorious under our King-Priest, Yeshua, in Jerusalem during the Millennium!

> *"And from Yeshua, who is the faithful witness . . . Unto Him that loved us, and washed us from our sins in His own blood, and hath made us Kings and priests unto God, and His Father; to Him be glory and dominion forever and ever."(Rev. 1:5-6)* Hallelujah!

Number 13—Sin/Rebellion—There are thirteen evil things from within, out of the heart of man: Evil thoughts, adulteries, fornications, murders, thefts, covetousness, wickedness, deceit, lasciviousness, an evil eye, blasphemy, pride, and foolishness which defile a man. (Mark 7:21-23)

The word "Dragon" (Satan) who rebelled against God is found thirteen times in the book of Revelation. In Chapter 13 the world is seen worshipping Satan (the dragon) who gives great power to the beast (one-world government led by the antichrist) who is also worshipped.

"And they worshipped the dragon which gave power unto the beast, and they worshipped the beast."(Rev. 13:4)

Number 14—Salvation—(Lev. 23:5) *"In the fourteenth day of the first month [Nisan, March-April of God's calendar], at evening is the Lord's Passover."* The date of the Passover feast was set by God on the *fourteenth day* of Nisan. The sacrificial lamb was to be killed on that specific day and his blood applied to the doorposts of the Israelites' houses. It was the day of salvation for the children of Israel. They kept Passover on the exact month, date and time (evening) that God had commanded.

From Exodus 12:25-27, we know that Yeshua was the Sacrificial Lamb crucified on the exact month, date and time as ordained by God, the *fourteenth day* of Nisan. His blood having been applied to the wooden beams, He died at 3:00 p.m. It was the day of our Salvation, purchased and secured as He cried, "It is finished". **"Gem"!**

Number 17—Victory—Yeshua became victorious over death when He arose from the grave after 3 days and 3 nights from the fourteenth of Nisan. He arose on the *seventeenth day* of Nisan (Feast of Firstfruits), securing our redemption and resurrection.

> *"And having spoiled principalities and powers,*
> *He made a show of them openly, triumphing*
> *over them in it."* (Col. 2:15)

In John 2:19-21, Yeshua used a symbolic statement: *"Destroy this temple, and in three days, I will raise it up."* He spoke of the temple of His body being victorious over death and the grave after three days and three nights.

Seventeen Greek words are found in this statement: *"These shall make war with the Lamb, and the Lamb shall overcome them, for He is the Lord of Lords and King of Kings."* (Rev. 17:14). **Amen!**

Number 20—Redemption—The young men of Israel were required to pay a *ransom* in *silver shekels* for every soul at the age of 20 and above. The silver was melted and used throughout Moses' Tabernacle to make sockets and hooks into which the boards (the framework fitly framed together) were set and secured to the Foundation. **"Gem"**!

Spiritually, all *twenty boards* (figurative of the redeemed) rested securely on the Foundation made for the boards as they were secured by the ransom price paid by Yeshua.**"Gem"**!

> *"And no one can ever lay any other real*
> *foundation than that One we already have,*
> *Yeshua HaMashiach [the Messiah]."* (I Cor. 3:11)

Number 30—*Blood of Yeshua*—Judas betrayed Yeshua for 30 pieces of silver, blood money.

> *"Then, Judas who had betrayed Him, when he*
> *saw that He was condemned, repented himself,*

and brought again the thirty pieces of silver to the chief priests and elders, saying, I have sinned in that I have betrayed the innocent blood."(Matt. 27:3-4)

The price of Yeshua's betrayal foretold by Zechariah:

"And I said unto them, if you think good, give me my price; and if not, forebear. So they weighed for my price thirty pieces of silver."(Zech. 11:12)

The good news: *"But God commandeth His love toward us, in that, while we were yet sinners, Yeshua died for us. Much more then, being now justified by His blood, we shall be saved from wrath through Him."* There are *thirty* Greek letters in the words, "being now justified by His blood."

Number 40—Trial or Tribulation—Yeshua was in the wilderness tempted by Satan for forty days. Israel was in the wilderness for forty years. Israel was tried forty days and nights while Moses was up on the mountain receiving the law. It rained forty days and nights while Noah was in the Ark.

One other interesting thing about the number forty (40) that I discovered in reading about Jacob's death is found in Genesis 50.

After Jacob died, Joseph commanded his servants, the physicians, to embalm his father. Even though it was against Jewish law to embalm, Joseph made an exception. Jacob had died in Egypt where it was the manner of the Egyptians to embalm, but there was another reason. Jacob's body needed to be preserved since Joseph, in honor of his father's request, promised to take Jacob's body to Canaan for a funeral and burial. Guess how long the embalming process was? Forty days! Never know what you'll find when digging deeper into the scriptures.

Number 50—Holy Spirit/Israel's Jubilee –The Number 50 is directly connected to the outpouring of the Holy Spirit and Pentecost (*Shavuot*, in Hebrew), meaning fiftieth (50th) in Greek.

Yeshua had told His followers to "tarry" and wait for the Holy Spirit whom He would send to fulfill His promise of the Comforter. How did they know how many days to tarry? The Jews *knew* the appointed times and days of God and *kept them*!

Yeshua's followers understood that they were to tarry forty-nine days from the Sabbath after Yeshua's resurrection, and on the *fiftieth day* (Pentecost/Shavuot*)*, the Comforter would come. They would have been *counting the omer* and in one accord. They would have brought thank offerings to the temple that evening and stayed the night in prayer, worshipping God and studying the Torah in preparation and anticipation of His arrival! "**Gem**"!

Seven weeks had gone by since the Sabbath after Yeshua's resurrection (forty-nine days), and when the Day of Pentecost (day fifty) had arrived, the disciples were gathered together and waiting for the promise of the Holy Spirit. According to Acts 2:1-4, we know that the Holy Spirit came in great power and glory and filled them all on that day!

Before looking at **"Jubilee,"** we need to understand the Sabbaths.

After the children of Israel first settled into Canaan, God required that after six years of sowing the land, the seventh year was to be a Sabbath of rest, meaning no sowing of crops. The seventh year was to be a Sabbath of *rest* for the *land*. It was called the "Sabbatical year." There was special consideration for the poor, the slave and the stranger. They could gather food or fruit still growing on its own accord from the previous year. Even the cattle and beasts of the land were fed.

At the end of the seventh year, called a "year of release," there was a cancelling of all debts to debtors, but this requirement was a principle that applied only to "brothers" (fellow Israelites), not to foreigners (those not belonging to Israel). It speaks of freedom, release and restoration to the people of God.

In a spiritual sense, we experience Jubilee (Yeshua) at salvation. Once we were slaves to sin, but have been set free by the blood of Yeshua. *"For whom the Son sets free is free indeed."*

Leviticus 25:9-11 refers to Israel's **Jubilee** at the end of every forty-nine years:

> *"And thou shalt number seven Sabbaths of years unto thee, seven times seven years, and the space of the seven Sabbaths of years shall be unto thee forty-nine years . . . And you shall hallow the fiftieth year, and proclaim liberty throughout all the land unto all the inhabitants thereof; it shall be a jubilee unto you, and you shall return every man unto his possession, and ye shall return every man unto his family."*

After every forty-ninth year, the **50th year** was a **Jubilee**. The trumpet (shofar) was blown at that time with a loud, long blast that rang out all over the land! Liberty was proclaimed throughout the land. Jubilee was a time of "returning to one's initial possession".

> "Thou shalt cause the trumpet of the Jubilee to sound on the 10th day of the seventh month in the day of atonement shall ye make the trumpet sound throughout all your land. And ye shall hallow the fifteeth year and proclaim liberty throughout all the land...For it is the jubilee. It shall be holy unto ye. Ye shall eat the increase thereof out of the field." (Lev. 25:12)

The above scripture speaks of the Trumpet of Jubilee sounding on the Day of Atonement. When Yeshua returns to earth on the future Day of Atonement, Israel's Jubilee will take place and Israel's possession of all the land promised to her by God (from border to border) will become hers! The Nation of Israel is a central part of the Millennium. She will bless all nations under her King at that time in fulfillment of God's plan for her and her future glory! **"Gem"**!

Jubilee (meaning "to bring back") also foreshadows God's *ultimate restoration* of **all** things in heaven and earth at His return!

It will also be a day of freedom and release (Jubilee) for all peoples from all of the suffering in this present world during the Millennium. What Satan meant for evil and man's destruction will be for made anew! Heaven and earth will be made new, and a restored Garden of Eden too! **"Gem"**! **Hallelujah!**

"For on that day, the creature itself shall be delivered from the bondage of corruption into the glorious liberty of the children of God. For we know that the whole creation groaneth and travaileth in pain together until now." (Romans 8:21-22) **Amen!**

I hope the few Numbers we have covered are enough to stress the significance of Numbers in the Word of God. Also, the importance of God's Cycles cannot be underestimated.

CHAPTER 11

PROPHETIC MESSAGES

God's *prophets* and their *messages* ring out throughout the Word of God. The **prophetic messages** of His prophets are most important and were given by the inspiration of God. Many times they were proclaimed in most *unique or unusual methods*. They proclaimed God's will to Israel and to the Gentile nations. The prophets revealed God's ways and moral precepts, warned of coming judgments for sin, revealed His plan of redemption through the coming Messiah and His Kingdom, and predicted future events.

In this Chapter, we will look at *some unique methods* and *unusual ways* used by God in getting His message across to the people through His prophets. I think you will find them very interesting! I consider each Messenger a **"Gem"**!

All of the **prophets' messages** (Old and New) spoke of the love, grace and mercy of God, as well as His judgments. God is gracious and always warns before He brings judgment. I wonder how many warnings it will take before America turns back to God, or will this nation turn back?

Why should we study the messages of the Old and New Testament prophets? They were **all** given by *inspiration of God* and therefore profitable as is all scripture.

> *"All scripture is given by inspiration of God, and is profitable for doctrine, for reproof, for correction, for instruction in righteousness. That the man of God may be perfect, thoroughly*

furnished unto all good works."(2 Timothy 3:16-17)

Sometimes the prophets spoke *straight forward pronouncements* with great conviction, and sometimes they used an allegory, or parable. God also gave open visions and dreams to many prophets, and angels assisted sometimes in revealing prophetic messages. Sometimes, God spoke directly to the prophet.

In this chapter and the following chapter, we will cover the prophets in the portion of the Old Testament called the *"Prophetic Books"*. The prophets are designated as *"major"* and *"minor"* prophets.

Isaiah through Malachi cover all of the **"Prophetic Books"**.

Isaiah, Jeremiah, Ezekiel and Daniel are called the **"major prophets"** of the *"prophetic books"* because of the length of their books.

Hosea through Malachi are called the **"minor prophets"** of the *"prophetic books"* because of the brevity of their books. Personally, I do not like designating them as "major" or "minor". They are all so important and all their messages are inspired by God.

When the Old Testament prophets reference the "Northern Kingdom" and/or the "Southern Kingdom," understand that the prophets were speaking to a divided Israel. Under the rule of King Solomon's son, Rehoboam, the secession of ten tribes (all but Benjamin and Judah) took place. The ten tribes established a separate state northwardly that became known as "Israel" with Samaria as its Capital. The remaining two tribes, Benjamin and Judah of the Southern Kingdom are called "Judah". They remained in Jerusalem, their Capital City.

Both kingdoms eventually became very wicked and were taken captive by the Assyrians and Babylonians. In the meantime, God's prophets were sent to warn both the Northern and Southern Kingdoms of God's coming judgments if they didn't repent and turn back to God. The Kingdoms had become rebellious, wicked, immoral and idolatrous by mingling with the pagans and worshipping other gods.

Isaiah which signifies "Salvation of the Lord". The prophet **Isaiah** was an example of *"playing out a prophecy"* when he was commanded to walk around in his undergarments and barefooted for three years! This depicted the humiliation the people of Judah would experience if they continued in their wicked ways. (Isa. 20:2)

Isaiah pleaded with Judah (Southern Kingdom) to turn from her wickedness, as did Ezekiel and the other prophets. God promised good things if they repented, but Isaiah told of a terrible punishment if they refused to repent.

Did you know that Isaiah prophesied around 688 B.C. that a King of Persia named Cyrus would be used by God to assure the return of a remnant of exiled Jews to Jerusalem to rebuild the temple? This prophecy was made before Cyrus was even born. The fulfillment took place in 538 B.C. (Isaiah 44:28) We have an all-knowing God!

Isaiah is called the "Messianic prophet" because he gives so much detail about the coming of Messiah. He prophesied of the birth, character, life, death, resurrection, and the second coming of the Lord. He also had visions from God, and he saw God "high and lifted up" in the Throne Room in one vision. Isaiah not only prophesied much about the coming Messiah, but also His coming rule and government:

> *"For unto us a child is born, unto us a Son is given; and the government shall be upon His shoulder, and His name shall be called Wonderful, Counselor, The Mighty God, the Everlasting Father, The Prince of Peace."*(Isaiah 9:6)

Isaiah prophesied of the Messiah's suffering and death in Chapter 53, with which most of us are familiar:

> *"And He made His grave with the wicked, and with the rich in His death . . . ."* (Isaiah 53:9)

> *"He was wounded for our transgressions, He was bruised for our iniquities, the chastisement of our peace was upon Him; and with His stripes we are healed . . . He was oppressed, and He was afflicted, yet He opened not His mouth . . . ."*(Isaiah 53: 5, 7)

Also in the 53rd Chapter of Isaiah, there is a beautiful prophetic reference to Yeshua's accomplishment in taking our sins upon Himself for our salvation:

> *"And when He sees all that has been accomplished by the anguish of His soul, He shall be satisfied; and because of what He has experienced, my righteous Servant shall make many to be counted righteous before God, for*

*He shall bear all their sins . . . He was counted as a sinner, and He bore the sins of many and He pled with God for sinners." (*Isaiah 53:11, 12)

Isaiah's vision of the Throne Room in Chapter 6 speaks of its glory: *"God was sitting upon a throne in the heavenly temple filled with His glory, and angels of fire were singing in a great antiphonal chorus, 'Holy, holy, holy is the Lord God Almighty; the whole earth is filled with His glory'."*

Such glorious singing it was! Isaiah described it as shaking the Temple to its foundations, and suddenly the entire sanctuary was filled with smoke. I can only imagine such a glorious scenario! Then Isaiah heard the voice of the Lord, saying, *"Whom shall I send, and who will go for us?"* Then, Isaiah replied, *"Here am I; send me."* Are we willing to give that answer to our Messiah in total submission like Isaiah?

In the last Chapter of Isaiah, the prophet prophesies to Israel of God's faithfulness in preserving them. *"For as the new heavens and the new earth, which I will make, shall remain before me, saith the Lord, so shall your seed and your name remain."* (Isaiah 66:22)

Jeremiah signifies "Raised up by the Lord". Jeremiah was a most compassionate and tender prophet, called the "weeping prophet." He suffered much heartbreak and shed many tears in proclaiming his people's destruction. He ministered for over 40 years without his people heeding his warnings. He was persecuted by his own people and forced to go to Egypt. He was stoned to death there.

Jeremiah played out a prophecy of the breaking of Judah. He took a clay jar in his hands and called for the elders to accompany him to a worthless plot of land. The plot of land was a place where potters dumped their broken pieces of pottery. Jeremiah emptied the jar he had taken there and smashed it to pieces, solemnly declaring that God would break Judah; that He would break them in the same manner if they continued to dishonor Him.

Jeremiah also made a miniature city and acted out the coming of enemy soldiers to besiege their city. Through Jeremiah, God promised to forgive the peoples' sins if they would repent and turn from their sins. If they did not turn from their sins, God would destroy them. Jeremiah prophesied that the people would spend seventy years in Babylon before God would bring them back to their homeland. (Jeremiah 29:10) The people were taken captive for exactly seventy years in Babylon before returning to Jerusalem.

Jeremiah prophesied the glorious coming of the Messiah and King by proclaiming the coming of the "Righteous Branch" (Yeshua). Jeremiah proclaimed that the "Righteous Branch" would be called the "Lord of Righteousness" and that His earthly Kingdom would be established in the thousand-year Millennium:

> *"Behold the days come, saith the Lord, that I will raise up unto David a Righteous Branch, and a King shall reign and prosper, and shall execute justice and righteousness in the earth."*(Jer. 23:5)

Ezekiel, our next prophet, signifies "God strengthens." He was translated in the Spirit of God many times and to many places.

> *"And he said unto me, son of man, stand upon thy feet, and I will speak unto thee. And the Spirit entered into me when he spoke unto me and set me upon my feet."* (Ezek. 2:1,2)

Ezekiel uses *metaphors* in describing Israel's backslidden condition. Through Ezekiel, God speaks of Jerusalem (Judah) as a "harlot," as a wife that commits adultery and that takes strangers as her husband. The prophet describes the Jewish nation as playing the whore with the Assyrians and worshipping its gods.

> *"How weak is thine heart, saith the Lord God, seeing thou doest all these things, the work of an imperious whorish woman . . . But as a wife that committeth adultery, which taketh strangers instead of her husband."*(Ezekiel 16:30,32)

Another "great harlot" is seen in the book of Revelation, Chapter 17 and described by Apostle John. She also represents spiritual idolatry in a false religious system in the last days. The system's practices in the last days will be much like the worshipping of idols and false gods in ancient Assyria and Babylon. The harlot is riding on the back of the beast in the book of Revelation. Most scholars believe the beast is the one-world system led by the antichrist, and the harlot is a false religion system. The two will form a church-state coalition as in the days of the old Holy Roman Empire.

> *"So He carried me away in the Spirit into the wilderness, and I saw a woman sit upon a scarlet colored beast* [antichrist]*, full of names of blasphemy having seven heads and ten horns*

> *. . . And upon her forehead was a name written, mystery Babylon, the great, the mother of harlots and abominations of the earth* [false religious system]*."* (Rev. 17:3,5)

Ezekiel was a priest and prophet in the Temple at Jerusalem (Southern Kingdom) before being taken captive to Babylon by King Nebuchadnezzar. Daniel was also taken captive in Babylon. Ezekiel was about twenty-five years old while Daniel was only a teenager. Ezekiel had many *visions.* This prophet foretold judgment upon both kingdoms, Judah and Israel. He also foretold of judgments upon enemy nations, and his role as watchman for Israel. God began giving Ezekiel visions while he was captive in Babylon.

The familiar vision and prophecy in Ezekiel 37 of the dry bones coming together to form an army speaks of the Jews' re-gathering and returning to Israel as a nation. This vision seemed almost impossible after their scattering throughout the world and especially after the Holocaust. I believe this could also have been a vision of the Holocaust. The vision also revealed to Ezekiel that the Nation of Israel would rise up again. The Jews not only survived, but became a nation once again in 1948 and are a strong nation again today. What a mighty God we serve!

Ezekiel, however, did not see the bones at first with a spirit, but with only flesh. As captives and slaves, their future looked dismal even then. In the vision, after God's breath was breathed into them, the *Ruach HaKodesh* (*Ruach* meaning "breath" or "wind") they lived. I believe this was a prophecy of many believing Jews receiving the Holy Spirit (*Ruach HaKodesh*). Did Ezekiel also see the outpouring of the Holy Spirit (*Ruach*

HaKodesh) at *Shavuot* (Pentecost) in the New Testament? I believe he did!

Ezekiel not only prophesied against all of Israel (both Kingdoms) for their rebellion, but he prophesied of their restoration and the coming "Prince" (Messiah) who would rule over His Messianic Kingdom. The promised Prince was born about six hundred years after Ezekiel told of His coming. Ezekiel includes many chapters on the last days and the glorious Temple of the Millennium in Chapters 40-48. In Chapters 38-39, according to Ezekiel, the war of "Gog and Magog" is the next forthcoming war of this generation.

A most dramatic and effective presentation of the prophetic message of a prophet was the "act" of playing out a prophecy. It signified that Ezekiel bore the guilt of the iniquity of Israel and Judah.

God commanded Ezekiel to lie on one side for 390 days, each day representing a year (390 years) of punishment for the House of Israel (the Ten Tribes). Then, he was to lie on the other side for 40 days representing 40 years of punishment for Judah (two tribes, Judah and Benjamin). Ezekiel laid on each side only certain hours of the day. Ezekiel was also struck dumb, shut himself up in his house, and shaved his head and his beard (shameful for a priest and prophet).

Ezekiel also had a vision of the Glory-Cloud of God's presence departing from the Temple of the Nation of Israel.

He saw the Glory-Cloud (God's manifest presence) over the Cherubim on the Ark of the Covenant in the Holy of Holies leave. He saw the Cherubim lift up their wings and fly away. It depicted that the presence of God no longer rested in the

Temple of the Jewish Nation because the nation had turned away from Him.

> "Then the glory of the Lord departed from off the threshold of the house..." (Ezek. 10:18)

God was saddened to withdraw His Glory in the Temple from Israel because of their sin and rebellion. He had given them so many chances to repent and turn from their idolatrous ways, but they would not. It sounds like America as she grows more wicked and rebellious every day. If we ever needed to pray for America to turn back to God, it is now.

God's presence would not be seen filling the Temple in Jerusalem as it did in Moses' Tabernacle or in Solomon's Temple. The last Temple, which was destroyed in 70 A.D, did not see God's Glory-Cloud appear over the Ark of the Covenant in the Holy of Holies either.

The removal of God's *Sh'chinah* Glory from the Nation of Israel, however, was only for a time. God has not turned His back on Israel forever. He still has a plan for the Nation of Israel and God has never stopped loving the first Nation of people with whom He made a covenant.

By no means has God abandoned His plans for yet a glorious return of a remnant of the Jewish nation during the last days. At their return, the Glory-Cloud will again appear in the Temple in Jerusalem, not the literal third temple, but the glorious Temple during the Millennium. From there, the *Sh'chinah* glory will never depart again! **"Gem"**!

Ezekiel also gave a promise of God to the whole House of Israel: *"Thus shall they know that I the Lord their God am with them, and that they, even the house of Israel, are my people."*

Ezekiel ends with the prophecy of the extending of the reestablished boundaries of the land of Israel during the time of the Messianic Age and Israel's future glory!

"...And the name of the City from that day shall be, **"***the Lord is there"***. Glory!*

We must not forget **Daniel.** He was the prophet out of the Tribe of Judah. His name signifies "God's judgment". He was taken captive by the Babylonians when he was only a teenager. God called him "greatly beloved." He had dreams and visions and was known as "interpreter of dreams". He stayed true to God during the seventy years of Israel's captivity in Babylon.

Babylon was a wicked pagan nation with an atmosphere of loose morals, standards and idolatry. Daniel and Ezekiel were true to God when evil was all around, and they never defiled themselves by partaking of its evil. They did not worship its gods or bow down to its pagan King, Nebuchadnezzar. They had no fear of man. They knew and trusted God with all of their heart. What great faith and steadfastness they possessed! May we be found faithful and steadfast in these last days as well!

God showed **Daniel** in a vision the four earthly kingdoms that would rule before the establishment of the Everlasting Kingdom, and the coming of Yeshua who would destroy the last evil kingdom.

Daniel 12 prophesies of the "times of the end" and great tribulation. Many will suffer persecution, prison and death, especially the remnant of all Israel. The remnant will be faithful servants and witnesses for their Messiah in the last days. Daniel saw their names being written in the Lamb's book of life. Here is a word about the faithful remnant in the last days: *"Those who are wise will shine like the brightness of the heavens, and those who lead many to righteousness, like the stars forever and ever."*(Daniel 12:3)

King Nebuchadnezzar had a terrifying dream while Daniel was captive in Babylon. The King was so terrified by the dream when he awoke that he couldn't' remember what it was he had dreamed. When his magicians and astrologers could not tell him what he had dreamed or give an interpretation of the dream, he became very angry. He threatened to have them destroyed and would have if Daniel had not come forth to interpret the King's dream.

Daniel had prayed and asked God to show him what the dream was and its interpretation. God answered Daniel's prayer, for he was a righteous man, and God's word tells us that the prayer of a righteous man availeth much.

Daniel told the King that none of his wise men could interpret the dream, but then said to Nebuchadnezzar: *"But there is a God in heaven that revealeth secrets, and maketh known to the King what shall be in the latter days."* Daniel then proceeded to interpret the dream. (Daniel 2:28)

Nebuchadnezzar's pagan world was made up of many images and statutes, so that's the way he saw the four Kingdoms in his dream, like the huge statute of a man: the head of fine gold (Babylon), the breast and arms of silver (Medo-Persian Empire), its belly and thighs of brass (Greek Empire), and its legs of iron (Roman Empire). Its two legs represented its two capitals, one in the east (Constantinople) and one in the west (Rome). The 10 toes also represented the breaking up of the old great Roman Empire into 10 regions. These 10 regions were later ruled by a church-state coalition called the Holy Roman Empire. The statute's two feet and ten toes of iron and clay is said to represent the revived Holy Roman Empire in the last days.

> *"And whereas thou sawest the feet and toes, part of potters' clay, and part of iron, the Kingdom shall be divided; but there shall be in it of the strength of the iron, foreasmuch as thou sawest the iron mixed with miry clay. And as the toes of the feet were part of iron, and part of clay, so the Kingdom shall be partly broken."* (Daniel 2:41-42)

It is believed by many bible scholars that the feet of iron and clay mixed (in our present day) could be church-state rule again as in the days of the Holy Roman Empire. Could iron represent the one-world government under the revived Holy Roman Empire and clay represent the one-world religious system? Are we seeing the stage being set today for a world system like the Holy Roman Empire?

The Roman Empire and the Roman Church, even though they formed an alliance, could never really "cleave" to one another. I think it is interesting that the word, "cleave" in reference to the "iron and clay" of the last earthly Kingdom seen in Daniel 2:43 states: *". . . but they shall not cleave one to another."*

We have already seen the global government in place, and are aware that the charter for a universal religious system is in the process of being written. All faiths would come together under one religious system and be required by law to abide by its Charter. There is also discussion today of a one-world government with all nations being divided into ten categorized regions. Under this system, each region would have a Chief Leader (Ruler). Very interesting!

In relation to Nebuchadnezzar's dream, the statute he saw was only one part of his dream. The King saw a stone hewn out of a mountainside supernaturally (without hands) and hurling toward the statute. It crushed the feet of iron and clay, smashing it into pieces. Then the whole statute collapsed into a heap of iron, brass, silver and gold. All of its pieces were so crushed that they were blown away by the wind as chaff. The Stone symbolized Yeshua who crushes the last earthly Kingdom to pieces.

After the Stone *symbolizing* Yeshua crushes the last earthly Kingdom, Yeshua sets up His Heavenly Kingdom which shall never be destroyed. *"His Kingdom shall not be left to other people again, and it shall stand forever."*(Daniel 2:44)

King Nebuchadnezzar was so grateful to have his dream interpreted, he said: *"Truly, O Daniel, the King said, Your God is the God of gods, ruler of Kings, the revealer of mysteries, because He told you this secret."*

In **Daniel's prayer** of thanksgiving to God for the interpretation of the dream, he praised God, saying, *"Blessed be the name of God forever and ever, for He alone has all wisdom and all power, and He changeth the times and the seasons; He removeth Kings, and setteth up Kings; world events are under His control . . ."* What a comforting word for us in these last days!

In the first year of Belshazzar, King of Babylon, **Daniel** had a vision in the night of four beasts, each representing a kingdom. They were the same kingdoms of the earth as in Nebuchadnezzar's dream. Daniel saw the kingdoms from God's view as "beasts" (God's view of earthly kingdoms) rather than a golden statute or idol, Nebuchadnezzar's mindset and lifestyle of idol worship. **Gem!**

The four beasts seen by Daniel were: (1) lion with eagle's wings (symbol of Babylon); (2) bear and a two-horned Ram (symbol of coalition of Medes and Persians); (3) a four-headed leopard with four wings (symbol of Greece, Alexander the Great and his four Generals); (4) the ten-horned terrible beast with iron teeth (symbol of the Roman Empire); and a "little horn" (believed to describe Antiochus IV of Syria, a tyrant, who desecrated the Temple at Jerusalem).

The "little horn" arose from the ten-horned beast. Horns in God's word usually mean "power"; the more horns, the more power. (Daniel 7:1-7)

Some bible scholars today see the four beasts in the Book of Revelation as the following four nations (Kingdoms) ruling in the *last days*: Great Britain (represented by the lion) and the United States (represented by the wings of an eagle) who broke away from Great Britain; Russia (represented by the bear); Germany (represented by the leopard); and the revived Roman Empire (represented by the ten-horned terrible beast).

According to Daniel, all nations under the last-day revived Roman Empire will be represented by ten rulers. Right now there are 28 nations in the European Union. Could they be pared down to 10 in the near future? Many believe that Germany will head up the organization of the ten rulers. We do see Germany rising in economic and political power today. As prophesied in Daniel 7, Revelation 13 and Revelation 17, the beastly empire will consist of "ten Kings" (Rulers).

Daniel continued to ask God about the fourth, most ferocious ten-horned beast with iron teeth which horns he saw in *two phases*. A "little horn" arose from this beast twice and at different times.

The first horn, believed to be Antiochus IV, and the other "little horn" (the last-day antichrist) came out of the same ten-headed beast (Roman Empire and Revived Holy Roman Empire). Both antichrists are cruel and brutal. The second last-day antichrist is seen as *exceedingly* dreadful, very brutal and shocking.

Daniel prophesied that this ferocious beast will be the fourth and last world power with ten Kings (Rulers) over it, and the latter "little horn" (antichrist) out of the last Ten-King Kingdom will defy the Most High God. He will be more terrible than all the other Kings, who will devour the whole earth, treading it down and breaking it into pieces.

> "... I saw in the night visions, and behold a fourth beast, dreadful and terrible, and strong exceedingly; and it had great iron teeth; it devoured and brake in pieces and stamped the residue with the feet of it; and it was diverse from all the beasts that were before it; and it had ten horns."(Daniel 7:7)

> "I beheld, and the same horn made war with the saints, and prevailed against them; Until the Ancient of Days came, and judgment was given

> to the saints of the most High; and the time came that the saints possessed the Kingdom."(Daniel 7:21-22)

The last-day antichrist is also described in Daniel 11:21: *"And in his estate shall stand up a vile person, to whom they shall not give the honor of the Kingdom; but he shall come in peaceably, and obtain the Kingdom by flatteries."*

According to Daniel, during the "Great Tribulation" (last half of a 7-year period), the antichrist will set up an image or idol of himself in the third Temple in Jerusalem. Daniel calls this the "abomination of desolation." The antichrist will also cause the animal sacrifices to cease mid-way the seven-year covenant/agreement period.

> *"He will confirm a covenant with many for one seven. He will put an end to sacrifice and offering. And on a wing of the temple, he will set up an abomination that causes desolation, until the end that is decreed is poured out on him* [antichrist].*"(Daniel 9:27)

Evidently, the conditions of the seven-year covenant between the Jews and the Palestinians will be broken after three and a half years. Within a few days of that time, the Great Tribulation will begin. It appears that the agreement will allow Israel to rebuild the third temple on the Temple Mount. The Jews will be able to resume animal sacrifices for a time prior to the beginning of the Great Tribulation. The Great Tribulation ends with the second coming of Yeshua! (Daniel 9:24-26)

Daniel had many visions and foretold the first and second coming of the Messiah. Daniel saw the succession of the worldly kingdoms and their Rulers, and events during and at the end of the Great Tribulation.

In Daniel 12, the Great Tribulation period is described by Daniel as a *"time of distress such as has not happened from the beginning of nations until now."*

Many things revealed to Daniel of the last days were also revealed to the Apostle John in the book of Revelation. The Great Tribulation period is referred to as "forty-two months" in the book of Revelation rather than "years." The comparison of the last-day events in Daniel, Ezekiel and Apostle John in the Book of Revelation are amazing to say the least!

Daniel not only saw the Son of Man coming in the clouds, he saw forward to the setting up of the 1,000-year Millennium. Talk about God revealing secret things to His faithful servant!

Daniel prayed often and walked to please God in the midst of a wicked, immoral nation, refusing to bow to the King or its idols. Could we be nearing a time when we will be required to make a stand for God in the midst of a wicked nation? Will we be able to refuse to bow or take the mark of the one-world government under the last antichrist? If so, may there be many like Daniel!

Daniel prophesied that the little horn's power (last-day antichrist) will be taken away by Yeshua. The anti-christ's kingdom will be destroyed at the end of the Great Tribulation. Daniel is told by the Lord that the kingdoms of the earth will then be turned over to the saints of the Most High. The Most High's Kingdom will be an everlasting Kingdom!

> *"And the Kingdom and the dominion, and the greatness of the Kingdom under the whole heaven shall be given to the saints of the Most High, whose Kingdom is an everlasting Kingdom, and all rulers will worship and obey Him."* (Daniel 7:27)

Isaiah prophesied that the time of the end would be a *"time cruel both with wrath and fierce anger."* (Isa. 13) Some Bible scholars believe that the New Testament believers will be "raptured" at the beginning of the seven-year period or that they will escape the last half, the Great Tribulation.

Jeremiah also referred to the Great Tribulation period as *"the time of Jacob's trouble,"* and he added that Israel (a faithful remnant) would be saved out of it. (Jer. 30:4-7)

In Matthew 24, Yeshua refers to the *first half* of the Tribulation period as the "beginning of sorrows." Then, He proceeds to describe the Great Tribulation up until His coming at the end, "immediately after the tribulation".

I have one question about a pre-tribulation or mid-tribulation "rapture." What if that is wrong and believers do not escape the seven-year tribulation? I will share my belief in a later chapter.

The stage is certainly set for the seven-year tribulation period to begin in our day. Some Bible scholars believe we have already entered the 7-year period.

Israel has become a Nation and is back in her own land. That had to happen before a covenant/ agreement could be made. The Jewish people, against all odds, have once again become a strong nation after nearly being annihilated so many times. In "one day" (1948) they were declared a nation called Israel just as Isaiah prophesied thousands of years ago. God's hand has certainly always been upon His beloved Jewish people.

Outside of the "prophetic books" of the *Old Testament*, let's close this Chapter by looking at the prophetic message of John the Baptist in the *New Testament*.

John the Baptist was the first great prophet in the New Testament. He was the *"voice of one crying in the wilderness, 'Make straight the way of the Lord' . . . The next day John seeth Yeshua coming unto him, and saith, 'Behold the Lamb of God which taketh away the sin of the world.'"* John the Baptist lived to *see* and *baptize* the One of whom he prophesied! **"Gem"**! (John 1:23,29)

Yeshua was and is the greatest Prophet. Look at this amazing prophecy in Deuteronomy of the One likened unto the great prophet, Moses:

> *"I will raise them up a prophet from among their brethren, like unto thee, and will put my words in His mouth; and He shall speak unto them all that I command Him."*(Deut. 18:18)

All of the prophets spoke with many different methods, but all of their messages were given by inspiration of God for our benefit. Let us keep the faith, be true to God and heed His messages through His prophets, especially Yeshua!

Let us look forward to the second coming of the greatest Prophet, Yeshua. The following words of wisdom and encouragement are found in the book of Titus.:

"For God's grace, which brings deliverance, has appeared to all people. It teaches us to renounce godlessness and worldly pleasures, and to live self-controlled, upright and godly lives NOW, in this age; while continuing to expect the blessed fulfillment of our certain hope, which is the appearing of the Sh'chinah of our Great God and the appearing of our Deliverer, Yeshua the Messiah!" (Titus 2:11-13)
Amen and Amen!

CHAPTER 12

THE TWELVE MESSENGERS

In this Chapter, we will look at the **Twelve Messengers** of God who are called "**minor prophets**" of the "Prophetic Books" of the Word. Each Book is a **"gem"** in itself!

Through the words of these prophets, as with all of the prophets of God, we learn more about God, His ways, His character, and His redemptive plan. Over and over again, God's messengers (prophets) foretold the coming of Yeshua, the hope of salvation for all mankind. All of the prophets' messages contained *God's grace, mercy and salvation*.

Let's look at the "**gems**" found in the messages of these "twelve" from Joel through Malachi, and how they still carry a word for us today.

Remember, all prophets relayed God's messages for the people's benefit *locally* and of *future events* for generations.

Since I cannot include everything in each book of the twelve prophets, I will condense each book into a short-story version, highlighting some of its main message or theme. Even though the prophets boldly pronounced God's word to the people, many of the people refused to listen and obey.

To me, God used one of the *most unusual methods* in relaying His message to Israel through His prophet, **Hosea.** His name means "to save". Hosea was sent to Israel, the Northern Kingdom. The method God used to relay His message through Hosea was by a family *metaphor*. God spoke His message directly to the prophet, for the first words of this book are:

"The word of the Lord that came to Hosea . . . .". Hosea was commanded by God to take an unchaste woman as a wife, who committed adultery and gave herself to other men.

The book of Hosea employs a family metaphor (husband and unfaithful wife) to express the relationship between God and Israel. Israel was the unfaithful wife committing spiritual adultery by worshipping other gods. She forgot and failed to see the goodness and faithfulness of her husband, God. This is a love story allegorically portraying God's unconditional love for Israel. It also speaks of God's unconditional love for all of His people.

Hosea's *theme* is the unconditional love of God. Hosea was a prophet to the Northern Kingdom, called Israel, but also had messages for the Southern Kingdom, called Judah. The time was during the reign of Jeroboam the Second. Jeroboam was a very wicked ruler. He set up golden calves for nature worship, child sacrifices and other evils. The Israelites became a part of his evil empire, turning away from God and worshipping false gods and becoming part of the pagans' evil, wicked ways.

As we know, Hosea was instructed by God to take a harlot for a wife whose name was Gomer. Even though his wife was unfaithful to him, God instructed Hosea to love her unconditionally. God used Hosea's tragic marriage to show Israel that He would always love her. God had remained faithful to the marriage covenant at Mt. Sinai as she (Israel) went a-whoring with other gods. God told Hosea to go and love his adulterous wife even though she was unfaithful. The following are God's words to Hosea concerning Gomer:

> *"The Lord said to Hosea, Go take unto thee a*
> *wife of whoredoms and children of whoredoms;*

> *for the land hath committed great whoredoms, departing from the Lord." (Hosea 1:2)*

> *"Then said the Lord unto me, go yet, love a woman beloved of her friend, yet an adulteress, according to the love of the Lord toward the children of Israel, who look to other gods, and love flagons of wine."(Hosea 3:1)*

Through Hosea, God pleaded for backslidden Israel to return unto Him. *"Come, and let us return unto the Lord, for He hath torn, and He will heal us; He hath smitten, and He will bind us up."(Hosea 6:1))*

Hosea reminded the people many times of God's love and that it was He who had blessed them and provided their abundance and prosperity. He warned them that their failure to repent and return to their God would force Him to impose judgment upon them. God even warned the people through Hosea that He would use their enemies as His instrument of judgment.

Hosea's message is of Israel's abandonment of God by her rebellion and spiritual idolatry. Hosea warned Israel (Northern Kingdom) of her apostasy and unfaithfulness to God who loved her in spite of her unfaithfulness. Hosea called for her to repent and return unto her husband (God).

Over and over again, God forgave Israel's backsliding and was eventually left with no choice but to bring judgment. Israel is eventually punished by God, and become captives of the Assyrians. However, allegorically speaking in this story, Hosea also prophesied of a future reconciliation between God and His wife, Israel, a time when she will love God and remain a faithful wife.

> *"Afterward shall the children of Israel return, and seek the Lord their God, and David their King, and shall fear the Lord and His goodness in the latter days."* (Hosea 3:5)

In this story, Hosea marries Gomer, a harlot, in obedience to God. God even told Hosea what to name his children to further emphasize the prophetic message to Israel of her unfaithfulness:

(1) "Jezreel," his firstborn, was to be named after the old battlefield on which the Kingdom (Israel) was about to fall. Jezreel means the "punishment is come." This foretold the breaking up of Israel and its power as an independent Kingdom in the Valley of Jezreel about 25 years later when they were conquered by the Assyrians.
(2) Then there was a daughter (who may not have been fathered by Hosea, to be named, "Lo-ruhamah," meaning, "no more mercy."
(3) The third child (who may not have been fathered by Hosea either), was a son, to be named, "Lo-ammi," meaning "no longer my people, or not mine."

God also spoke through Hosea that one day in the future Israel would again prosper and become a great nation. Then, instead of saying to them, "I will have no more mercy" or "You are no longer my people," He will say, "You are my sons, children of the living God."

The names of Lo-ruhamah and Lo-ammi are repeated in Chapter 2:1, but without the "Lo" part of the name, which predicts the later time when Israel would become God's faithful people. God will say, "I will have mercy" and "You are my people."

Gomer came to a place that she was no longer desired by her men friends and was placed on a slavery block to be sold for practically nothing (of little worth), but Hosea bought her for a price. He took her back once again even though she had played the harlot. Hosea was commanded by God to take her back, forgive her and love her. This portrays God's forgiveness, mercy and love for Israel who kept breaking her covenant (vow) with God.

> *"Then the Lord said to me, "Go, and get your wife again and bring her back to you and love her, even though she loves adultery. For the Lord still loves Israel though she has turned to other gods and offered them choice gifts."*

Hosea prophesied that Israel would return to God and call Him *"Ishi." "Ishi"* means "my husband" instead of *"Baali"* which means "my master." Normally, Gomer would have called Hosea *"Baali"* (her master) after being purchased from the slavery block where she was being sold. Hosea said, however, that she was to call him *"Ishi"* (my husband) for he would love her as a husband anyway. This was *prophetic* of God receiving Israel back after her captivity, and her eventual restoration and faithfulness to Him in the last days.

Concerning the reconciliation between God and the Jewish Nation, we find this prophecy:

> *"And I will betroth thee unto me forever; yea, I will betroth thee unto me in righteousness, and in judgment, and in loving kindness, and in mercies. I will even betroth thee unto me in faithfulness; and thou shalt know the Lord."* (Hosea 2:19-20)

This is a beautiful *allegorical love story* of unconditional love and it has a happy ending. It is a picture of backslidden Israel returning to accept her Messiah and becoming part of the faithful bride in the last days.

Hosea prophesied of the time when other nations would be called the "people of God." Did you know that Hosea prophesied many years ago that we Gentiles would be called the "people of God"? Look at the following scripture quoted from Hosea by Paul in the New Testament, meaning the extended gospel to the Gentiles.

Hosea is quoted in the New Testament by Paul:

> *"Remember what the prophecy of Hosea says? There God says that He will find other children, who are not from the Jewish family, and He will love them, though no one had ever loved them before. And the heathen of whom it once was said, 'You are not my people,' shall be called 'sons of the Living God.'"* (Romans 9:25) What a loving God He is of all of His people!

In Hosea, Chapter 14, we see a powerful call to the backslidden Israel to repent, and to all backsliders: *"Return, O Israel unto the Lord, thy God; for thou hast fallen by thine iniquity."*

> *"Bring your petition. Come to the Lord and say, O Lord, take away our sins; be gracious to us and receive us, and we will offer you the sacrifice of praise. Assyria cannot save us, nor can our strength in battle; never again will we call the idols we have made 'our gods'; for in you alone, O Lord, the fatherless find mercy."*
> Amen.

Hosea's last words speak a message to us all: *"Those who are wise understand these things; those who are discerning know them. For the ways of the Lord are right, and the upright walk in them, but transgressors shall stumble in them."*

There is an eerie parallel between Israel during Hosea's days and America today. America has removed God in so many ways from our country. America has backslidden so far from her Provider who blessed and prospered her. America has already begun in forcing God to impose His judgments. Why? Like Israel, America has forgotten her Maker. *"For Israel hath forgotten her Maker . . . ."* (Hosea 8:14)

> *"O Israel, thou hast destroyed thyself; but in Me is thine help."* (Hosea 13:9) Yes, only in God alone is our hope for America.

In Hosea, God continues to call Israel to repent. He tells her that He will forgive and take away all iniquity and receive her back with love.

> Hosea said to Israel: *"Take with you words, and turn to the Lord; say unto Him, take away all iniquity, and receive us graciously, so we will render the offerings of our lips."* (Hosea 14:2)

Then, God's reply: *"I will heal their backsliding. I will love them freely; for mine anger is turned away from them."*

This book of Hosea is an example of the backslider who repents, returns to God and receives mercy and forgiveness. Pray for our nation to return to God!

Joel: "Jehovah is God" is the meaning of Joel's name. His main theme and focus was "the Day of the Lord" and His coming at the end of the age. He also forewarns of coming judgment upon Judah, the Southern Kingdom of Israel for their sins.

Joel gives a call to the people to return to the Holy One of Israel with fasting, prayer and lamenting. This warning could certainly be for America today. We are witnessing the judgments of God already. He is beginning to shake many nations including our nation, and it is only the beginning.

Joel prophesied of a devastating plague of locusts that would strip the land bare, destroy the grain, the fruit trees and grapevines. There would be no rain, so that even the animals would suffer as the land and rivers would be dry. He warned the people to repent and turn back to God. Locust plagues were a natural phenomenon and a part of Israel's history. In times of Israel's backslidings God used locust plagues as a call to repentance.

In Joel's prophecy of the locusts, some scholars say it could also have referred to invading enemy armies from the north since locusts usually come from the south. Joel describes four species of locusts: cutter-locusts, swarmer-locusts, hopper-locusts and stripper-locusts. These could be an allegory for four future conquerors of Israel: the Babylonians, Persians, Greeks and Romans. The plague of locusts could also be prophetic of the last days typical of those found in Revelation 9:1-11.

> "And there came out of the smoke locusts upon the earth; and unto them was given power, as the scorpions of the earth have power."(Rev. 9:3) Some believe these are spiritual demon armies loosed from *Sheol*.

Joel prophesied that in the last days a great outpouring of the Holy Spirit (*Ruach HaKodesh*, Hebrew) would take place prior to the day of the Lord's judgment upon enemy nations. Joel also prophesied of God's great mercy to "whosoever calls on the name of the Lord." In the New Testament, Peter quotes Joel :

> "But this is that which was spoken by the prophet Joel; And it shall come to pass in the last days, saith God, I will pour out my Spirit upon all flesh; and your sons and daughters shall prophesy, and your young men shall see visions, and your old men shall dream dreams; . . . The sun shall be turned into darkness, and the moon into blood, before that great and notable day of the Lord come: And it shall come to pass, that whosoever shall call on the name of the Lord shall be saved." (Acts 2:17-21; Joel 3:15-16)

For Joel, it was a prophecy that meant God's judgment on the enemies of his day. But Joel also saw beyond his time to the end times. He prophesied of the last great harvest of souls before the great battle of Armageddon. God showed Joel the largest and strongest armies ever to be assembled against

Israel. At that time, God will utter His voice from Jerusalem, and the heavens and earth will be shaken. The wicked will be destroyed, and Yeshua, the Lion of Judah, will roar out of Zion, His holy mountain, to rule and reign.

> *"Multitudes, multitudes in the valley of decision [judgment], for the day of the Lord is near . . . the sun and the moon shall be darkened, and the stars shall withdraw their shining. The Lord shall also roar out of Zion, and utter His voice from Jerusalem; and the heavens and earth shall shake; but the Lord will be the hope of His people, and the strength of the children of Israel. So shall you know that I am the Lord your God dwelling in Zion, my holy mountain, then shall Jerusalem be holy."* (Joel 3:14-17).Amen!

As we see the signs of the last days approaching in our generation, let us apply the words of Joel:

> *"And rend your heart, and not your garments, and turn unto the Lord your God; for He is gracious and merciful, slow to anger, and of great kindness, and anxious not to punish you."* (Joel 2:13)

Amos, prophet of Judah means "Burden" or "Burden Bearer." He carried a great burden for Israel (Northern Kingdom) and the Southern Kingdom (Judah). He was from Tekoa, a wilderness area about eight miles from Jerusalem. David sought refuge from Saul there. Amos was a herdsman, a dresser of sycamore trees and a man of the fields. Although Amos was from Judah, the Southern Kingdom, he was sent to Bethel, which was across the border in Israel. Amos had no prophetic background, but God gave him a strong call to go to Bethel with His message of forthcoming judgment. Bethel was the cultic center of calf-worship and wickedness under Jeroboam II.

Amos began to preach in Bethel, the first city of consequences for the peoples' wickedness. He also preached of judgment concerning several other nations that would follow in the future. Amos prophesied of a future restoration for all of Israel and the future glory of the coming of the Messiah and His Kingdom.

The Northern Kingdom under King Jeroboam II had enlarged and Israel was in a state of prosperity, but brazen in its idolatry and moral rottenness. It was a land of stealing, oppression, adultery, robbery and murder. It had been about 200 years since the ten tribes had set up the Northern Kingdom with calf-worship and Baal worship. They had waxed worse and worse, and Israel's accountability was greater than the enemy nations. Israel had had greater privileges and knowledge of the Word of God and therefore held more accountable.

It appears that America may find itself in the same category as old Israel if it doesn't turn back to God. No other nation on this earth besides the Nation of Israel has had the great privileges and knowledge of God's Word than America. No other nation has been more blessed by God either.

God had already sent Elijah, Elisha and Jonah to proclaim God's warning to the Israelites, but they ignored the warning. The people were steeped so deep into idolatry and wickedness that their hearts had been hardened. That is a grave danger of not being able to return to God. God sent Amos in a final effort to save Israel from destruction. Hosea was a coworker with Amos and may have been in Bethel at the time of Amos's visit who was also warning the Nation.

*"Prepare to meet your Go*d" for "*He is coming to judge*" became the theme of the warning. The people seemed to be willing to offer sacrifices to God, but not to reform and mend their heathen lifestyle. Amos warned them of God's judgment for their sins and of intolerable sufferings about to befall them, but to no avail. May it not be so for America!

God also warns before He brings judgment. Have you seen the warning signs in America in 9/11, the floods, hurricanes, fires, extreme weather, tornadoes, etc.? Prophets of today are calling for America to repent, turn back to God and His principles. Seemingly, it appears to be to no avail. America seems to be waxing worse and worse. Surely this is a time for believers to wake up and cry out to God for this Nation to turn around. We have already begun to see His judgment upon America, but it is only the beginning if we don't turn around soon.

Amos lamented under a great burden for all of Israel and interceded for them over and over again. God forgave and relented many times, but finally Israel's final warning came. Amos had previously seen a vision of locusts descending on Israel as approaching judgment. He interceded for Israel, and God relented.

Amos also had a vision of a great fire consuming Israel that would have destroyed vegetation, people, and creek beds. Amos' intercession stayed God's judgment once again. God then showed Amos a "plumbline" and said: "*Behold I hold a plumbline in the midst of my people Israel: I will not again pass by them anymore. I will no longer turn away from punishing* . . .

." That would mean Israel's doom and neighboring nations as well.

God also showed Amos a basket of summer fruit, which was a symbol that Israel was ripe for ruin, and their future captivity foretold. Amos reiterates their sins of greed, dishonesty, and mercilessness towards the poor. Their captivity came to pass within thirty years when judgment came through the Assyrians. The fierce and cruel warriors captured the Northern Kingdom, deported its citizens, scattering the ten tribes of Israel which ended the ten tribes as a nation. Are we headed for the falling of our great nation?

It is sad to admit that America has become like the rotten summer fruit ripe as we see ungodly, heathen practices and sexual immorality. Wickedness and violence is taking precedence in our nation over God's principles and His law. TV and computers in some cases have become one of the worst idols in America. Even commercials on T.V. are filled with abominations to God. It is a crucial time for believers to guard their minds and eyes.

Amos helps us to understand that God's judgment comes to those who live *contrary to His Word*. On the other hand, Amos shows that God is longsuffering and merciful, giving space for repentance before administering punishment, especially when the righteous are interceding. Amos shows the importance of *intercession*. It does stay the hand of God for a time.

Amos's last words speak a message of hope and encouragement to Israel that God would gather them back to their land in the future. He promised to restore them as a nation, never to be scattered or driven out of their land again.

We are witnessing that ingathering and their return today. The Jews in Israel will never be driven out of their land and scattered again.

> *"And I will plant them upon their land, and they shall no more be pulled up out of their land which I have given them, saith the Lord thy God."*(Amos 9:15).

Amos also saw the glorious days of Yeshua's Kingdom when *all the Body of Believers will dwell in Jerusalem* in the land of Israel. Hallelujah!

> *"After this I will return, and will build again the tabernacle of David, which is fallen down; and I will build again the ruins thereof, and I will set it up: That the residue of men might seek the Lord, and all the Gentiles, upon whom my name is called, saith the Lord, who doeth all these things. Known unto God are all His works from the beginning of the world."*(Amos 15:16-18)

Obadiah's name means "Servant of the Lord." Obadiah was from the Southern Kingdom. His *theme* was the "doom of Edom" and the Edomites, descendants of Esau. Petra, carved high in a huge cliff, was its capital. Even though the Edomites were relatives of the people of Judah and Israel, they sided with the enemy.

Obadiah prophesied that the Edomites would be "cut off forever" and "be as though they had not been" and that the "Kingdom of Judah's God would prevail." Obadiah warned Edom that God was about to avenge Judah for the treachery and cruel treatment perpetrated upon them by the Edomites. Pleasing the Babylonians by bringing calamities upon their brother Judah would bring swift and final judgment from God. Edom laughed at Judah's calamity and even ambushed Jewish escapees and turned them over to the Babylonians.

Obadiah brought words of encouragement to Judah that a remnant would be saved, and the Kingdom of Judah's God would prevail. Many believe that the Jews will flee to Petra for safety from their enemies in the last days. Petra still exists today.

Because of Edom's treatment to Judah, the Edomites would suffer a cruel fate. Historical research indicates that the Nabateans overran the region of Edom and destroyed the Edomites. They seemed to have disappeared from history after that. They lost their land, their society and bloodline as descendants of Isaac. If only they had repented and loved their brothers, they could have shared in the blessings of Jacob and received an everlasting inheritance.

Obadiah ends the book by *foretelling a restoration and ideal future for Israel:* "*I will restore my people Israel . . . and I will plant them upon their soil, nevermore to be uprooted from the soil I have given them.*"

The recognition of Israel as a Nation in 1948 was the first step in the fulfillment of this prophecy. We look forward to the final return and restoration of the Nation of Israel to her God.

> "*But upon Mount Zion shall be deliverance, and there shall be holiness; and the house of Jacob shall possess their possessions.*"(Obadiah 17)

Speaking to the enemies of Israel, God said through Obadiah:

> *"For the day of the Lord is near upon all the heathen; as thou hast done unto Israel, so it will be done to you. Your acts will return upon your own head!"*(Obadiah 1:15)

Obadiah declared that the enemy nations would be destroyed as stubble is burned, but that the Israelites would return and be victorious. It sure sounds like the same fate that the endtime enemy nations of Israel will meet at the battle of Armageddon yet to be fulfilled.

> In Genesis 12:3, we read: *"Those who bless Israel shall be blessed, and those who curse Israel shall be cursed; and in that nation shall all families of the earth be blessed."*

Be careful, America! Right now as I write this book, America is making deals with Iran and other enemy nations of Israel. He who blesses Israel is blessed. He who curses Israel will be cursed. I pray America will continue to heed this message!

Jonah's name means "A Dove." The *theme* is a mission to Nineveh, the capital of the Assyrian empire and Israel's enemy. It is in narrative form, a story of an errand of mercy to Nineveh. Jonah isn't too happy about Israel's God's concern and interest in Israel's enemies, and tries to run away from his call.

Most know the story of Jonah who was fleeing by boat to Tarshish in Spain. It was more than 2,000 miles west in the opposite direction from Nineveh. He was thrown overboard and swallowed by the great fish. Jonah stayed in the fish's belly for three days and three nights before being vomited up on the shore near Joppa. Jonah records his cry from the belly of the fish:

> *"I cried by reason of mine affliction unto the Lord, and He heard me; out of the belly of hell cried I, and Thou heardest my voice."* (Jonah 2:2)

Jonah even records in his story that water and seaweed were wrapped around him in the belly of the fish.

> *"The waters compassed me about, the weeds were wrapped about my head."* (Jonah 2:5)

After Jonah's "resurrection" out of the belly of the fish, he went in obedience to God on a mission of mercy to Nineveh. Jonah preached repentance to them concerning their wickedness. Jonah probably went with witnesses to verify the miracle of the fish story. His "fish story," however, was not "fishy" at all, but very true and would surely have gotten the people's attention!

The people of Nineveh became afraid of the God of Jonah and repented, much to Jonah's disappointment. He wanted God's punishment to fall upon them, but God delayed judgment because of their repentance. Yeshua refers to this prophet's mission in Luke 11:32: *"The men of Nineveh repented at the preaching of Jonah."*

Yeshua Himself also attested to this story and miracle as a historical fact. He quoted it as a prophetic picture of His own resurrection on the third day after His burial.

> "... For as Jonah was in the great fish for three days and three nights, so I, the Messiah, shall be in the heart of the earth three days and three nights." (Matt. 12:40)

Jonah was upset with God because He renounced punishment upon the people of Nineveh. Jonah is grieved over it even though he professes *"that God is a compassionate and gracious God, slow to anger, abounding in kindness, renouncing punishment."*

Jonah was so upset that he went off and sat down to have a pity party on a very hot day. God provided him with shade from the hot sun with a ricinus plant. The plant supernaturally grew up over Jonah. Jonah was very happy for the plant and its shade until God placed a worm on the plant. The plant withered and died. The sun, along with the sultry east wind that God sent, caused Jonah to grow faint and beg to die.

I really see a sense of humor in this story. Can you imagine Jonah sitting under the plant enjoying its shade not knowing that a worm was eating away at it? It wasn't long though before the sun started beating down upon Jonah's head as the worm finished his meal. Who would have created such an event but God to illustrate a point to Jonah? Sorry, but I just can't help myself from chuckling over this story.

God reminded Jonah that he had not created the plant nor planted it. God had provided it because He cared for Jonah. So, God asked him a question: *"Should I not care about Nineveh in which there are more than 120,000 who do not yet know their right hand from their left?"*

The scriptures do not give us Jonah's answer. It's not always easy to show mercy and forgiveness to those who have wronged us. Regardless, it is required of us to forgive as children of God.

There is a large mound in the ruins of Nineveh (in Iraq) called *"Yunas,"* the native word for "Jonah," where his tomb lies. It is also called the "Jonah Mound." It covers forty acres, and is one hundred feet high. It is so sacred that no large-scale excavations have been permitted there for years.

This is also a story of evangelism to a lost and dying world. Jonah began to dishonor that command by not obeying, and instead tried to run away from God's divine call. We know that he did obey later.

That divine call to every Believer today is to carry the good news of the gospel to the lost. Our response to God reveals our heart. Will we go, even if it is to our enemy?

Yeshua told His followers: *"Go ye into all the world and preach the gospel to every creature."*

Nahum's name means "Consolation" or "Comfort." He was from the Southern Kingdom of Judah. The *theme* is the pronouncement of doom against Nineveh. Nahum went to Nineveh with a message of doom about 150 years after Jonah. God had prolonged the day of judgment because of Nineveh's previous repentance.

Years later after Nineveh had repented, they grew to great power and had limitless wealth. They became very cruel to other nations, including Israel. It became an exceedingly wicked, sinful and politically oppressive nation. Its rulers were powerful oppressors of the people and other nations. Nahum encourages the people of God to hope and trust in Him even when being oppressed. God did bring Nineveh down, and their destruction is told in graphic detail.

Our political structure in America is changing rapidly. We are seeing our leaders making decisions that are anti-God. We see increased anti-Semitism and socialistic values rather than democracy. Many are suffering economically, and it may get worse. May we hold fast to our hope and trust in God. He alone is our hope and strength in times of trouble and oppression.

Nahum prophesies that God is jealous (zealous) over those He loves, and takes vengeance on their adversaries. He reserveth wrath for their enemies, and will not acquit the wicked. (Nahum 1:2-3) People surely need to be careful how they treat the people of God!

Nahum prophesied the certainty of judgment upon Nineveh: *"Nineveh lies in utter ruin. Yet no one anywhere regrets your fate!"* Her fierce cruelty to other nations, especially to Israel, caused the nations to clap their hands for joy at Nineveh's total ruin. However, God does not send His wrath speedily upon a person or nation. He is slow to anger, but will not acquit the wicked, and they cannot escape His judgment. God delays judgment because He is not willing that any should perish. (2 Peter 3:9) Nineveh certainly had every chance to stay true to God.

> *"The Lord is slow to anger, and great in power, and will not at all acquit the wicked . . . ."*
> (Nahum 1:3)

> In reference to Nineveh: *"There is no healing for your wound, it is far too deep for cure. All who hear your fate will clap their hands for joy, for where can one be found who has not suffered your cruelty?"* (Nahum 3:19)

Nineveh's destruction was so complete that the site looked as though there had never been a city there. Its walls and luxurious palaces were totally destroyed. The glory of the great Assyrian Empire and its capital, Nineveh, vanished into oblivion exactly as Nahum had prophesied. Archeologists have unearthed numerous parts of the palaces in ancient Nineveh that showed evidence of a fire. Statutes also found had split from a great heat.

Sometimes it seems as though the wicked are prospering while the righteous suffer, but God is a just God. God says that "vengeance is His." He will repay.

The evil kingdom of Satan will also vanish into oblivion at the great day of the Lord's vengeance against enemies of His Kingdom. All of the people of God will rejoice, *". . . for who has not suffered from Satan's constant malice?"* The devil and those of his kingdom will have their due. Until then, a merciful God gives unbelievers "time to turn to the Lord" and backsliders space to repent.

> *"The Lord is not slow in keeping His promise, as some people think of slowness; on the contrary, He is patient with you; for it is not His purpose that anyone should be destroyed, but that everyone should turn from his sins."* (2 Peter 3:9)

In the midst of God's judgment upon the wicked, God is a stronghold to those that trust in Him: *"The Lord is good, a strong hold in the day of trouble; and He knoweth them that trust Him."* (Nahum 1:7)

Help us Lord to trust you in the coming days of Tribulation, and we will have ultimate triumph in the midst of it. Praise the Lord!

Habakkuk's name means "To Embrace or Be Embraced." Habakkuk was from the Southern Kingdom. His main *theme* is a complaint and question to God concerning the Chaldeans' destruction of Judah. Judah had become very wicked and deserved punishment for her sins. Habakkuk did not warn Judah, but saw Judah's destruction coming. He asked God why He would allow Judah to be destroyed by a people more wicked, the Chaldeans.

God answered that He Himself had a purpose in the conquests of Judah by the terrible Chaldean armies. God continues with His answer by saying that the Chaldeans (Babylonians) are drunk with the blood of other nations and shall in His time be destroyed. The enemy's triumph over Judah would be temporary and God's justice would be served in the end. So, both Judah and the Chaldeans would be judged for their sins. Habakkuk was to live by faith, believing that justice would be served at God's appointed time.

> *"For the vision is yet for an appointed time, but at the end it shall speak, and not lie; though it tarry, wait for it; because it will surely come, it will not tarry. Behold his soul which is lifted up is not upright in him; but the just shall live by his faith. "* (Habakkuk 2:3)

Habakkuk believed and had confidence in God that He would indeed see to the eternal security and blessings of His people. He was a man of faith, and even though he saw the dark days ahead, he could only await God's deliverance while trusting totally in God. Can you see how this can speak to us today?

A very encouraging word is spoken to Habakkuk in this scripture of the endtime:

> *"For the earth shall be filled with the knowledge of the glory of the Lord, as the waters cover the sea."*(Habakkuk 2:14)

Habakkuk was sure that God would triumph in the end and he sang a prayer of triumph.

> *"Oh, Lord, I have heard your report, and I worship you in awe for the fearful things you are going to do. In this time of our deep need, begin again to help us as you did in years gone by. Show us your power to save us. In your wrath, remember mercy."*

Then Habakkuk recalled many things and times when God moved in power to save His people (Chapter 3). We pray for mercy, Lord, in your judgment of America in these evil days.

Habakkuk ends with this beautiful song of thankfulness, praise and faith. Let us sing!

> *"Although the fig tree shall not bloom, neither shall fruit be in the vines; the labor of the olives shall fail, and the fields shall yield no meat; the flock shall be no herd in the stalls; yet I will*

> *rejoice in the Lord, I will joy in the God of my salvation. The Lord God is my strength, and He will make my feet like hinds' feet [sure and swift], and He will make me to walk upon mine high places."*

What faith this man had! What confidence in God he had! Can we sing this song no matter how dark the days may seem in the future? We must keep a song of praise in our hearts and rejoice always in the God of our Salvation. Habbakuk's theme was to *trust God* and *live by faith, not by sight*.

Zephaniah means "Treasured of God." He was the great-grandson of Hezekiah and of royal blood. He prophesied about the wrath of God upon Judah a few years before her doom.

Over and over again, God announces severe judgment, the impending doom of Judah and other nations, and their last chance to repent. Judah was later taken captive along with the cities of the Philistines, Ethiopia, Assyria, Egypt, and Nineveh.

Jerusalem (Judah's capital) had become polluted with idolatrous priests, and the people were worshipping false gods of Baal and Molech, who sacrificed babies. God called them "filthy and polluted."

> *"Woe to her that is filthy and polluted, to the oppressing city (Jerusalem)! She obeyed not the voice of God; she received not correction; she trusted not in the Lord; she drew not near to God . . . Her prophets are treacherous persons; her priests have polluted the sanctuary, they*

have done violence to the law."(Zephaniah 3:1,3-4)

A call by God is given for the people to gather together. He called the nation to a solemn assembly for the sake of acknowledging sin, repenting, and seeking God's mercy. Zephaniah gave three directives to those who desired to repent and be saved from the wrath of God. Zephaniah also encouraged the faithful remnant of Judah.

"Seek ye the Lord, all ye meek of the earth, which have wrought His judgment; seek righteousness, seek meekness; it may be ye shall be hid in the day of the Lord's anger."(Zephaniah 2:3)

Never before have we seen such flaunting of abominations in the face of God in our churches today. There are increased false teachings and false doctrines, and ungodly practices by priests, bishops, pastors and teachers. Many are polluting God's house having their consciences seared with no respect or fear of God. They are "filthy and polluted" in God's eyes.

Zephaniah also prophesied that a remnant in their return from captivity would speak a "pure language." The Jewish people have been scattered to different nations and spoken many different languages. We know now that in Israel today the returning Jews are learning to speak the original language of Hebrew in schools there. This prophecy is another one that has been fulfilled in our generation.

Chapter 3:9:"For then will I turn to the people a pure language, that they may all call upon the name of the Lord, to serve Him with one consent [in one accord]."

Zephaniah prophesied of the "day of the Lord" (day of wrath) for the wicked at His second coming:

> "That day is a day of wrath, a day of trouble and distress, a day of wasteness and desolation, a day of darkness and gloominess, a day of clouds and thick darkness."(Zephaniah 1:15)

Zephaniah ends the book prophesying a message of hope and joy in the future concerning the remnant of Israel. *"Wait upon me,"* God says. God will destroy the wicked nations, but He will redeem those who have trusted in Him. Zephaniah prophesied of a complete restoration under the Messiah:

> "At that time will I bring you again, even in the time that I gather you; for I will make you a name and a praise among all people of the earth, when I turn back your captivity before your eyes, saith the Lord."(Zephaniah 3:20)

The following scripture from Zephaniah speaks of a faithful remnant being secure in Jerusalem at the coming of Yeshua:

> "The Lord thy God in the midst of thee is mighty; He will save, He will rejoice over thee with joy; He will rest in His love, He will joy over thee with singing."

Once Yeshua wept over Israel's rejection of Him, but one day soon He will rejoice and sing over them as they say, "Blessed is He who comes in the name of the Lord." He shall also rejoice and sing over all of His faithful remnant, both Jew and Gentile, and the earth will resound with the praise of all of His people at His coming.

All of the redeemed of the Lord should be echoing the proclamation of Zephaniah: *"Sing, shout and rejoice for He has saved us and is mighty in the midst of us."***Amen!**

Haggai's name means "Festal" or "Festive". Haggai's *theme* was the joyous return of the Jewish exiles from Babylon to rebuild the Temple in Jerusalem. Haggai prophesies that the glory of the latter Temple shall be greater than the former.

Haggai was one of the Jewish exiles who returned to Jerusalem under Zerubbabel, Governor of Judah, in about 536 B.C. Haggai helped the Jews to rebuild the Temple at Jerusalem, which had been demolished and burned as Zephaniah had predicted. Haggai, along with Zechariah and the people, began rebuilding the temple. However, they stopped shortly after building the foundation because of the opposition by neighboring people.

For about fourteen years after that, the people concentrated on building their own homes, planting their fields, and tending to personal concerns. They had lost their focus and neglected the building of the Temple of God.

Apathy and neglect kept God's blessing from them. The people's crops were poor and not producing. Haggai, speaking for God, told the people the reason for the poor crops was that they had abandoned the building of God's Temple. Comfort and encouragement is given to the people by Haggai in telling them to keep their hearts right with God. Then, He would take away the famine and restore them with plenty. The following words of encouragement were spoken by Haggai:

> *"Yet now be strong, O Zerubbabel, saith the Lord; and be strong O Joshua, the high priest; and be strong all ye people of the land, saith the Lord, and work; for I am with you, saith the Lord of Hosts. According to the word that I covenanted with you when ye came out of Egypt, so my Spirit remaineth among you: fear not."*(Haggai 2:4,5)

Then as God spoke encouragement to the people through Haggai, their spirits were stirred and they began work again on the Temple. King Darius gave them permission to build and even sent supplies and provisions to help them. Then at Haggai and Zechariah's urging the building of the temple began again, and its construction was completed in about four years. Zechariah also wrote several predictions about Israel during his time there with Haggai. These two witnesses, Haggai and Zechariah, brought much encouragement to the people of Israel.

Haggai had visions of the future Temple that they were building, but the vision went beyond that Temple. The vision looked to another Temple, a greater and more glorious Temple in Jerusalem at the Lord's coming!

> *"The glory of this latter house shall be greater than of the former, saith the Lord of Hosts; and in this place will I give peace, saith the Lord of Hosts."*(Haggai 2:9)

Zerubbabel was encouraged by the word of the Lord through Haggai when he became concerned about ruling over the few Jews as Governor of Judah. Zerubbabel was concerned about the threat of hostile neighbors. God told Haggai to go to him and *"tell him it shall be well with him and his remnant."*

The word of the Lord came again unto Haggai and gave him these prophetic words to speak to Zerubbabel:

> *"I am about to shake the heaven and the earth, and to overthrow thrones, and destroy the strength of the Kingdoms of the nations . . . but when that happens, I will take you, O, Zerubbabel, my servant, and honor you like a signet ring upon my finger; for I have specially chosen you, says the Lord Almighty."* A signet ring represents great power and authority by a King and was used to seal legal documents.

Those words encouraged Zerubbabel not only to look at the present, but to gaze forward to the day of the future glory of a new temple. Zerubbabel's crowning and reign was used *symbolically* by Haggai with a *prophetic* reference. The reference was to another Ruler who would come from Zerubbabel's royal line, Yeshua.

God's words through Haggai pointed to Yeshua, the Chosen Servant with a signet ring (symbol of a King's power and authority) seated at the right hand of God. Yeshua has all power and authority to shake the heaven and the earth. Such a shaking there will be when Yeshua returns! Yeshua is the sole builder of God's glorious future temple. Figuratively speaking, Satan and his kingdom's fate are already sealed with the Signet Ring of the King of Kings. **Gem!**

We too are servants of the Most High, a chosen generation of kings and priests. Let us be encouraged and not grow weary in these last days. Let us be strong and work, for His Spirit is in the midst of us. Fear not, for He is with us.

> *"Then spake Haggai the Lord's messenger in the Lord's message unto the people, saying, "I am with you, saith the Lord."* (Haggai 1:13)

Zechariah's name means "God Remembers." He was the prophet with Haggai during the four years of re-building and completing the Temple at Jerusalem, a theme of this book. After the first eight chapters, the theme turns to the second coming of Yeshua. Zechariah refers to "The Lord of Hosts" over and over again, so it appears he received messages directly with Yeshua.

Zechariah gave Judah, who had returned from exile in Babylon, a warning. He warned her that if she did not repent and turn to God, that He would turn from her. Zechariah told the people that they should listen to God's prophets and keep a good relationship with God lest they suffer His judgment. Zechariah had a series of night visions and offered encouragement to the builders of the temple. He pointed out that the key to a right relationship with God was obedience. God would settle for nothing less. And so it is.

Here we see angels assisting to bring the message from God by talking back and forth with Zechariah. What an experience that must have been! Can you imagine?

Zechariah reminded the people of how displeased God had been with their fathers and says:

"Thus saith the Lord of Hosts, turn you to me saith the Lord of Hosts, and I will turn to you, saith the Lord of Hosts."

Visions and revelations of the Lord were given to Zechariah to encourage the workers who had returned to Jerusalem to rebuild the Temple. The visions helped the people look beyond the present Temple and focus on a glorious future for the Nation of Israel. The visions helped the workers to realize God's plan for Israel, its coming Messiah and King, His glorious Temple and His Everlasting Kingdom.

Zechariah had many visions. He had eight visions in one night which were explained to him by an angel. Due to the lack of space and time, we will not be able to cover them, but will cover another vision that followed.

It was a vision of the coronation of Joshua as high priest. Joshua was chosen by God to be high priest who was worthy of the office. He was found worthy to intercede for the sinfulness of the people. This was *prophetic* of Yeshua our High Priest and Intercessor. Yeshua was chosen by God and is more than worthy of His office!

Zechariah was also told to take the silver and gold brought back from Babylon and make a crown. Then, he was to set the crown on the head of Joshua and pronounce, *"Thus speaketh the Lord of Hosts, saying,* **Behold the man** *whose name is The Branch". (Zech. 6:12)* Emphasis added. This prophesied of Yeshua's crowning as King. Yeshua (called The Branch) will soon be crowned King of Kings and Lord of Lords!

Zechariah's vision also revealed that the two offices of High Priest and King would be merged into one office with one

Ruler. It was *prophetic* of Yeshua as High Priest and King. Many prophets predicted a King who would reign in righteousness from the royal stock of King David like unto the Melchizedek order of one office, King-High Priest.

"The Branch" meant an offshoot (offspring) from Zerubbabel's Kingly lineage of King David. It meant that the Messianic line would be preserved through Zerubbabel. It pointed to Yeshua, who is called "the Branch" in Isaiah 4:2 and Jeremiah 23:5.

Zechariah prophesied that God would bring forth His Servant the Branch: *"Hear now, O Joshua, the high priest, and thy fellows that sit before thee . . . behold, I will bring forth my servant the branch."*(Zech. 3:8)

As to the words **"Behold the man"** in Zechariah 6:12, these same words were prophetic and spoken by Pilate when Yeshua was brought before him:

> *"Then came Yeshua forth, wearing the crown of thorns, and the purple robe. And Pilate said, 'Behold the Man'."*(Zech. 3:8;6:12) Awesome prophecy and **"Gem"**!

There is another interesting thing about Yeshua being called "the Branch." Did you know that Nazareth was a small village of only a few hundred humble people who worked hard for a living? We know that Yeshua lived and worked in Nazareth as a carpenter and stone mason. The little Town of Nazareth during Yeshua's childhood was known as the "Branch Village" because of its small size and population. Not only was Yeshua the Branch that sprang forth from the lineage of King David,

"Yeshua of Nazareth" was from the little Town called the "Branch." Very interesting!

Zechariah also saw visions of the judgment of God upon neighboring nations and Israel's struggle against their enemy nations. Zechariah saw the restoration of God's scattered people in the last days, and the setting up of Messiah's Kingdom on earth.

Chapter 11 is in parable form of two shepherds. It tells of Israel's rejection of the "good shepherd", the smitten shepherd. He is the shepherd who cared for His flock even though He was destined for death. The flock despised and rejected Him. In breaking His covenant, the flock was left vulnerable to the cruel onslaughts of the enemy nations. The good shepherd turned His rebellious flock over to the foolish "idol shepherd" that scattered and slaughtered them. Zechariah saw Israel's rejection of the Messiah and her struggle with enemy nations for generations.

> "And I took my staff, even Beauty, and cut it asunder, that I might break my covenant which I had made with all the people."(Zech. 11:10)

Zechariah prophesied that Jerusalem in the last days would become a burdensome stone to the nations. Many nations will be gathered against Israel in the last days. They will be destroyed at Yeshua's coming. At His coming, Zechariah prophesied that the Jews will look upon Yeshua whom they pierced, and there will be great mourning in Jerusalem. (Zech. 12:3,9-11)

Zechariah saw so many visions and glimpses of Yeshua, which also included His entry into Jerusalem on a colt ((Zech.

9:9). Zechariah is quoted in Matthew 21:5:*". . . Behold, thy King cometh unto thee, meek, and sitting upon an ass, and a colt the foal of an ass."*

Zechariah prophesied that Yeshua's body at His crucifixion would be pierced with a spear: *"And they shall look upon me whom they have pierced . . ."*(Zech. 12:10)

Zechariah prophesied of Yeshua's betrayal by Judas for thirty pieces of silver. The good shepherd asked for His pay in Zechariah 11:12:

> *"And I said unto them, if ye think good, give me my price; and if not forebear, so they weighed for my price thirty pieces of silver. And the Lord said, cast it unto the potter in the house of the Lord. And I took the thirty pieces of silver, and cast them to the potter in the house of the Lord."*

The Good Shepherd was betrayed for thirty pieces of silver. The fulfillment is seen in Matthew 27:3:

> *"Then Judas, which had betrayed Him, when he saw that He was condemned, repented himself, and brought again the thirty pieces of silver to the chief priests and elders, saying, I have sinned in that I have betrayed the innocent blood . . . "*

Zechariah prophesied many things about the coming Messiah and His Kingdom to the Jewish exiles to give them hope of better days. Zechariah saw Messiah's first coming into

Jerusalem, and His second coming to Jerusalem when His feet shall stand upon the Mount of Olives.

> *"And His feet shall stand in that day upon the Mount of Olives, which is before Jerusalem on the east, and the Mount of Olives shall cleave in the midst thereof toward the east and toward the west,* and *there shall be a very great valley; and half of the mountain shall remove toward the north, and half of it toward the south . . . and the Lord thy God shall come, and all the saints with Thee."*(Zech. 14:4-5)

Did you know that there is a fault in that mountain today just waiting for an earthquake to happen? Will Yeshua's feet cause the bursting open of that fault?

Zechariah's prophecies end with final visions of God's victory over Israel's enemies in the last days. Zechariah saw Yeshua's universal reign in the House of God and His rule over all the earth from Jerusalem. Zechariah also prophesied that the nations will come up from year to year to Jerusalem to worship the King and to keep the Feast of Tabernacles.(Zech. 14:16)

Since that Feast is still being celebrated in the future Messianic Kingdom, shouldn't we be celebrating it now in anticipation of the future day when we will celebrate it in the presence of our King?

Listen to Zechariah's closing words in relation to the last days, especially to us:

> *"Watch, for the day of the Lord is coming soon! . . . The sun and moon and stars will no longer*

shine, yet there will be a continuous day; only the Lord knows, but it shall come to pass that at evening time it shall be light . . . And the Lord shall be King over all the earth: in that day shall there be one Lord, and His name one."(Zechariah 14:1,6,7,9)

Prepare the way for the King is coming!

Micah means "Who is Like the Lord?" His *theme* is the promised Deliverer to come from Bethlehem to set up His Kingdom. He warned Judah, the Southern Kingdom in Jerusalem and Israel, the Northern Kingdom of God's judgment upon their sins. He also gave counsel to Kings Uzziah, Jothan, Ahaz, and Hezekiah. Micah's home was about 10 miles southwest of Jerusalem.

Samaria, the Capital of the Northern Kingdom (Israel), was an evil, wicked, idol-worshipping nation. God had sent several prophets to warn them of coming doom if they didn't repent, but to no avail. Micah predicted the doom of Samaria, and he lived to see the predictions come true. The Assyrians conquered northern Israel, and Samaria ended up in ruin. Micah also pronounced the doom of the Southern Kingdom Judah whose capital was Jerusalem.

Micah describes a vision of a happy, warless, and glorious time in the future in the Messianic Kingdom. Then suddenly, he reverts back to the doom of Jerusalem, announcing that the people would be carried away captive to Babylon. This prophecy was given a hundred years before the Babylonian empire. The prediction, however, took place exactly as Micah had prophesied. Years later, Assyria was overthrown by the Babylonians, Jerusalem was conquered by the Babylonians and the people taken captive to Babylon.

After the prophecy of doom, the prophet reverts back to visions of peace ahead after many days of trouble and distresses for the Jewish nation, and a promise of the coming Deliverer from Bethlehem. He describes the place of birth of this Deliverer, of His Kingdom's advancement, His protection of His people and His victory over His enemies. Micah prophesied that this Deliverer would be a glorious Prince and His subjects would be very happy under His government. He is none other than Yeshua, our soon coming Prince of Peace who will reign on earth over the Kingdom of God during the Millennium.

> *"They shall beat their swords into plowshares, and their spears into pruning hooks; nation shall not lift up a sword against nation, neither shall they learn war anymore."* (Micah 4:3)

Through Micah, God calls for the people of Israel to heed His warning of judgment and expresses His displeasure with the sins of the people. Their sins of ingratitude, religious pretense, idolatry and dishonesty were displeasing to God.

Micah lamented their decay, their prevailing violence, treachery and blood-thirstiness. Anguish poured from Micah's heart as he cried, *"woe is me."* He prayed to God for mercy for *the "flock of God's heritage,"* and that God would take care of them in captivity. Micah prayed that they might feed in their own country again as in the days of old. That prayer has been answered as we see the Jews occupying their land again today.

God's answer: that He would show them marvelous things and would repeat the wonders and miracles again as in the days of their coming out of Egypt. It would amaze the present age!

> *"According to the days of thy coming out of the land of Egypt will I shew unto thee marvelous things. The nations shall see and be confounded at all their might: they shall lay their hand upon their mouth, their ears shall be deaf. They shall lick the dust like a serpent, they shall move out of their holes like worms of the earth: they shall be afraid of the Lord our God, and shall fear because of thee."* (Micah 7:15-17)

Micah gives a thankful acknowledgment of God's mercy:

> *"Who is like unto thee, that pardoneth iniquity, and passeth by the transgression of the remnant of His heritage? He retaineth not His anger forever, because He delighteth in mercy. He will turn again, He will have compassion upon us; he will subdue our iniquities; and thou will cast all their sins into the depths of the sea. Thou wilt perform the truth to Jacob, and the mercy to Abraham, which thou hast sworn unto our fathers from the days of old."* (Micah 7:19-20)

No Lord, there is none like unto Thee, Oh God. You will show marvelous things and repeat wonders and miracles in these last days for your faithful remnant. God has always had and will always have a faithful remnant.

Malachi means "My Messenger." His *theme* is the final *recorded message* in the Old Testament to a disobedient people. Malachi was from Jerusalem. Many metaphors are used in the book of Malachi. After God had brought His people back from Babylon, He raised up Malachi to speak the last recorded Old Testament prophetic message. The Jews had declined spiritually again at that time. Their priests were corrupt, the men were committing adultery with no conviction and social and sexual evils abounded. The worship of God had become hypocritical and meaningless. The people were offering impure sacrifices and withholding their tithes. God warned that He will surely punish those who are disobedient.

Between Malachi and the next prophet there would be four hundred years called "the silent years" because there is no other recorded prophetic message until the New Testament.

Several times in Chapter 4, Malachi sweeps forward to the end time "day of the Lord" (the day of God's wrath). It seems to point to Yeshua's coming at the end of the seven-year tribulation at the battle of Armageddon:

> *"For lo! That day is at hand, burning like an oven. All the arrogant and evil doers shall be straw, burnt to ashes. But for you who revere my name a sun of victory* [son of victory] *shall rise 'to bring healing' . . . the wicked shall be dust under your feet on the day that I am preparing, saith the Lord of Hosts."*

The prophet warned the people to remember and be mindful of the teachings of God's servant, Moses. For us today, that is Yeshua. These are encouraging words to those who do: *"He will bring healing and bless the faithful."*

Malachi predicted the coming of one like Elijah in the spirit and power of Elijah who would usher in the beginning of the coming Messiah's ministry. He would prepare the peoples' hearts for Yeshua's arrival. He was prophesying of John the Baptist.

> *"And He shall turn the heart of the fathers to the children, and the heart of the children to their fathers. "Behold I will send you Elijah the prophet before the coming of the great and dreadful day of the Lord, lest I come and smite the earth with a curse."*(Malachi 4:5-6)

This prophecy was fulfilled about 400 years later at the birth of John the Baptist, who preceded Yeshua by six months. John the Baptist ushered in the arrival of Yeshua. Another awesome prophecy!

> Luke quotes from Malachi: *"And he shall go before Him* [Yeshua] *in the spirit and power of Elijah to turn the hearts of the fathers to the children, and the disobedient to the wisdom of the just; to make ready a people prepared for the Lord."*(Luke 1:17)

In the New Testament, when the angel appeared to Zacharias in the temple, it was to announce the birth of his son, John the Baptist. The angel described John the Baptist as a *"man of rugged spirit and power like Elijah, the prophet of old,"* and that he would precede the coming Messiah. The angel told Zacharias that his son would persuade many Jews to return to God. Over and over again in the New Testament we see quotations, references and prophecies from the Old Testament, which tie the two Testaments together.

Malachi denounced Israel's evil ways and practices and challenged them to begin *honoring* and *obeying* God. He warned them to repent of their sins before the great and dreadful day of the Lord that would come after Great Tribulation. This is also a challenge, **a must** for our generation. We are much, much closer to this day that Malachi prophesied of than any other generation.

> *"Watch now, the Lord Almighty declares, the day of judgment is coming, burning like a furnace. The proud and the wicked will be burned up like straw; like a tree, they will be consumed, roots and all. But for you who fear my name, the Sun of Righteousness will rise with healing in His wings and you shall go forth, and grow up as calves of the stall."* (Malachi 4:1-2)

The prophet Malachi gave the final *recorded* Old Testament prophetic message and warning to a disobedient and rebellious nation. He warned the nation of a coming day of judgment. His warning still rings true for America or any other nation that turns away from God or turns on Israel.

Even though God's prophets pronounced judgment for sin and rebellion, they always gave hope and encouragement of forgiveness through repentance. We have seen a long suffering and merciful Father who warned over and over again before bringing judgment. The prophets revealed God's plan of redemption through the coming Messiah. Yeshua is the Central Theme of Hope and Encouragement by the prophets of God to all people.

By the way, God also called prophetesses like Deborah, Miriam, Huldah in the Old Testament and Anna and the daughters of Phillip in the New Testament.

Even though the *Twelve Apostles* are not part of the "prophetic portion" of the Word, let's not forget them. Although not much of their history is known, it is believed that they were all martyred except the Apostle John. They are:

Andrew, Thomas, Peter, John (son of Zebedee, James (son of Zebedee), James (son of Alphaeus), Matthew, Simon Zelotes, Phillip, Thaddaus, Judas Iscariot and Bartholomew. Judas Iscariot was replaced by Matthias. Yeshua chose them to spread the gospel message, and gave them His authority to rule and reign in the Kingdom of God. That includes all born-again believers in the Body of Yeshua too!

God showed His great love for mankind by sending His prophets and His Only Son, the Greatest Prophet, to bless us and turn us from sin.

> *"Unto you first, God, having raised up His Son, Yeshua, has sent Him to bless you, in turning away every one of you from your iniquities."*
> (Acts 3:26)

CHAPTER 13

THE CATCHING AWAY

First of all, I realize that this may be a very controversial chapter in relation to the second coming of Yeshua. The big question is: Will believers go through all or any part of the seven-year tribulation period before Yeshua comes? Is there a **"rapture" ("catching away")** *before* the tribulation, in the middle or at the end of the age? I believed for many years that believers would be raptured (caught away) before the tribulation period began.

After finding some interesting scriptures and historical facts on the subject, I have changed my pre-tribulation belief. However, I still respect the belief of those who believe differently. Of course, this is my view that has recently changed based on the following information shared in this chapter.

First of all, did you know that Yeshua's followers and their congregations never taught that there would be a pre-tribulation "rapture"? Not one word in their early history or literature refers to a silent coming of the Lord to "catch away" believers before Yeshua's return. Instead, for almost nineteen centuries, believers wrote of Yeshua's second coming with a great shout and the sound of the trumpet (*shofar*). The Word states that every eye will see Him coming in the clouds.

The "rapture" ("catching away") before the end of the age (the seven-year tribulation) was not a belief by the early believers. There is a "catching away," but it is always referred to at the same time that the dead in Yeshua and the remaining living are caught up together (resurrected).That occurs at His second coming, and it is not a silent coming. The ultimate trumpet sound and shout is recorded:

> *"For the Lord Himself shall descend from heaven with a shout, with the voice of the archangel, and with the trump of God: and the dead in Christ shall rise first: Then we which are alive and remain shall be caught up together with them in the clouds, to meet the Lord in the air; and so shall we ever be with the Lord."*(I Thess. 4:16-17)

There is an interesting and important thing about the word "meet" in Verse 17. The Greek translation is *"apantesin."* That word means to go out to meet an official visitor then "return with him." In Acts 28, the same meaning applies when the brethren go out to meet Paul and then return to the city with him. Very interesting! The saints meet Yeshua in the air and return with Him later to Jerusalem. **"Gem"!**

When does this meeting take place according to the Word? Three times in John 6, Yeshua says He will raise up every believer *"at the last day"*:

> *"And this is the Father's will which hath sent me, that of all which He hath given me, I should lose nothing, but should raise it up again at the last day. And this is the will of Him that sent me that everyone which seeth the Son, and believeth on Him, may have everlasting life; and I will raise him up at the last day."*(John 6:39-40)

> *"Whoso eateth my flesh, and drinketh my blood, hath eternal life, and I will raise him up at the last day."*(John 6:54)

In the parable of the wheat and the tares, the saints are on the earth with the wicked until the harvest at the end of the age. Our Lord gathers His wheat (saints/sheaves) unto Himself and judges the wicked at the end of the age.

> *"Let both grow together until the harvest; and in the time of harvest I will say to the reapers , gather ye together first the tares, and bind them in bundles to burn them; but gather the wheat unto my barn . . . the harvest is the end of the age; and the reapers are the angels."* (Matt. 13:30,39)

Yeshua promised His disciples (followers) that He would be with them unto the end of the age.

> *"Teaching them to observe all things whatsoever I have commanded you; and lo, I am with you always even unto the end of the age."* (Matt. 18:20)

Yeshua was referring to His presence with all saints until the end of the age. Then, they will be *"caught up together"* with Him forever. There is no record of two different comings for His saints. I do not believe there is a silent coming for those before the tribulation. The scriptures use the word "together" when referring to the saints being resurrected. The Word seems to indicate one event. The scripture always speaks of His coming with a shout, the sound of the shofar (trumpet) and visible to every eye.

> ***"Immediately after the tribulation*** *of those days...And they shall see the Son of Man coming in the clouds of heaven in power and great glory. And he shall send his*

angels with a great sound of the trumpet, and they shall gather his elect from the four winds from one end of heaven to the other." (Matt. 24:30,31)

So, where did this theory of a *silent coming* for the saints *before the tribulation* originate? It originated from a young girl named Margaret McDonald in 1830 from Port-Glasgow, Scotland. She supposedly had a vision from God. She claimed to have received a "new revelation". The "new revelation" was that believers would be resurrected before the seven-year tribulation and *secretly*. What about the following scripture?

"Behold, He cometh with clouds; and every eye shall see Him, and they also which pierced Him, and all kindreds of the earth shall wail because of Him. Even so, Amen." (Rev. 1:7)

Why would anyone take the vision of a young woman to be the "gospel" when it was absolutely anti-biblical? It was not biblical according to the teachings for centuries by the early believers. The apostles did not teach anything without reservation to its validity by Yeshua Himself. Is that one reason Yeshua said that deception and false doctrine would be so subtle that if it were possible even the "elect" would be deceived? Could one example be the pre-tribulation rapture doctrine?

I believe this young girl's theory may be a tool of great deception and may cause many believers to be caught unaware of the truth. If it proves to be false, and I believe it will, many believers will be unprepared and become afraid.

The early believers always believed from the teachings of Yeshua and the Apostles that He would return after the seven-year tribulation. They believed the overcomer who *"endured to the end"* would see Him at His second coming. Apostle Peter in the following passage distinctly states that the end is identified with the appearing of Yeshua:

> *"Wherefore gird up the loins of your mind, be sober, and hope to the end for the grace that is to be brought to you at the revelation (unveiling, appearing) of Yeshua."* (I Peter 1:13)

Other scriptures like the following indicate enduring to the end:

> *"But he that shall endure unto the end, the same shall be saved."* (Matt. 24:13)

> *"Behold, I show you a mystery. We shall not all sleep, but we shall all be changed. In a moment, in the twinkling of an eye, at the last trump; for the trumpet shall sound, and the dead shall be raised incorruptible, and we shall be changed."* (I Cor. 15:51-52)

Here again is the sound of the trumpet ("last trump") and "catching up" of the saints in connection with the return of the Lord for believers as one event. Is this a secret or silent catching away of the saints? No.

When God blew the trumpet (ram's horn) at Mt. Sinai, the people trembled with fear. They thought they were going to die from the earth-shaking sound! Apostle John also heard the Lord's voice as the sound of a loud trumpet!

Revelation 4:1:

"I John saw a door standing open in heaven, and the same voice I had heard before that sounded like a mighty trumpet blast, spoke to me, and said, 'Come up here and I will show you what must happen in the future!'"

Many pastors, teachers and believers use this scripture to say this is where the present-day "church" is raptured. Since the word "church" isn't used after Chapter 4:1, they assume that the present-day "church" is no longer on the earth. The truth is that John was merely translated in the Spirit to heaven for future revelation concerning the **universal** body of Yeshua, outside of the seven churches first addressed.

There is a good reason why the word *"ekklesia"* or "church" doesn't appear after the end of Chapter 3 of Revelation. The revelation of future events is to the **"universal"** Body of Yeshua. Yeshua is no longer speaking to the **literal** congregations.

The universal Body of Yeshua is referred to over and over again, called by many names after Revelation 4:1:

"fellow servants," "servants of God," "ones who come out," "those who keep His commandments," "saints," "redeemed," "those who follow the Lamb," "firstfruits," "my people," "chosen," etc.

If one believes John's calling up to the throne room in heaven is actually the rapture, then there must be several raptures. Apostle John changes locations from earth to heaven and vice versa several times during the visions.

I don't think Revelation 4:1 should be taken *literally* as a fact that it symbolizes the rapture of the present-day church. It is only assumed by theorists that believers are raptured in Revelation 4:1. John is translated to and from heaven and earth specifically to view and record future events that occur in heaven and on earth in reference to the servants of Yeshua. Some scholars believe that Revelation 14 refers to the "catching away".

Some examples of John's translation from earth to heaven and from heaven back to earth are:

Rev. 10:8: John viewing things on earth

Rev. 11:1: John viewing things from heaven

Rev. 13:1: John back on earth

Rev. 14:1: John on Mt. Zion (earth)

Rev. 17:3: John in the wilderness

Rev. 18: John on earth

Rev. 22:1: John in heaven again

Preceding the "catching away" of the saints, I believe the last days will be like the Israelites' exodus out of Egypt. However, the Body of Yeshua will experience the greatest outpouring of the Holy Spirit and fire ever seen! It will be a glorious time for God's faithful remnant! It will be the greatest Pentecost (Shavuot, Hebrew) ever!

> *"And it shall come to pass afterward, that I will pour out of my spirit upon all flesh; and your sons and your daughters shall prophecy, your old men shall dream dreams, your young men shall see visions...And I will show wonders in the heavens and in the earth, blood, and fire and pillars of smoke. The sun shall be turned into darkness, and the moon into blood, before the great and terrible of the Lord's coming."* (Joel 2:28-30)

Yeshua will have many faithful followers (Jew and Gentile) who will be preaching the Gospel of the Kingdom of God worldwide and manifesting the power, love and glory of God! They will be *united as one in the Spirit* (Jew and Gentile) a powerful army that will not break ranks! Yeshua prayed for this *unity* amongst His followers before His death:

> *"Neither pray I for these alone, but for them also which shall believe on me through their word. That they all may be one; as thou, Father art in me, and I in thee, that they also may be one in us; that the world may believe that thou hast sent me. And the glory which thou gavest me, I have given them; that they may be one, even as we are one..."* (John 17:20-22)

The Body of Believers in the last days of Tribulation will be a great light in a dark place; the sick will be healed, the blind will see, the lame will walk and demons will be cast out! Signs and wonders will follow them in the worldwide revival even though there will be great persecution and opposition. God's Glory Cloud will follow the faithful remnant, and they will perform the "greater works" spoken of by Yeshua!

Yes, there will be martyrdom, but also a Goshen too. God will supernaturally protect His people like He did when His people left Egypt during the plagues upon the earth. I believe the Body of Believers will be here when the plagues are poured out before the catching away at Rosh Hashanah. The vials of wrath that follow will be poured out *after* the saints have been resurrected and translated to the other side and looking down upon the judgment of the wicked. They will be destroyed just as Pharaoh's army, after God's people are safely on the other side! **"Gem"!**

> *"But he that shall endure unto the end, the same shall be saved. And this gospel of the Kingdom shall be preached in all the world for a witness, unto all nations; and then shall the end come."* (Mt. 24:13,14)

In 2 Thessalonians 2:4-8, Paul continues to refer to the Lord's coming and the *"catching away"* at the end of the tribulation period at which time the antichrist is destroyed. Verse 8 reads: *"And then shall that Wicked One be revealed whom the Lord shall consume with the spirit of His mouth, and shall destroy with the brightness of His coming."*

Another reference to the "last day" being the resurrection (catching away) of the righteous is when Martha said to our Lord: *". . . I know that he (Lazarus) shall rise again in the resurrection at the last day."* (John 11:24)

The Word states that many will be deceived because they do not receive the love of the truth (the Word of God). Their consciences will be seared and they will no longer have ears to hear or have the will to obey the Holy Spirit who convicts. Therefore, God will send them strong delusion so that they believe the lie of the antichrist. They will eventually be judged for delighting in unrighteousness. (2 Thess. 2:10-12)

The coming antichrist will deceive many too. He will come as a wolf in sheep's clothing.

> *"Even him* [man of sin]*, whose coming is after the work of Satan with all power and signs and wonders and lying wonders."* (2 Thess. 2:9)

This is not a time to be complacent. It's certainly a time to wake up and be sober for the Bridegroom is soon coming to "catch away" His Bride!

The Bride will not know the day or the hour, but she should know the season. Her Bridegroom will come with the sound of the trumpet. What feast and at what season will it be?

It will be a future *fall season*, during the **"Feast of Trumpets"** (Yom Teruah, Hebrew), also called Rosh HaShanah. This Feast is *prophetic* of the return of the Bridegroom for His Bride. What a glorious "catching away"!

> *"Behold, I shew you a mystery; we shall not all sleep, but we shall all be changed, in a moment, in the twinkling of an eye, at the last trump; for the trumpet shall sound, and the dead shall be raised incorruptible, and we shall be changed."* (I Cor. 15:49,51-52)

Where is the Bridegroom now? What is He doing? What did He say to the disciples when He left? Why would He tell them that He had to go away, but would return for them at a later time? Remember this scripture?

> *"In my Father's house are many mansions. If it were not so, I would have told you. I go to*

prepare a place for you. And if I go and prepare a place for you, I will come again, and receive you unto Myself; that where I am, there ye may be also."(John 14:2-3)

Did you ever relate that scripture to the ancient Jewish tradition of betrothal and marriage between a bride and her bridegroom? The disciples would have immediately understood where Yeshua was going, why He was going and that He would return for them. They knew because they understood the Jewish betrothal and marriage tradition. It is a prototype of the betrothal and marriage between Yeshua and His Bride. Get ready for some "**gems**"!

In Jewish tradition, there are two phases to marriage; the betrothal and then marriage. When a Jewish man and woman become betrothed, it is so binding that they are *considered married*. However, they do not actually wed for at least a year. That is why Mary and Joseph were considered married even though they were only betrothed to one another. The bride was to keep herself pure and faithful to her bridegroom until the marriage was consummated. It was a terrible disgrace for her to become pregnant, especially if it wasn't by her soon-to-be husband. She was to remain a virgin.

The Jewish bridegroom after the betrothal goes to prepare a place for the bride. While the bridegroom is away, the bride-to-be stays at home with her family preparing for her wedding day. When the bridegroom returns for his bride, he takes her to the marital home for their wedding ceremony.

The Jewish bridegroom-to-be and his father would have negotiated a price to be paid for the bride. Yeshua and the

Father negotiated the price for His bride. The price Yeshua paid for His Bride was His life. Once the terms had been made, a betrothal ceremony would take place in front of witnesses.

At the "betrothal ceremony", the bride and bridegroom always shared a cup of wine at the end of the meal. This sharing of the cup symbolized their betrothal and commitment to each other. The bridegroom would drink first from the cup and then pass it to his bride.

Another meal and cup of wine is drunk at the "marriage ceremony" sometime later to *seal* the marriage contract (covenant). That is the meal and cup that Yeshua referred to in stating that He would not partake of until the **fullness** of the Kingdom of God has come, referring to the Marriage Supper of the Lamb! **"Gem"**!

How awesome when viewing from a Jewish perspective!

> *"With desire I have desired to eat this Passover with you before I suffer: For I say unto you, I will not any more eat thereof until it be fulfilled in the Kingdom of God. And He took the cup, and gave thanks, and said, take this and share it among yourselves: For I say unto you, I will not drink of the fruit of the vine, until the Kingdom of God shall come."* (Luke 15-18)

According to Jewish tradition, there are four (4) cups drank at the Seder, plus one set aside for Elijah. The four cups are based upon four promises ("I will") made by God to Israel at Mt. Sinai in bringing them out of Egypt. These promises also apply *spiritually* to believers who have come out of the world (Egypt) and received Salvation.

> *"I am the Lord, and I will bring you out from under the yoke of the Egyptians. I will free you from being slaves to them, and I will redeem you with an outstretched arm and with mighty acts of judgment. I will take you as my people, and I will be your God..."* (Exo. 6:6,7)

(1) *Cup of Sanctification (Salvation)* – "I will bring you out from under the yoke of the Egyptians." Spiritually, at salvation believers experience a setting apart from the world (Egypt) and are consecrated unto the Lord. He is our Salvation. His yoke is easy and His burden light.

(2) *Cup of Freedom or Cup of Plagues* – "I will free you from being slaves." At salvation, believers are freed from the bondage of sin and Satan. They come out of darkness into the Light and know the liberty and freedom in Yeshua. I believe this also speaks of the bitter cup that Yeshua drank in the Garden of Gethsemane full of dregs, not His own, but ours to save us from the penalty of sin.

(3) *Cup of Redemption* – "I will redeem you with an outstretched arm" (transfers ownership of believers to God) by the blood of the Firstborn Son of God, the Passover Lamb. By His blood, He purchased us at a great price. This cup is the new

blood covenant "cut" in Yeshua's blood sealing our redemption.

(4) *Cup of Praise* – "I will take you as my people, and I will be your God." This points to "oneness" with God through **covenant**. The Israelites rejoiced at their escape from Egypt and their becoming a nation (peoples) chosen of God. As believers, we have much reason to rejoice as chosen children of God and citizens of His Kingdom! Let our praises resound to the Father, Son and Holy Spirit!

There is another cup set at the end of the table for Elijah. It is filled with a cup of wine, but not partaken of at the Seder. Only Elijah is to drink of this cup. Non-Messianic Jews believe that the prophet, Elijah, is literally coming back to earth to drink of that cup as forerunner to the Messiah's coming and announce His coming.

Of course, most Gentile believers and Messianic Jews know that John the Baptist (the one Yeshua spoke of as having already come) was the forerunner to the Messiah's first coming. Some Bible teachers teach and believe that Elijah will literally be one of the two witnesses that comes back during the tribulation period and to announce the Messiah's return! Interesting!

However, I like to think of that cup of wine as the cup awaiting Another, the Bridegroom. He is coming soon to share the cup of wine with His Bride at the marriage supper of the Lamb that seal the marriage covenant! Look for the next fall Feast yet to be fulfilled. It is the *fifth feast* of the Lord's seven feasts.

The **"Feast of Trumpets"** is called **"Yom Teruah"** in Hebrew. "Yom Teruah" means the "Day of the Blasting" (of the Shofar). That is the Biblical name. It also means "awakening blast", and can also be translated "shout"!

"Awake" is an idiom of this feast. It falls on the first day of the **seventh month** (mid-September to mid-October) on the **religious** calendar, Tishrei. All of God's *end time* Feasts are celebrated in the last, *seventh month of His calendar*. Remember, the *fall feasts* are holy convocations for a *future, ultimate fulfillment* at Yeshua's second coming!

This Feast is about preparation for the meeting between Yeshua and His Bride at His appearing!

> "In the seventh month [Tishrei], on the first day of the month, you shall have a Sabbath rest, a memorial of blowing of trumpets, a holy convocation. You shall do no customary work on it."(Lev. 23:23-25)

> "And that, knowing the time, that now it is high time to awake out of sleep: for now is our salvation nearer than when we believed." (Rom. 13:11) Amen!

In modern day Judaism, this Feast is also known as **"Rosh Hashanah"**, and is celebrated as the Jewish New Year. Rosh Hashanah means "year" or "head of the year", or the beginning. It falls on the **first month** (mid-Sept. to mid- Oct.) of the *Jewish* **civil** *calendar*.

This Feast is a *part* of the season of repentance called "Teshuvah" (repentance). This season speaks to all believers in Messiah. They are called to examine their lives and repent of sin. It is a time for all of us to search our hearts and make ready for the coming of our Bridegroom. The sound of the shofar is blown many times as a warning signal to wake up and make ready BEFORE the appearing of Yeshua at "Yom Teruah" (Feast of Trumpets!

Rosh Hashanah at this same time is believed by the Jewish people to be the beginning of creation, or the birthday of the world. They believe that creation began at this time and that Adam may have been created on this day. It is traditionally celebrated with the wish for a good, sweet and healthy year ahead. Sliced apples are dipped in honey. The apples represent God's provision for the next year, and the honey represents a sweet and healthy New Year.

Rosh Hashanah is also called **"the hidden day"** because no one, especially Satan is to know the day or the hour of Yeshua's coming. It is celebrated for *two days* in relation to the appearing of the new moon. That makes it even harder, however, for one to know which day Yeshua will come. Only the Father knows the day and hour when the trumpet of Rosh Hashanah at the Feast of Trumpets (Yom Teruah) will sound! It **will be** on a new moon!

> *"Blow up the trumpet in the new* moon, in the time appointed, on our solemn feast day." (Ps. 81:3)

This Feast is also called the **"Day of Remembrance"**. It is a day to remember the loud, long sounding of the Shofar ("first trump") blown by God at Mt. Sinai. It announced God's manifest presence! Let us be reminded of a day coming sooner than we might think when God's Shofar announces Yeshua's manifest presence as He breaks through the clouds in great splendor and glory! Hallelujah!

> *"For the Lord Himself will descend from heaven with a shout, with the voice of the archangel and with the trumpet of God, and the dead in Christ will rise first."* (I Thess. 4:16)

On the other hand, it will be a dreadful day for many. It will be a day of judgment. It will be a dark and frightening day for those who waited too late to prepare for Yeshua's second coming. It will be a very sad day for those like the five virgins who were not ready to meet the bridegroom. We must be preparing and making ready now!

> *"But of that day and hour knoweth no man, no, not the angels of heaven, but my Father only. But as the days of Noah were, so shall also the coming of the Son of Man be. For as in the days that were before the flood they were eating and drinKing, marrying and giving in marriage, unto the day that Noah entered into the Ark. And knew not until the flood came, and took them all away; so shall also the coming of the Son of Man be."*(Matt. 24:35-38)

> *"Therefore let us not sleep, as do others; but let us watch and be sober."*(I Thess. 5:6)

Joel 2:1-2 tells us to *"blow the trumpet in Zion"* for Yeshua's coming is nigh at hand. It is more relevant for us today than ever before!

"Blow the trumpet in Zion, sound the alarm in my holy mountain; let all the inhabitants of the land tremble, for the day of the Lord cometh, for it is nigh at hand: A day of darkness and gloominess, a day of clouds and thick darkness, as the morning dawn spread upon the mountains; a great people [hostile] and strong; there has never been the like, neither shall be anymore after it, even to the years of many generations."

Our mouths can also be *symbolic* of blowing the trumpet. We need to be sounding the alarm as a trumpet, warning and announcing that Yeshua is coming soon! Of course, we should examine ourselves first. I have written this book to sound the alarm. It is my way of "blowing the trumpet"!

Do you realize that by keeping this Feast that our minds and hearts will be on Yeshua's coming at His appearing? If we are keeping this Feast, we will be focused and prepared for His appearing as we are *literally* celebrate **this** Feast! "**Gem**"!

We must be busy about Yeshua's work to bring in the lost and backslidden souls. The day of His coming is fast approaching whether it pre-trib, mid-trib or post-trib. Most importantly, NOW is the time to be preparing for His coming!

"Therefore, be ye also ready; for in such an hour as ye think not, the Son of Man cometh." **Selah!**

The Bridegroom's return is very near, even at the door! Let us not be complacent, but watch the signs of the time, pray and seek the Lord before the blasting sound of the *Shofar* (Ram's horn)!

The cry will soon go out: *"Behold the Bridegroom cometh!"* **Be ready!**

The following are a few of the short phrases read at this Feast:

May the sound of the shofar shatter our complacency and make us conscious of the corruption in our lives.

May the sound of the shofar awaken us to the magnitude of our sins and the vastness of the Lord's mercy toward those who turn to Him.

May the sound of the shofar stir our hearts to obey the Lord our God, for blessed are those who hearken to His call.

May the sound of the shofar inspire us to wholeheartedly seek and devote ourselves to the One and only True God.

The following is a *prophetic reading* for the Feast of Trumpets (Yom Teruah) and Rosh Hashanah:

"Listen, I tell you a mystery; we will not all sleep, but we will be changed in a flash, in the twinkling of an eye, at the last trump. For the trumpet will sound, the dead will be raised imperishable and we will be changed." (I Cor. 15:51,52)

CHAPTER 14

WHY STUDY PROPHECY?

Prophecy is approximately one-third of the Word and is a very important **Gem** in the Word of God, as we have already seen. Personally, I love studying prophecy.

One of the most important reasons to study prophecy is that **Yeshua** is the One toward whom all prophecy points. Through prophecy we know that Yeshua is *"truly the Messiah."* Prophecies of His first coming have been fulfilled exactly as foretold. We can be assured that His second coming will be fulfilled exactly as foretold, including the loud blast of the shofar.

It is important to know that prophecy is closely connected to symbolism and figures of speech that have literal meanings, especially seen in the books of Isaiah, Jeremiah, Ezekiel, and Daniel. The Book of Revelation in the New Testament probably has the most symbolism.

Prophecy is also to make us aware of future events and understand God's actions before they happen. Prophecy is especially important to us in these last days prior to His second coming. By the signs and wonders prophesied, we need not be caught unaware or ignorant of God's actions. Didn't He say to Abraham, *"Shall I hide from my servant Abraham that thing which I do?"*

The Book of Revelation is especially an important book of prophecy to read and study in these last days. It is the only book of prophecy that promises a blessing to the reader. It does appear that many more pastors and evangelists are looking closer at the book of Revelation today.

> *"The revelation of Jesus Christ, which God gave him to show to his servants what must soon take place; and he made it known by sending his angel to his servant John, who bore witness to the word of God and to the testimony of Jesus Christ, even to all that he saw. Blessed is he who reads the words of the prophecy, and blessed are those who hear, and who keep what is written therein; for the time is near."* (Rev. 1:1-3)

Prophecy not only teaches us of past and future events, it also assures us that God's Word is true and accurate in every word and every little detail. The findings of the archeologists are still proving the truth and accuracy of His Word today. The more they dig, the more truth they find. Towns, cities, people and events existed exactly as stated in the Word. Their findings prove that God is an all-knowing, all-seeing, all-powerful God who reigns over the past, present and future .Amen!

Last but not least, studying **prophecy** is important in that we might hearken and be challenged as believers to live holy and be obedient to God. In an unholy world we need to see that God is in control and aware of all events. Most importantly, prophets of God were moved by the Holy Spirit (*Ruach HaKodesh*), thereby relaying their messages directly from God. Look at this scripture in Peter:

> *"Knowing this first, that no prophecy of the scripture is of any private interpretation. For the prophecy came not in old time by the will of man, but holy men of God spake as they were*

moved by the Holy Spirit [Ruach Hakodesh]." (2 Peter 2:20-21)

Let's begin with the prophets Isaiah and Micah revealing prophecies of the Messiah's birth:

"Therefore, the Lord Himself shall give you a sign; Behold, a virgin shall conceive, and bear a son, and shall call His name "Immanuel" [meaning, "God with us"]. (Isaiah 7:14)

In Micah 5:2, we are told by the prophet Micah where Yeshua's birthplace would be:

"O Bethlehem Ephrathah, you are but a small Judean village, yet you will be the birthplace of my King who is alive from everlasting ages past."

Why didn't the prophet say "Bethlehem" instead of "Bethlehem Ephrathah"? There were several towns called "Bethlehem" at the time of Yeshua's birth. The prophet had to be specific about a particular one where Yeshua was to be born. The prophecies of the word are completely accurate, down to every little detail. The word "Bethlehem" means "house of bread".

In the book of Genesis, the Word tells us that the Messiah would come from the Tribe of Judah, meaning "praise", and would be from the royal/Kingly line of King David:

"The scepter shall not depart from Judah until Shiloh [Messiah the Prince] comes, who all people shall obey." (Gen. 49:10)

When an angel appeared to Joseph, who was engaged to Mary, the angel referred to Isaiah's prophecy:

> *"Don't be afraid to take unto thee Mary thy wife; for that which is conceived in her is of the Holy Ghost. And she shall bring forth a Son, and thou shalt call His name, 'Yeshua', [meaning 'Salvation' or 'God saves'] for He shall save His people from their sins. This will fulfill God's message through the prophet of old."*

Did you know that even the stars speak a prophetic message of the Messiah? The prophets prophesied of a "star" that would appear in the sky at the time of the Messiah's birth:

> *"Where is he that is born King of the Jews? For we have seen his star in the East and are some to worship him."* (Matthew 2:2)

It was by the "star" that had been prophesied so many years before that the wise men knew Yeshua had been born!

The wise men (Magi) were learned men who were advisors to the Kings of Babylon. They studied the stars and their movements very closely. They were Jewish Rabbis, teachers of Jewish law. Many Jews lived in Babylon after their captivity. They were very familiar with the prophecies of their coming Messiah.

The Magi would have been familiar with Balaam's prophecy of Israel's influential place through the star. The star would come "out of the East" and their King's coming as the "bright and morning star."

When the wise men saw the star appear at the time of Yeshua's birth, the scriptures state that they were "exceedingly joyful" at the sight of the star. It led them for months over a thousand miles as they made their way to Bethlehem. The scriptures do not tell us how many men there were, but they arrived in caravans with many armed men. They not only brought gold, frankincense and myrrh, but many other gifts to the newborn King.

Did you know that the star led them to the exact location (house) where Yeshua lived? The star "hovered" over the house!

> "...and lo, the star, which they saw in the East, went before them till it came and stood over where the young child was. When they saw the star, they rejoiced with exceeding great joy!" (Matt. 2:9-10)

There is another interesting thing about the treasures that the wise men brought to Yeshua. Some biblical scholars say that they had been entrusted with the treasure for safe-keeping for about five hundred years.

The prophet Daniel had accumulated many riches while in Babylon. Since Daniel had no heirs, It is believed that Daniel before his death designated the treasures be kept and given to the Messiah upon His birth. It was another important reason that the Magi observed the sky for the appearing of the "star out of the East" announcing that the King had been born. It would then be time to take the treasure to the newborn King whose was then between one and two years of age.

Did you know that the gifts were brought at the **very time** that Joseph and Mary needed them for their journey to Egypt? Herod had ordered all children two years and under to be killed in hopes of killing the newborn King. God was way ahead of Herod, for the angel had already appeared to Joseph telling him to take the flight to Egypt! The gifts provided by the wise men were all the provision needed for the journey and for settlement in Egypt by the royal family! **Awesome God! "Awesome Gem"!**

There is another interesting thing about the treasures that the wise men brought. Some biblical scholars say that they had been entrusted with the treasure for safe-keeping for about five hundred years.

The prophet Daniel had accumulated many riches while in Babylon. Since Daniel had no heirs, It is believed that Daniel before his death designated the treasures be kept and given to the Messiah upon His birth. It was another important reason that the Magi observed the sky for the appearing of the "star out of the East" announcing that the King had been born. It would then be time to take the treasure to the newborn King whose was then between one and two years of age, the time that Herod was killing those under two years of age! **"Gem"!**

Now, before we go any further, know that the Zodiac is not evil or of the occult or of the devil. God created the heavens, the earth and the stars. He even named them in order to proclaim the gospel message across the sky for all to see. The Zodiac is a beautiful prophetic picture-story of redemption from Yeshua's birth to His victorious overthrowing of Satan and his Kingdom.

The gospel story is told by the position, names and movement of the stars in the Zodiac. There are twelve (12) signs, with each one revealing a phase of the plan of redemption and its fulfillment by Yeshua. It would be of great benefit and a blessing to you, the reader, to obtain a book revealing the picture/story of redemption in God's Zodiac.

> "The heavens declare the glory of God; and the firmament sheweth His handiwork. Day unto day uttereth speech [a message], and night unto night sheweth knowledge." (Psalm 19:1)

> "He alone spreads out the sky and walks on the waves of the sea. He made Arcturus, Orion, the Pleiades and the hidden constellations of the south. He does great, unsearchable things, wonders beyond counting." (Job 9:8-10)

Satan has perverted and twisted this part of God's creation. He has used horoscopes, etc. to deceive and counterfeit God's purpose of displaying the gospel message. The last sign, Leo, shows Satan's final fate by the Lion of Judah. Leo means "He that rends or tears asunder." The chief star in that sign is "Rigel" which means "treading underfoot". The serpent's head is seen beneath the paw of the lion. The Lion of Judah is seen crushing (bruising) the head of the serpent as foretold in the book of Genesis. What a **"Gem"** in the stars!

Yes, even after the crushing of Satan and his kingdom, the stars reveal the serpent's end as he is cast into the abyss! It is no wonder that Satan doesn't want the story in the stars to be seen!

Virgo is the first sign in the Zodiac in the Hebrew month of Tishrei (mid-September to mid-October). It shows a woman holding a child. His head is above hers indicating His greatness. The brightest star in Virgo is "Spica", meaning "seed" and reveals the season of the Seed's birth! The second brightest star is called "Prometheus", meaning "deliverer who comes".

The three decans in Virgo are:

(a) "Coma", meaning "the desired son" or "the longed for";
(b) "Centaurus", meaning "King/ruler", but also meaning "dual nature" (God-Man); and
(c) "Bootes", meaning "to come", or "the coming one." Amazing!

How is that for starters in relation to the "stars" in the Zodiac?

Yeshua prophesied that there would be signs in the sky and in the earth revealing His return. God communicates with us through signs in the heavens and the earth. He conveys messages, including warnings through them. Signs before Yeshua's second coming will not only be seen in the stars, but in the moon and the sun. The blood moons are an example in these last days of God's communicating a message, especially concerning the Nation of Israel and other Gentile nations.

A "blood moon" was seen at Passover on April 14, 2014, and another on the Feast of Tabernacles on October 8, 2014. Other blood moons appear on Passover and Feast of Tabernacles in 2015. Watch for them and the national events surrounding or following them. Other signs of the last day appear on the earth by fire, wind and earthquakes.

> *"And I will show wonders in heaven above, and signs in the earth below; blood and fire and vapor of smoke. The sun shall be turned into darkness and the moon into*

blood before that great and notable day of the Lord come." (Acts 2:19-20)

The "notable day of the Lord" in the above scripture, as I understand it, is the future **Day of Atonement** when Yeshua, High Priest and soon-coming King, comes to fight for Israel. He will set His feet upon the Mount of Olives which causes a great earthquake. It is near the end of the Great Tribulation.

This Day is called **"Yom Kippur"** in Hebrew. "Yom" means "Day" and "Kippur" means "Atonement". It is kept on the tenth day of Tishrei (mid-Sept to mid-Oct) annually. It has not yet been fulfilled. It is the sixth annual *fall feast* celebrated between Rosh Hashanah/ Feast of Trumpets and the Feast of Tabernacles.

"Also, the tenth day of this seventh month [Tishrei] shall be the Day of Atonement...you shall afflict your souls [fast] and offer an offering made by fire to the Lord. And you shall do no work on that day, for it is the Day of Atonement for you before the Lord your God..." (Lev. 23:26-28)

Lev. 23:26-28 speaks of "afflicting the soul", "fasting" and "self-denial". This refers to the *command* God gave to the Nation of Israel to keep the Day of Atonement. Israel *corporately* as a nation keeps this Day once a year with fasting, repenting of sins and prayer. It is **not** the same as Passover.

Passover celebrates *individual salvation for all*. The Day of Atonement (Yom Kippur, Hebrew) is more of a communal or corporate salvation. "Atonement" means "at one with God". The Biblical name for Yom Kippur is "Yom HaKippurim" meaning "the covering, canceling, pardoning, returning or reconciling, especially in reference to the Nation of Israel.

> *"And so all Israel shall be saved: as it is written, There shall come out of Zion the Deliverer, and shall turn away ungodliness from Jacob: For this is my covenant unto them, when I shall take away their sins."* (Romans 11:26-27)

> *"On that day a fountain will be opened to the house of David and the inhabitants of Jerusalem, to cleanse them [Israel] from sin and impurity."* Emphasis added. (Zech. 13:1)

There are ten (10) days between the Feast of Trumpets/Rosh Hashanah and the Day of Atonement. These ten days are known as "days of repentance" or "days of awe". Most Jewish people believe that the gates of heaven are opened at Rosh Hashanah to usher in the righteous. They believe that the Lamb's Book of Life will be opened at the future Feast of Trumpets. Then, the Day of Atonement takes place after the ten (10) days of awe.

The Word of God doesn't tell us what takes place during those ten days after the gates are opened. Some believe that Yeshua's coronation will take place during that time in heaven. Others believe that the righteous stand before God to be judged. Yeshua, their Mediator is present. The righteous are **not** judged for sin because Yeshua's blood has cleansed them from sin. Rather, it is said that they receive their rewards for their work on earth. As stated before, the Word doesn't tell us. God chose to leave it a mystery. That still doesn't seem to stop inquisitive minds like mine!

Since it is the only day that a fast is *commanded* by God for the Jewish nation, it is sometimes referred to as the **"Great Fast"** called **"The Day"** (Day of Forgivensess").

The **high priest** is a **central figure** on Yom Kippur, and points to Yeshua, our High Priest. *Passover* pointed to Yeshua who came as the *Sacrificial Lamb*. *Yom Kippur* points to Yeshua, as *High Priest*, who is coming back as King to rule and reign on earth. Since there are so many ceremonies performed on this day, we will *focus* on Yeshua, High Priest and soon-coming King.

The Day of Atonement at the time of the Temple in Jerusalem, was the *one day a year* that the high priest went behind the veil into the Holy of Holies with the blood of atonement. He would apply it first for himself and his family, and then again for the sins of the nation (Israel).

On that Day, the people of Israel waited anxiously outside as the high priest entered the Holy of Holies to sprinkle the blood upon the mercy seat of the Ark of the Covenant. His garments would have been sprinkled with the blood of the sacrificial animals. Their fate depended upon God's acceptance of the high priest and the blood sacrifice. If the offering wasn't acceptable, the high priest died and the people's sins remained unforgiven. They would be doomed and die without God's grace and forgiveness. Seeing their high priest come out from the Temple alive was a joyous sight! They knew God had showed mercy and grace again!

God has accepted the Offering, and surely, He has shown His grace and mercy to us through Yeshua! It will be a joyful and glorious sight when Yeshua, our High Priest, comes out from the Heavenly Tabernacle to set up His kingdom on earth! **"Gem"**!

As the high priest sprinkled the blood on the mercy seat of the Ark of the Covenant, it is said that he came *"face to face"* with God on that day. That is why this day is known by the phrase **"face to face"**.

Yeshua our High Priest, has already stood face to face with God and sprinkled His own blood on the Mercy Seat for each believers' *individual* atonement at Passover after His death and resurrection. On this future Day of Atonement Yeshua will return to save the remnant of the **Nation of Israel**. I understand this to be at the end of the great tribulation period at the Battle of Armaggadon.

> *"But the Messiah being come an high priest of good things to come, by a greater and more perfect tabernacle, not made with hands, that is to say, not of this building; Neither by the blood of goats and calves, but by his own blood he entered in once into the holy place, having obtained eternal redemption for us."* (Heb. 9:11,12)

> *"And he was clothed with a vesture dipped in blood; and his name is called The Word of God. And the armies which were in heaven followed him upon white horses, clothed in fine linen, white and clean. And out of his mouth goeth a sharp sword, that with it he should smite the nations..."* (Rev. 19:11,13-15)

The language "vesture dipped in blood" identifies Yeshua with the high priest's garment of white linen splattered with the blood of sacrificial animals on the Day of Atonement.

The Nation of Israel will be fasting and praying on Yom Kippur when He appears. They will **know Him** immediately when they see the blood on His garment. They will know that He is their **High Priest**, that their **Messiah** has come before, died, and been resurrected.

Yom Kippur is *prophetic* of Yeshua's coming to fight for Israel on that day **and** to judge the nations. He comes with the clouds shining brilliantly in all of His glory! *Every eye* will see him *"face to face"*!

> *"Look! He is coming **with** the clouds! Every eye will see him, including those who pierced him and all the tribes of the Land will mourn him.* (Rev. 1:7)

Have you ever thought that the *"clouds"* could be the millions of saints dressed in white linen coming with Him?

It is also said that the high priest on that day saw God's presence as a *brilliant cloud* hovering over the mercy seat ("kapporet", Hebrew) from the root word "kaphar". Kaphar is the Hebrew word for "atonement". Yeshua is our Atonement and has already entered the Holy of Holies in the heavenly tabernacle *once* and for all, but many Jews and Gentiles have not yet believed.

Since there is no temple or human high priest to present the blood, the Jewish people fast and present *themselves* before God to repent of their sins on this Day each year. The unbelieving Jews do not realize that Yeshua, their High Priest, has already come, entered into the Holy of Holies with His blood **once** and for all. Many are still looking for a temple and a human high priest so they can continue with their sacrifices and offerings as before when there was a Temple.

There will also be great mourning in Jerusalem that Day. The Jewish Nation will realize that the prophecy by Zechariah of that Day is being fulfilled.

> "I will gather all the nations to Jerusalem to fight against it; the city shall be captured, the houses ransacked, and the women raped; half of the city will go into exile, but the rest of the people will not be taken from the city. Then shall the Lord go forth and fight against those nations, as when He fought in the day of battle. And His feet shall stand in that day upon the Mount of Olives, which lies before Jerusalem on the east, and the Mount of Olives shall be split in two from the east to the west by a great valley; and half of the mountain shall remove toward the north and half of it toward the south." (Zech. 14:2-4)

> "On that day I will set out to destroy all the nations that attack Jerusalem. And I will pour out on the house of David and the inhabitants of Jerusalem a spirit of grace and supplication. They will look on me, the one they have pierced, and they will mourn for him as one mourns for an only child, and grieves bitterly for him as one grieves for a firstborn son. On that day, the weeping in Jerusalem will be great like the mourning at Hadad Rimmon in the plain of Megiddo." (Zech 12:9-11)

Do you realize that when Yeshua returns, His feet will touch the Mount of Olives where He ascended? He told the disciples that He would return in like manner to this same Mount of Olives! **"Gem"!**

Yeshua will come in great fury and power and pour out His wrath upon those nations that surround Jerusalem to destroy it. Yeshua will totally destroy those nations. It will be a day of reckoning for all the nations that have come against Israel! Isaiah prophesied of this Day too:

> *"So shall he startle and sprinkle many nations; the Kings shall shut their mouths because of him; for that which has not been told them shall they see, and that which they have not heard shall they consider…"* (Isa. 52:15)

Yeshua prophesied of this day (Day of Atonement) when He told the Jews in Jerusalem that they would not see Him again until they said, *"Blessed is He who comes in the name of the Lord."* Yeshua was speaking more to the religious leaders in His day, many of whom rejected Him as their Messiah, rather than the people. The remnant will cry and welcome Him on that day! **Yes, Lord!**

The Jews believe that the gates of heaven that opened at the Feast of Trumpets/Rosh HaShanah are closed on the last day of the Day of Atonement. The final service is called the "neilah" service.

The blast of the *great trumpet* (shofar) or "Shofar HaGadol" (Hebrew) is heard at the end of the final service. At that time, according to Jewish tradition, the last of the saved are inscribed in the Lamb's Book of Life and the gates of heaven are closed. That is why the Jews on the Day of Atonement (Yom Kippur) say, *"May your name be inscribed in the book of Life.*

In Judaism, there are three main *trumpets (shofars)* that mark major events in God's redemption plan. They are: The "first trump" associated with Shavuot (Pentecost) and the giving of the law at Mt. Sinai; the "last" trump sounded at Rosh Hashanah associated with the "catching away" of believers in the Messiah; and the "great trumpet", "Shofar HaGadol" on the Day of Atonement.

The gates that opened at Rosh HaShanah will close on the last day of Yom Kippur. There will be no more time or opportunity to receive salvation, and Yeshua begins to rule over the thousand-year Millennium. All of the people of God will go rejoicing to the Feast of Tabernacles! It will be the time for all of the saints to build a succah!

Do Gentiles have to observe the Day of Atonement? Why shouldn't we? It is a perfect opportunity to show our love and support for the Nation of Israel on this special day that God has set aside for Israel's restoration. It is a time to fast and pray for the Nation of Israel and the Jewish people who do not yet believe that their Messiah has come.

It is also a good time to search our own hearts, fast and repent of our sins and start the following year afresh. Believers can also keep this Day as a *memorial* in remembering the One who has already atoned for our sins and for Israel. It is a good day to praise the Lord that there is no more need for any *human high priest* to apply the blood for us!

It is also the future **Day** our **Atonement (Yeshua)** comes back with His army of saints riding upon white horses to rule and reign on earth with our King! **"Gem"**!

> " And the armies which were in heaven followed him upon white horses, clothed in fine linen, white and clean...And he hath on his vesture and on his thigh a name written. KING OF KINGS AND LORD OF LORDS." (Rev. 19:14,16) **Hallelujah!**

Watching events concerning Israel and Jerusalem are significant to us today. The Lord would not have us ignorant and blind. We are living in the end-time days. The biggest, most obvious sign was the establishment of the Nation of Israel in 1948 in one day, and prophesied by Isaiah.

> "Who hath heard such a thing? Who hath seen such a thing? Shall the earth be made to bring forth in one day? Or shall a nation be born at once...?" (Isa. 66:8)

Have you ever seen a nation blossom and prosper like Israel since the Jewish people returned to their land? Shortly after their return, the desert began to turn green and blossom with flowers. Water bubbled up from the ground and now waters the many vegetables and fruit trees growing in the land. Just recently, oil and gas were discovered in abundance. Their scientists are some of the smartest in the world. Even their military might and power is amazing.

It seems the land and nature itself knows the Jewish people have returned and are rejoicing, just as prophesied! This scripture, however, will have its complete fulfillment during the Millennium.

> "The wilderness and the solitary place shall be glad for them; and the desert shall rejoice, and blossom as the rose. It shall blossom abundantly, and rejoice even with joy and singing . . . they shall see the glory of the Lord, and the excellency of our God." (Isaiah 35:1-2)

Then there was the miraculous six-day war won against several nations against all odds in 1967 when the Jews took back their territory including Jerusalem. In just six days, Israel captured the Sinai Peninsula from Egypt, the Golan Heights from Syria, the West Bank from Jordan and the old city of Jerusalem. Once again the city of God belonged to the Jews and still does.

God supernaturally moved on behalf of Israel in the 1967 war, and many testimonies came forth of supernatural happenings. Jewish soldiers stood praying and crying at the Western Wall, and Defense Minister Moshe Dayan said, "We have returned to the most sacred of shrines never to be parted again." God's eye is turned on Israel and so is the world's eye today.

God loves the Jewish people and has supernaturally kept them and given them Jerusalem "for such a time as this!" He has not fulfilled His plan for Israel and her glorious future!

God has surely turned His attention towards Israel and has begun to move forward in accomplishing His plan for her restoration. Can you believe that so much of prophecy concerning Israel and the last days is unfolding right before our eyes in this generation? Keep watching prophecy concerning Israel and Jerusalem!

Israel and Jerusalem are a key reference to understanding the end time fulfillment of God's plan for Israel. He has not abandoned His plan by any means. It is the major area to watch for future fulfillments spoken of by the prophets of old, by Yeshua, and by the Apostles of the New Testament. It's time to wake up, shake ourselves and look, listen and watch events around us. It's time to pay attention to the prophecies being fulfilled in our present day as a "light shining in a dark place." He that hath an ear let him hear and heed. Peter further states:

"Yes, we have the prophetic word/prophecy made very certain, and we will do well to pay attention to it as a light shining in a dark place, until the day dawns and the Morning Star rises in your hearts. No prophecy of scripture has come as a result of human will, but rather of people moved by the Holy Spirit speaking the message from God."(2 Peter 1:19-21)

After Israel became a nation in one day in 1948, the fulfillment of this prophecy began: *"And He shall set up an ensign for the nations, and shall assemble the outcasts of Israel, and gather together the dispersed of Judah from the four corners of the earth."*(Isaiah 11:12)

Jeremiah 23:3 prophesied that a great increase of Jews would return to Israel just before the return of the Lord, and we are seeing that happen today. *"And I will gather the remnant of my flock out of all countries whither I have driven them again to their folds; and they shall be fruitful and multiply."*

As mentioned earlier, according to the book of Daniel, a peace agreement will mark the beginning of the seven-year tribulation period, a sign for which believers should be watching.

In any case, we are witnessing today the attempt to get a peace agreement between Israel and the Palestinians. It could be made before I finish this book. John Kerry, Secretary of State, said he planned to have an agreement signed by April 29, 2014.It didn't happen. A blood moon had appeared on April fourteenth. It is interesting to note that the planned agreement between Israel and the Palestinians fell apart after the blood moon had appeared. The blood moons are signals and warnings from God, especially in relation to Israel.

Remember, Daniel also predicted that a coming prince (not Yeshua, but the antichrist) would bring about the signing of the pact (treaty) to bring peace (a false peace) and would break it at midpoint (after three and a half years).After that, the last three and one-half years begin , called the "Great Tribulation".

> *"And he shall confirm the covenant with many for one week* [prophetic week, seven years]*; and in the midst of the week* [half of prophetic week, three and a half years]*, he shall cause the sacrifice and the oblation to cease, and for the overspreading of abominations he shall make it desolate, even unto the consummation . . . ."*(Daniel 9:27)

Yeshua even referred to the prophecy in Daniel about the "abomination of desolation." That's when the antichrist stands in the Temple at Jerusalem mid-way the seven-year tribulation(beginning of "Great Tribulation").The antichrist will shut down the altar and sacrifices of the third (next) Temple and set up an image to be worshipped.

> *"Forces from him* [antichrist] *will arise, desecrate the sanctuary fortress, and do away with the regular sacrifice. And they will set up the abomination of desolation* [image].*"*(Dan. 11:31)

Concerning this prophecy, Yeshua Himself said:

> *"When ye therefore shall see the abomination of desolation, spoken of by Daniel the prophet, stand in the Holy Place, then let them which be in Judaea flee into the mountains . . . for then shall be 'Great Tribulation,' such as was not since the beginning of the world to this time, no, nor ever shall be."*(Matt. 24:21)

By the way, did you know that Daniel gave one of the most amazing prophecies in relation to Yeshua's baptism and the beginning of His ministry?

> *"Know therefore and understand, that from the going forth of the commandment to restore and to build Jerusalem unto the Messiah the Prince shall be seven weeks, and*[plus]*threescore and two weeks*[sixty-two weeks]*; the street shall be built again, and the wall, even in troublesome times."*(Daniel 9:25)

In the above scripture, Daniel prophesied that the Messiah the Prince would come at the end of the first seven weeks plus sixty-two more weeks (a total of sixty-nine weeks, or 483 years) from the decree to rebuild Jerusalem.

So, our starting point to calculate the year of the Messiah is by counting from the year of the decree. The decree took place during the reign of Artaxerxes, King of Persia. The book of Ezra gives us the time:

> *". . . and the King granted Ezra all his request . . . And there went up some of the children of Israel, priests, Levites, singers, porters, and the*

Nethinims unto Jerusalem in the seventh year of Artaxerxes the King."(Ezra 7:6-7)

We know from historical records that this King began to reign in 464 B.C. So, the seventh year of Artaxerxes would have been 457 B.C., the time of the decree.

This first seven weeks (forty-nine years) was a time period from the decree that allowed the Jewish people to rebuild the Temple in Jerusalem until its completion in 408 B.C. (forty-nine years from 457 B.C.)

Sixty-two more weeks (434 years) from the completion of the temple in 408 B.C. brings us to 26 A.D., a total of sixty-nine weeks (483 years).However, when changing from B.C. to A.D., we have to add one year. Guess what year that brings us to? The year 27 A.D., the very year that Yeshua the Messiah was baptized, anointed and began His ministry as Israel's Messiah! How's that for an awesome **"Gem"**?

Lastly, Daniel saw another Temple in Jerusalem in the last days. There is no Temple in Jerusalem at this time. All of the architectural plans and preparations have been made, however, to hold services in a new anticipated temple. The news media last year showed the Jews gathering smooth stones at the shores of Galilee to make the altars.

As I write this book, everything is ready, including the high priest's garment and other priestly garments for ministering in the temple. Since the original Ark of the Covenant for the Holy of Holies has not been found, a duplicate has been made. But who knows, the original may be found before the temple services begin. Many believe that it is in a tunnel under the Dome of the Rock. Some believe it could be under Mt.

Nebo. If it is found, there will be the biggest ingathering of Jews into Jerusalem in history!

The last thing needed and not yet found is the "red heifer," whose ashes are necessary in the old cleansing ceremony for the cleansing of all Israel. There is a search continuing to this day for a red heifer without blemish or any white hair. Many red heifers are being bred today in hopes of finding that perfect one by the time the third temple is built. However, it is possible, according to some Rabbis, that a vessel containing ashes saved for years from a previous heifer may be found.

There have been suggestions of the Jews and Palestinians sharing the Temple Mount where the present Dome of the Rock is located. Past President Bill Clinton was one to make the first suggestion. It is being considered today with the U.N. having control over the Temple Mount. It would set the stage for the "man of perdition" (antichrist) to stand in the newly built temple. He could be there to stop the animal sacrifices that will be offered again to God by the Jews.

According to prophecy, we know that the antichrist will stand in the temple and show great signs and wonders. That will be the beginning of the Great Tribulation.

Yeshua warned the Jewish people in Judea (West Bank area) of the time that the antichrist would stop the sacrifices and set up an image in the temple. They are told to flee quickly from Judea at that time. Many living there today are being informed of this prophecy and are told they should consider leaving now.

Yeshua Himself refers to Daniel's prophecy concerning Judea:

> "When ye therefore shall see the abomination of desolation spoken of by Daniel the prophet, stand in the holy place, then let them which be in Judea, flee into the mountains."(Matthew 24:15)

The scriptures state that the Lord will shorten the time of the Great Tribulation for the elect's sake.

> "For then there will be great distress, unequaled from the beginning of the world until now—and never to be equaled again if those days had not been cut short, no one would survive, but for the sake of the elect, those days will be shortened."(Matt. 24:22)

Cosmic disturbances are one of the *last signs* that precede Yeshua's coming for the elect near the **end** of the Great Tribulation before His wrath is poured out. Yeshua prophesied of the cosmic disturbances and the gathering of the elect in the following scripture:

> "Immediately after the distress of those days, the sun will be darkened, and the moon will not give its light; the stars will fall from the sky, and the heavenly bodies will be shaken. At that time the sign of the Son of Man will appear in the sky, and all the nations of the earth will mourn . . . He will send an angel with a loud trumpet call, and they will gather His elect from the four

winds, from one end of the heavens to the other."(Matt. 24:29-31)

Daniel used the words, "the distress of those days" in reference to the Great Tribulation. Yeshua used the same words, "distress of those days" in referring to the same time just prior to His appearing.

I know there are pre-tribulation, mid-tribulation and post-tribulation believers. Even though there are different views, one thing all can agree upon is being ready to meet Yeshua at whatever time He comes. Amen?

The following scripture describes saints who have come out of "Great Tribulation":

"After this I looked and there before me was a great multitude that no one could count, from every nation, tribe, people and language, standing before the throne and in front of the Lamb. They were wearing white robes and were holding palm branches in their hands. they cried out in a loud voice: "Salvation belongs to God who sits on the throne and to the Lamb." (Rev. 7:9-10)

"Then, one of the elders asked me, these in white robes—who are they, and where did they come from?"(Rev. 7:13)

"And he said, these are they who have come out of Great Tribulation; they have washed their robes and made them white in the blood of the

> *Lamb . . . and serve Him night and day in His temple."* (Rev. 7:13-15)

The good news is that during the Tribulation Period many will turn to God, cry out to Him and find salvation. God sends judgment to turn people from sin and bring them to repentance and salvation. Many Jews and Gentiles will be saved and many backsliders will return to God during the tribulation days. They will welcome the coming of Yeshua. He will come in great power and glory for His saints!

Ezekiel 38 and 39 prophesies of nations gathering against Israel which starts a third world war in the last days. We are witnessing these prophecies being fulfilled today, and World War III is very near and may have already started.

Nuclear weapons and nerve gas are already being used to destroy man and nations. Threats of destruction are being made from Iran and other nations against Israel and the United States in particular. There are wars and rumors of war everywhere. The Islamic movement is growing larger every day. The terrorists' attacks are increasing in every nation. Many nations are turning against Israel because it is defending itself against its enemies. Ezekiel prophesied that Russia would lead the attacks in the next war with other nations. The aggressiveness of Russia and its army is taking place in Europe this very day.

> Yeshua's words ring loud and clear today that *"nation shall rise against nation, kingdom against kingdom: and there shall be famines, and pestilences, and earthquakes in divers places . . . and many false prophets."* (Matthew 24:7-11)

Signs of God's shaking are all around us. Our weather is unpredictable and the floods, fires, ice and snow are devastating. Earthquakes are increasing in number and intensity. Crime and violence are increasing. Could these signs be the early stages of the seven-year tribulation described in Matthew 24?

However, God would not have us be fearful of the coming days. The prophecies must be fulfilled by Yeshua before He comes. As we see the prophecies coming to pass, we know that His coming is soon. Let these words of encouragement in Isaiah encourage us:

> "Fear thou not; for I am with thee, be not dismayed; for I am thy God: I will strengthen thee; yea, I will help thee; yea, I will uphold thee with the right hand of my righteousness.(Isaiah 41:10)

When I was writing this book several years ago, Pope Benedict XVI just resigned as Pope. Pope Frances has taken His place. According to an ancient prophecy concerning Popes by Saint Malachy, many believe the last Pope who will serve with the antichrist will be called "Peter of Rome."

Saint Malachy's prophecies concerning the past reigning Popes, especially the names of each pope have been very accurate. The Popes always have a name other than their birth name. If Saint Malachy's prophecy of a Pope named "Peter of Rome" is accurate, then according to a prophetic teacher I heard recently, Pope Frances' original name is "Peter", and that he is originally from Rome. If that is true, Pope Frances could be the Pope reigning when the antichrist appears. Again, only time will tell. Keep watching!

Revelation 17:16 depicts a woman (representing a religious system) riding upon the ten-horned governmental system of the antichrist (many believe this to be the European Union).

"Beasts" in the Word and in the book of Revelation represent governments. A "woman" many times represents the true or false church. Did you know that a new European Union coin just came out with a picture of a woman riding a beast on it? Also, in front of the European Union Headquarters there is a huge statute of a figure riding a huge animal.

On a brighter side, look at the increasing archeological sites and artifacts being uncovered in our day. I get so blessed when I see ancient ruins of places uncovered in the exact location as described in the Bible.

Recently, a synagogue was uncovered near the Sea of Galilee. It is a first century synagogue, and it is believed to be one in which Yeshua taught. One of the artifacts had the Menorah inscribed upon it.

Also for the past several years, archeologists have been digging up stony remains of the City of David, including its surrounding walls. Recently, the archeologists believe they have discovered part of the palace. If that is the case, then it probably won't be long before they find King David and King Solomon's tombs. Many Kings were buried under their palaces, and it is stated in the scriptures that David and Solomon were both buried in the city of David. Most likely, they were buried side by side. How awesome that will be if their tombs are discovered!

> "Then David slept with his ancestors and was buried in the city of David." (I Kings 2:10)

> "Then Solomon slept with his ancestors and was buried in the city of David his father . . ." (I Kings 11:43)

Another discovery was made several years ago on Mt. Ebal. It was made of stones measuring twenty-seven feet by twenty-one feet with sheep bones, ashes and dark blood stains. It was dated by Carbon 14 technique back to the time of Joshua's conquering of Canaan.

> "Then, Joshua built an altar to the Lord God of Israel at Mt. Ebal, as Moses commanded in the book of his laws: Make me an altar of whole stones, over which no man hath lift up any iron; and they offered thereon burnt offerings unto the Lord, and sacrificed peace offerings."(Joshua 8:30-35)

Joshua had won a victory over King Ai and the entire population of twelve thousand had been wiped out, and King Ai was hanged on a tree. At evening, Joshua took his body down and threw it at the gate of the city and piled up a great pile of stones over it. The huge pile of stones *"remaineth unto this day"* according to Joshua 8:25-29.

"Prime Time Live" in the early 1990's visited the old city of Babylon in Iraq. They took pictures of the rebuilt gates, palace walls and pagan temples within the walls. Saddam Hussein had spent billions to rebuild part of Babylon. One brick had the inscription upon it, "I am Nebuchadnezzar, King of everything from sea to sea."

Did you know that King Nebuchadnezzar was Saddam Hussein's hero? Saddam Hussein had a coin made with King Nebuchadnezzar's picture on one side and his own picture on the other. Not only that, but Saddam Hussein had a duplicate of King Nebuchadnezzar's gold chariot made with a picture of himself (Saddam) sitting in the chariot. Saddam Hussein really had a vision of rebuilding Babylon and reigning over it. Such vanity, but where is he now?

They found another brick on which Saddam Hussein had inscribed, "I am Saddam Hussein, president of the Republic of Iraq" in honor of himself.

As we discussed earlier, Babylon was a rich and powerful pagan nation, the Wonder City of the ancient world. It was a nation of sexual immorality and wickedness, a nation based on witchcraft and idolatry, with many gods and goddesses. It was called the "seat of Satan." Nimrod was the most outstanding leader between the flood and Abraham. King Nebuchadnezzar was ruling there when Daniel and Ezekiel became captives.

Let's look at a prophecy about old Babylon. In Isaiah 13:17-20, it is prophesied that Babylon would *"never be inhabited"* again. When Hussein started rebuilding it, he intended to complete it in his day, but was cut short. However, it was inhabited by him and others for a short while as they rebuilt it.

Jeremiah 50:13-40 prophesied that it would be *"wholly desolate,"* which is not true today, and has not come to pass.

Jeremiah 51:25,58,62 and 64 prophesied that there would be *"no stone left,"* and *"would never rise again."* That has not happened. Many of the stones left from the last destruction of Babylon remain, and some have been used to build cities around the area, e.i., City of Hallah. We have not seen the total destruction of the City of Babylon with *"no stone left"* yet.

The book of Revelation, Chapter 18:8-9-21 describes Babylon's *"utter destruction"* in the latter days. If this scripture is literal and referring to the rebuilt city, Babylon will be completed by someone. Could it become a great commercial and religious center and site of the world government once again? Will another leader continue the work that Saddam Hussein started? Time will tell.

According to Revelation, Babylon is called "Mystery Babylon," not "old Babylon." It is described as a very prosperous commercial city with merchants and countries receiving commodities from her. The merchants end up mourning her sudden destruction.

Of course, the prophecy could refer to a wicked "system" like Babylon rather than a literal re-built Babylon. Some Bible scholars of prophecy believe that it refers to a "wicked system" of world government like old Babylon. They believe it will operate from Rome in the last days as in the Holy Roman Empire. They believe that Rome will be the seat of "mystery Babylon," the mother of harlots (the apostate church, a false religious system). The false prophet will be the head of that apostate church during the tribulation period.

The location of this religious system is a seven-hilled city, which could refer to Rome. The beast that she sits upon is the wicked governmental system under the antichrist. They seem to form a coalition of false religion and a wicked world government as in the days of the Holy Roman Empire.

According to Timothy, two major things must happen in the last days before Yeshua's return: *"great apostasy"* and the *"antichrist revealed."*

> *"Let no man deceive you by any means; for that day shall not come, except there come a falling away first, and that man of sin, the son of perdition [antichrist] be revealed."* (2 Thess. 2:3)

> *"Who opposeth and exalteth himself above all that is called God . . . so that he as God sitteth in the temple of God, showing himself that he is God."* (2 Thess. 2:4)

Apostasy is infiltrating our churches at a fast pace. Apostasy has always been present, but never as it is today. The word "apostasy" comes from the Greek word *"apostacia"* meaning, "departing or defecting from the truth." Can't you see it in many denominations today more than ever? Denominations are splitting up or compromising the Word of God, especially on issues involving homosexuals and same-sex marriage.

We are warned of these things in I Timothy 4:1-2:

> *"Now the Spirit speaketh expressly, that in the latter times some shall depart from the faith, giving heed to seducing spirits, and doctrines of devils; speaking lies in hypocrisy; having their conscience seared with a hot iron . . . ."*

Never has there been a more important time to "try the spirits," and, if you are part of a church that teaches false doctrines or performs services contrary to the Word of God, get out! Remember Yeshua's words to His people who lived in a wicked Babylonian system:" . . . *Come out of her, my people, that ye be not partakers of her sins, so that ye receive not of her plagues."* (Rev. 18:4)

Our nation is a rich and powerful nation because of God's blessings, but it is removing Godly principles from its foundation. We have become a nation of sexual permissiveness, and immorality is being flaunted in God's face. Because our leaders are changing our laws contrary to God's Word, God, according to His pattern, may allow evil rulers to rule over our nation.

Persecution of Jews and Christians is increasing. As I am completing this book, thousands are fleeing for their life in Iraq and other surrounding nations. So many believers today are being tortured and killed in many countries, some by decapitation. Pastors of house congregations are being arrested and killed in foreign countries. Opposition to Christianity is on the rise in America too. At least one pastor has been arrested and fined for holding a Word study in his own home. This is becoming a time for God's people to stand together even if it means imprisonment or death. Did you ever think this would happen in America?

The "day of the Lord's wrath" will come to the unbelievers who say "everything is peaceful and secure," and are not looking for the Messiah. Yeshua will **not** come as a "thief in the night" to the believer.

Paul states that destruction will come upon the unbelievers (those in spiritual darkness) suddenly, **not** to believers. If we know the Word and know what signs to look for, believers will certainly know the season and when the time is very near. Praying, seeking His face and obeying the Holy Spirit is especially important. Believers must be faithful to the Lord and obedient to His Word in overcoming evil.

> *"But you, brethren, are not in the dark, so that that day should take you by surprise as a thief, for you are people who belong to the light . . . therefore, let us not sleep as do others, but let us watch and be sober."* (I Thess. 5:5)

Studying prophecy and listening to present-day prophets of God will also keep us aware of God's actions before they happen, so that we will not be overcome by fear or caught unaware!

The following scripture is a good word for us today:

> *"Let us draw near with a true heart in full assurance of our faith, having our hearts sprinkled from an evil conscience, and our bodies washed with pure water. Let us hold fast the profession of our faith without waivering, for He is faithful that promised; and let us love one another and do good works, not forsaking the assembling of ourselves together, but exhorting one another; and so much the more, as ye see the day approaching."* (Hebrews 10:22-25) Amen!

AUTHOR'S NOTE: This author has barely scratched the surface of the seven annual "Feasts of the Lord". This author has only covered the key themes and highlights of each Feast (literal and spiritual significance). It would be beneficial for you, the reader, to purchase a book with more details of each Feast . Let's continue with the *seventh* and *last* annual Feast of the Lord, the Feast of Tabernacles.

CHAPTER 15

FEAST OF TABERNACLES

The Feast of Tabernacles (called **"Sukkot***,*" in Hebrew), is celebrated in the fall months, Mid-September to Mid-October. It is the *largest and most joyous feast* in the yearly cycle of the seven "Feasts of the Lord." It is the culmination of the *summer harvest* (Feast of Shavuot) and the gathering of the *fall crops* into the barn before winter. *All* the *fruits* from the vintage such as the grapes, figs and dates had been gathered in as well.

Sukkot is a "thanksgiving feast" unto God for the great harvest of wheat and fruits. It also points spiritually to the great latter harvest of souls at the end of the age. It is a seven-day feast spilling over into a "special event" on the eighth day.

The **Feast of Tabernacles** is the most joyous celebration of all the feasts. The fall season of this feast is called the **"Season of Joy."** It is the only feast in which God *commands* everyone to rejoice. It is also called "Feast of Ingatherings" and "Feast of Nations." This Feast teaches us about the Millennial reign of Yeshua. This feast is to be celebrated by all of the saints of God and many nations during the Millennium.

> *"Celebrate the Feast of Tabernacles for seven days after you have gathered the produce of your threshing floor and of your winepress. And thou shalt rejoice in thy feast, thou, and thy son, and thy daughter, and thy manservant, and thy maidservant, and the Levite, the stranger, and the fatherless, and the widow, that are within thy gates. For the Lord your God will bless you in*

all your harvest and in all the work of your hands, and your joy will be complete." (Deut.16:14)

The Israelites after journeying in the wilderness for 40 years entered and settled into the Promised Land. During their wilderness journey, they built the temporary tabernacles/huts (called "succah") for rest and protection. They celebrated this Feast in the Promised Land by building the "succah" and still do at this Feast.

The succah were made of leafy branches of willows, myrtles and palm branches. The roof was left partially open so they could see the stars shining through as they lay down in them at night.

Many Jewish people live in them for seven days during the Feast of Tabernacles. It is a *memorial* to God in remembering how He protected them and brought them through the wilderness to the Promised Land.

Historically, this Feast reveals a *personal relationship* between God and the Nation of Israel during their journey. They experienced God's presence, His provision and His protection during their journey. God was the One they had to depend upon, and He was always there with them.

In celebrating this Feast today, many Gentiles also build succah and invite friends over to fellowship and celebrate God's blessings. This Feast points to the believers' *personal relationship, provision* and *presence* of God who never leaves nor forsakes us by the "indwelling of the Holy Spirit"! In a spiritual sense, we are temporary, living tabernacles (succah). Our bodies are temporary dwelling places during our journey here on earth. Soon, we will reach the heavenly Promised Land and dwell in glorified bodies during the Millennium! **Gem!**

This Feast was one of the three feasts in which God required all males to travel to Jerusalem to celebrate. The other two were the Passover (Pesach) and Shavuot (Pentecost).

Spiritually, this Feast is also *prophetic* of the greatest harvest or ingathering of souls at the end of this age and is also the *first feast* celebrated before the throne in the Millennium.

> *"And it shall come to pass that every one that is left of all the nations which came against Jerusalem shall even go up from year to year to worship the King, the Lord of Hosts, and keep the feast of tabernacles."* (Zech. 14:16)

Yeshua was the first **Living Tabernacle** in which God dwelt. God's great desire to dwell with man was manifested by the sending of His Son to dwell among us. God revealed Himself in the flesh through Yeshua. Yeshua said: *"If you have seen me, you have seen the Father."*

> *"The Word became flesh and made His dwelling among us. We have seen His glory, the glory of the One and Only, who came from the Father, full of grace and truth."* (John 1:14)

As Believers living in fleshly tabernacles where God dwells, we should celebrate His glory in us through the Holy Spirit with great joy and thanksgiving *every day*! **"Gem"**! What an awesome God we serve!

In the book of Revelation the redeemed dressed in white robes are seen celebrating this feast. They are waving palm branches and crying out words related to the feast's theme, Salvation.

> *"After this I beheld, and lo, a great multitude, which no man could number, of all nations, and kindreds, and people, and tongues, stood before the throne, and before the Lamb, clothed with white robes, and palms in their hands; and cried with a loud voice, saying, salvation to our God which sitteth upon the throne, and unto the Lamb."*(Rev. 7:9-10)

Yeshua, whose name means "Salvation" ("God saves"), is the Central Figure revealed in the Feast of Tabernacles, as in all of the feasts which also reveal God's plan of redemption and reconciliation to God through Yeshua. This feast includes two main ceremonies that reveal Yeshua:

(1) The "lighting ceremony," pointing to Yeshua as the Light of the World; and
(2) "drawing of water ceremony," pointing to Yeshua, the Well of Salvation out of whom Living Waters flow.

Part I. The Lighting Ceremony

In the temple courtyard during the lighting ceremony each night, there were four tall golden candlesticks (menorahs) set up with lamps atop each one, 50 cubits high, holding seven and a half gallons of pure olive oil. Each candlestick or menorah had a wick made of old worn priestly garments called "swaddling cloth." Tall ladders were used to enable the young priests to climb to the top, pour in fresh olive oil each evening and light the lamps atop each candlestick.

When the lamps were lit they illuminated the whole temple and courtyard. The great fire and smoke from them could be seen for miles around the whole City of Jerusalem. It was a spectacular light that represented the *Sh'chinah* Glory of God. The Temple at Jerusalem was known as the "Light of the World" at this Feast. A future temple will again be established in Jerusalem during the Millennium and called the "Light of the World. "**Gem**"!

The four golden candlesticks (menorahs) dispelled the darkness of night with their great light. The four candlesticks represented the Light (Yeshua) reaching out to the four corners of the earth. Remember the message to Peter in Acts 10:1-12 when he saw the sheet (could have been a Talit) with four corners? It was to show Peter that the gospel was for every nation, kindred, tongue and people, which included the Gentiles.

Historically, the fire and the smoke from the four huge candlesticks at the lighting ceremony of the feast would have reminded the Jewish people of their journey through the wilderness. They would have recalled the fire that led them by night, and the cloud that led them by day (Yeshua). They would have celebrated this ceremony with thanksgiving and praise to God for their deliverance from Egypt and His presence and protection in their journey through the wilderness.

The people would also have been reminded of the Menorah, the only light burning in the Holy Place of the wilderness tabernacle. It provided the light for the priests in performing their duties. The priests were *never* to let the light go out. The Menorah from ancient times has been and still is the central identifying **symbol** of Israel. It is the main symbol tying the Jewish nation to God and her calling to be a light to the world through her Messiah.

The Menorah (also called Candlestick/Lampstand) represents Yeshua, the Word, and the Light of the World. He is the Center Staff (Stem out of the root of Jesse), standing taller than the other branches of the Menorah. The six (6) branches stemming out from His side represent His Body of Believers. The Oil (Holy Spirit) flows out from the Center Staff (also called "Servant Branch") into the branches. Without the Oil, there would be no Light! Yeshua provides the Light by which the saints, also to be the light of the world, perform their duties! **"Gem"**! (See Rev. 1:13)

> *"Ye are the light of the world. A city that is set on an hill cannot be hid. Neither do men light a candle, and put it under a bushel, but on a candlestick; and it giveth light unto all that are in the house. Let your light so shine before men, that they may see your good works, and glorify your Father which is in heaven."* (Matt. 5:14-16)

At the lighting ceremony of the Feast each evening, the people danced with joy in the great light of the night. The Levites played all sorts of instruments including flutes, shofars and timbrels, while the Sanhedrin danced around carrying torches. All the people sang, danced and worshipped God well into the night.

This Feast lasted for seven days with a special grand finale on the eighth day. There was an atmosphere of "great joy and rejoicing" as God had commanded. This ceremony of the Feast celebrates Yeshua as the "Light of the World". It was in the morning on the seventh day of the ceremony, while the lighting ceremony from the previous evening was still on the peoples' minds, Yeshua stood and said:

> *"I am the Light of the World, whosoever follows me will never walk in darkness, but will have the Light of Life."* John 8:12) Amen!

> Later that day, He healed a blind man and said: *"While I am in the world, I am the light of the world."* (John 9:5)

> Now, every born-again believer is the "light of the world": *"Ye are the light of the world",* Yeshua said.

Part 2. Drawing of Water Ceremony

The second main ceremony was called "house of water drawing." It was also a very joyous ceremony. Each day of the feast, shortly after dawn, the high priest was dispatched down to the Pool of Siloam with a golden pitcher to draw water. The water was called "living waters of salvation." "Waters" is plural meaning ever-moving, ever-flowing, on and on, and never ending (like the Holy Spirit)."**Gem**"!

The high priest (prototype of Yeshua) drawing the living waters was called, "he who is sent" or "the sent one." *Historically*, it celebrated God's provision of life-giving water to the Israelites out of the rock in the wilderness. *Prophetically*, it foreshadowed Yeshua who was sent by the Father, and the Rock out of whom Living Waters flow! "**Gem**"!

In this water drawing ceremony, once the "living waters of salvation" were drawn from the Pool of Siloam, a flute player (called the "pierced one", figurative of Yeshua) played music while leading the procession back to the temple. The flute player accompanied the high priest with the golden pitcher (vessel, figurative of Yeshua) of Living Waters (figurative of the Holy Spirit). Yeshua spoke of the joy set before Him in relation to His sacrifice.

The joyful throng of people would follow the high priest back to the temple waving large willow branches and palm branches. The branches made a swishing sound like wind (figurative of the Holy Spirit). Can you see Yeshua, the Pierced One, the Sent One, the High Priest, and the Divine Vessel filled with Living Waters in this ceremony?

After arriving at the inner court, the high priest poured the water into a large basin. He was then joined by a priest carrying a silver pitcher. Silver is figurative of the "redeemed". The silver pitcher was filled with wine (figurative of Yeshua's blood).

Together, the two would each pour out the water and the wine into funnels that flowed down the side of the brazen altar. The brazen altar in the temple was the altar upon which sacrifices were made. The tree at Golgotha became the *brazen altar of sacrifice* for Yeshua who died for all peoples and nations.

As both pitchers, one of water and one of wine were poured out down the side of the brazen altar, they produced an outpouring appearing like water and blood. Water and blood flowed down the tree from the pierced side of Yeshua. What an awesome *prophetic* picture of the scene at Golgotha as blood and water ran out Yeshua's riven side for His priests who are redeemed by His blood. Awesome picture!

There was said to be 70 nations at that time, so 70 bulls, one for each nation was sacrificed during this Feast. That is one reason this Feast is also called the "Feast of Nations". It also points to the Millennium when the nations will celebrate the Feast of Tabernacles.

On the last day of the Feast ("Hoshana Rabbah") meaning "Great Hosanna", a greater outpouring of water was poured out from the altar. The "living waters" ran down the altar, through the temple and out to the streets. It pointed to the One possessing the Living Waters and the great outpouring of the Holy Spirit. Yeshua sat watching at this great outpouring of water on that day. He could sit silent no longer, knowing that the ceremony spoke of Him and the Holy Spirit. His cry is recorded by the Apostle John:

> "In the last day, that 'great day' of the feast, Yeshua stood and cried, saying: If any man thirst, let him come unto me and drink. He that believeth on me, as the scripture hath said, out of his belly shall flow rivers of Living Water."(John 7:37-39)

> "Indeed you know me! And you know where I am from. I have not come on my own! The One who sent me is real! I do know Him, because I am with Him and He sent me!...However, again, the One who sent me is still with me . . ."(John 7:14,28-29,38)

Yeshua quoted scriptures from the old Prophet Isaiah during this Feast in proclaiming Himself the Jewish Messiah, and the One possessing the Living Waters. The Jews would have been familiar with the following scriptures, and knew they spoke of the Messiah, but many failed to see that He had come. They missed His first visitation.

> *"Behold, God is my salvation, I will trust and not be afraid; for the Lord God is my strength and song, and He has become my Salvation. Therefore, you will joyously draw water from the springs of Salvation."* (Isa. 12:2,3)

> *"Ho, every one that thirsteth, come ye to the waters, and he that hath no money; come ye, buy wine and milk without money and without price."* [Salvation is free to all.](Isa. 55:1)

At His first coming in the flesh (Living Tabernacle, the dwelling place of God), Yeshua fulfilled the **main theme** of this Feast, "Salvation", and the **two main ceremonies**, "Light of the World" and "Well of Salvation out of Whom Living Waters flow"! **"Gem"!**

Part 3. The Eighth Day 'Special Event'

Immediately following the last day of this Feast (the seventh day called "Hoshana Rabbah") two more days, Tishrei 22, "Shemeni Atzeret", and "Simchat Torah" on the 23rd. Both days were considered *one long day*.

> *"On the eighth day ye shall have a solemn assembly: Ye shall do no servile work therein."* (Num 29:35)

"Shemini Atzeret" in Hebrew means "eighth day of assembly" and to "tarry" an *extra day* at the end of Sukkot. It concluded the festivities of the 7-day Feast. The Rabbis interpret this to mean that God asks all who have made a pilgrimage for Sukkot to stay another day. It is celebrated on Tishrei 22 and is a very joyful day.

The *most joyful day* following is called *"Simchat Torah"*, meaning "rejoicing in the Torah" on Tishrei 23rd. This celebration reached its crescendo with the loud, long blasting of the shofar. These days point to a time beyond time, one long eternal day! **"Gem"**!

This day is also the end of the *annual cyclical reading* of the Torah by the Jewish "civil" calendar, but also the recommencing of the Torah reading in Genesis. Therefore, it is continuous without actually ending (unending). It is very important to read the Torah over and over again. However, the *prophetic picture* is of Yeshua, the Living Torah, Who is everlasting and without end! Let us rejoice in the Living Torah, Yeshua, Who teaches us the ways of God! **"Gem"**!

The *ultimate fulfilling* of the Feast of Tabernacles is during the thousand-year reign of Yeshua when all the knowledge of God and the teachings of the Messiah will fill the earth. The greatest outpouring of the Holy Spirit will be experienced at that time.

> *"And it shall come to pass in the last days, that the mountain of the Lord's house shall be reestablished in the top of the mountains, and shall be exalted above the hills; and all nations shall flow into it. And many people will say, Come ye, and let us go up to the mountain of*

the Lord…and he will teach us of his ways, and we will walk in his paths; for out of Zion shall go forth the law, and the word of the Lord from Jerusalem. (Isaiah 2:2,3)

The Nation of Israel will also be a *central part* of the Millennium. Israel will be a great blessing to all of the nations!

Mary and Joseph thereby fulfilled the Law of God pertaining to all Jewish males at *eight days old*. I believe that Yeshua's circumcision was the *ultimate fulfillment* of God's blood covenant with Abraham in the ***flesh*** through His Son's circumcision! The promise that Israel's Messiah would come through the seed of Abraham and bless all nations was fulfilled and sealed forever! **"Gem"!**

> *"And in the eighth day the flesh of the manchild's foreskin shall be circumcised at eight days old."*(Lev. 12:3)

Not only was this the day of His circumcision, it was the day when His Jewish name "Yeshua" (Hebrew name meaning "Salvation" or "*Yah* (God) saves") became official. His name was given according to the instructions by the angel that appeared to Mary **before** Yeshua was even conceived. Isn't that awesome?

> *"On the eighth day, when it was time for His b'rit-milah, He was given the name Yeshua, which is what the angel had called Him before His conception."*(Luke 2:21, Complete Jewish Bible)

After forty days of *purification* for Mary as required by Jewish law, she and Joseph went to the Temple for Yeshua's dedication to the Lord. (See Lev. 12:2-4)

> *"And when the days of her purification according to the law of Moses were accomplished, they brought him to Jerusalem to present him to the Lord."* (Luke 2:22)

Simeon was there in the Temple in Jerusalem when Mary and Joseph brought the infant Yeshua that day. He had been led there by *Ruach HaKodesh* (Holy Spirit) who had revealed to him that he would not die until he had seen the Messiah. When seeing Mary and Joseph with the baby, he knew the baby was the promised Messiah. Simeon knew God had kept His promise and he must have been crying tears of joy as he took the baby, Yeshua, into his arms. He began to praise God with these words:

> *"Then took he Him up in his arms, and blessed God, and said, Lord, now lettest thou they servant depart in peace, according to thy word; for mine eyes have seen thy salvation, which thou hast prepared before the face of the people; a Light to the Gentiles, and the glory of thy people Israel."* (Luke 2:28-32)

Then, Simeon blessed Mary and Joseph and prophesied to Mary:

> *"Behold this child is set for the fall and rising again of many in Israel; and for a sign which shall be spoken against; Yea, a sword shall pierce through thine own soul, for this child shall*

be rejected by many of Israel and this to their undoing. But He will be the greatest joy of many others, and the deepest thoughts of many hearts shall be revealed."(Luke 2:34-35) **How true!**

Did you notice that this particular prophecy was to Mary alone? Why? Joseph was not the biological father of Yeshua, and he would not be living at the time of Yeshua's crucifixion. How accurate are God's prophecies! **"Gem"!**

Can you imagine how Mary's soul was torn with pain as she saw her innocent Son beaten, His flesh torn to pieces, and His mutilated body hanging on the cross at age thirty-three? No wonder the prophecy spoke of the piercing (heartbreak) of Mary's soul.

Anna, a prophetess, the daughter of Phanuel of the Tribe of Asher was also in the temple that day.

Anna was of great age, possibly around one hundred years old, and had been a widow for about eighty-four years (not 84 years old, but a widow for 84 years). She had never departed from the temple. She served the Lord there day and night with fastings and prayers. She heard Simeon's words over the infant the day Mary and Joseph came with Yeshua, and gave thanks unto the Lord. She immediately began telling everyone in Jerusalem who had been awaiting the coming of the Messiah that He had finally arrived. She continued to announce Yeshua's birth in Jerusalem. Can you imagine Anna, an old woman of "great age" evangelizing Jerusalem? I love it, not being a young chicken myself.

> *"And she coming in that instant* [of Simeon's prophecies] *gave thanks likewise unto the Lord and spake of Him to all them that looked for redemption in Jerusalem."*(Luke 2:38)

Do you realize that Simeon and Anna, after *tarrying an extra day* after the Feast (Shemini Atzeret), the eighth day and last day, that they were *rejoicing over the Living Torah* on "Shemini Atzeret" and "Simchat Torah" (considered one long day beyond time as we know it), the *most joyful day* of the Feast? Could it be prophetic of the day of eternity? **Gem!**

Believers too should rejoice over the Living Torah daily who teaches us God's ways through the Holy Spirit. Yeshua is also revealed in this Feast as the Light and the Well of Salvation of Living Waters. He is the Light that shines in us and the Living Waters that flow out from the midst of us (our belly)! **"Gem"!**

> *"He that believeth on me...out of his belly shall flow rivers of Living Waters."* (John 7:39)

> *"Let your Light so shine before men that they may see your good works, and glorify the Father which is in heaven."* (Matt. 5:14-16)

Until we *literally* celebrate this future Feast of Tabernacles in the Millennium, let Him shine out from us, and the Living Waters flow out of us! **Amen!**

CHAPTER 16

SEASON OF GREAT JOY

In this Chapter, we continue to look at the Feast of Tabernacles, but as the "season of **great joy**". Do the Scriptures give the actual date of Yeshua's birth? Keep reading!

In the Book of Luke, can we identify some details of Yeshua's birth with the themes and ceremonies of the Feast of Tabernacles? Is the terminology in relation to Yeshua's birth similar to the terminology of the Feast of Tabernacles?

Let's look at Luke, Chapter 2. Remember, the main *theme* of the Feast of Tabernacles is **Salvation**, and the *two main ceremonies*, the "light of the world" and "well of salvation" with living waters. This Feast is not only called the "season of joy," but is also called the "Season of **Great** Joy."

In comparing the themes and terminology of this Feast with terminology in Luke, Chapter 2, we find the following:

First of all, at Yeshua's birth, He was wrapped in **"swaddling clothes"**:

It was the same cloth made from old *"priestly garments"*, which were saturated with pure olive oil and used to light the tall, golden candlesticks at the *Feast of Tabernacles*.

> "And she brought forth her firstborn son, and wrapped him in swaddling clothes . . ."(Luke 2:7)

Yeshua was placed in a **manger**: It means "stall" or "booth", a place for hitching cattle. It is the same word used in

Genesis 33:17 where Jacob journeyed to Sukkoth and built "booths" or "stalls" for his cattle. The Hebrew word for "booths" is *"sukkah"* and associated directly with the Feast of Tabernacles when *"sukkah"* were built.

The sukkah (booths) would have been erected all along the roads, in the fields, on the rooftops, etc. for miles during the Feast of Tabernacles. So the word *"manger"* (meaning "stall" or " booths") where cattle were fed and watered are connected directly to the birthplace of Yeshua. "Manger" *does not* mean a "trough", even though a trough may have been Yeshua's cradle.

" . . . and laid him in a manger("stall" or "booth"); because there was no room for them in the inn." (Luke 2:7)

Some Bible scholars believe that the "manger" ("stall" or "booth") adjoined the house belonging to one of Joseph's relatives and served as a *sukkah*. It sure seems like a logical possibility to me.

Since all Jewish men (who took their families too) were required to attend this feast, there would have been thousands of Jewish people in and around Jerusalem for the feast: There was no room for Mary and Joseph in Jerusalem the night of Yeshua's birth. The crowd would have taken up every spare room in Jerusalem and surrounding towns. That's why Mary and Joseph couldn't find a place to stay and had to go to Bethlehem, where Joseph's relatives lived. **Gem!**

Shepherds kept night watches (all night) over the temple flocks (the special flocks used only for temple sacrifices) destined for sacrifice during the Feast of Tabernacles:

The many *shepherds* on the night of Yeshua's birth were *keeping night watches* over their flocks all through the night.

> *"And there were in the same country shepherd abiding [staying] in the field, keeping watch over their flock by night."*(Luke 2:8)

Was the Sacrificial Lamb without blemish *born* one night amongst the other sacrificial lambs without blemish destined for sacrifice? Yes!

The **angel** of the Lord **announced** to the shepherds in the fields the **"good tiding"** (the Hebrew is *"basar,"* meaning the "gospel") of **"great joy"**:

The *announcement* was of *"great joy"*, a theme of the Feast of Tabernacles.

> *"And lo, the angel of the Lord came upon them, and the glory of the Lord shone round about them; and they were sore afraid. And the angel said unto them, Fear not; for, behold, I bring you good tidings of great joy which shall be to the people."*(Luke 2:9-10)

Remember that **a great light** representing the ***Sh'chinah* Glory** of God shone forth from the golden candlesticks (lampstands) at the Feast of Tabernacles during this Feast.

The Glory of the Lord *(Sh'chinah glory)* as mentioned in the previous scripture, shone all around on the night of Yeshua's birth, a brilliant light **much brighter** than that of the golden candlesticks at the Feast of Tabernacles!

The Jewish shepherds who were out in the fields were filled with **joy**, and went immediately to Bethlehem to see the Savior. They became the first evangelists to spread the good news that was for all mankind at Yeshua's birth. Remember, another name for this feast was "Feast of Nations" (for all nations).

> *And the shepherds went with haste to Bethlehem: And they came with haste, and found Mary and Joseph, and the Babe lying in a manger. And when they had seen Him, they made known abroad the saying which was told them concerning this Child."*(Luke 2:16)

Now, to pinpoint the time of Yeshua's birth from the scriptures, let's begin at Luke 1:24:

> *"And after those days, his wife (Zacharias's wife), Elisabeth conceived and hid herself five months."*

Zacharias finished his priestly duty at the Temple in Jerusalem and returned home around mid-June.

And in the sixth month (of Elisabeth's conception, around mid-December)), the angel announced Mary's conception:

> *"And in the sixth month the angel Gabriel was sent from God unto a city of Galilee, named Nazareth..." Luke 1:26)*

> *"And behold thou shalt conceive in thy womb, and bring forth a son, and shalt call his name, Yeshua."* (Luke 1:31)

> *"And behold, thy cousin, Elisabeth, she hath also conceived a son in her old age; and it is the sixth month with her, who was called barren. For with God nothing shall be impossible."* (Luke 1:36.37)

Mary's response to Gabriel: *"And Mary said, Behold the handmaid of the Lord; be it unto me according to thy word. And the angel departed."* (Luke 1:36)

Can we reply to the Lord with those words? Do we have enough faith and love in God to trust Him in our life to that point?

Now, we know that Mary stayed with Elisabeth the last three months of her pregnancy:

> *"And Mary abode with her about three months, and returned to her own house. Now Elisabeth's full time came that she brought forth her son."* (Luke 2:56-57)

We know that John the Baptist was born at the time of Passover in the early spring (March-April). So, Mary would have been *three months* pregnant at the time of John the Baptist's birth in the early spring. If we count forward six months, Yeshua would have been born in the fall between mid-September to mid-October, the time of the Feast of Tabernacles. Yeshua was also the first living tabernacle (dwelling) of God not made with hands. What more appropriate time for His coming? **"Gem"**!

By the way, I had an interesting thought when reading about Mary helping Elisabeth before John the Baptist was born. I know Mary probably helped her with household chores since Elisabeth was old. However, I wonder if they also sewed or made clothes and blankets for their babies with Zechariah's old, worn priestly garments? We do know that Yeshua was wrapped in swaddling cloth. It must have been a joyful time of fellowship as Mary and Elisabeth talked about their miracle babies. How fitting that He would be wrapped in *priestly garments* at birth! **"Gem"!**

Remember, the Feast of Tabernacles is a seven-day Feast spilling over into an eighth day from the fifteenth day of Tishrei (mid-September to mid-October) to the twenty-third day of Tishrei. The *first day* and the *eighth day* were Sabbaths (Holy Days).

> "*Also in the fifteenth day of the seventh month* [Tishrei] *when ye have gathered in the fruit of the land, ye shall keep a feast unto the Lord seven days; on the first day shall be a Sabbath, and on the eighth day shall be a Sabbath.*"(Lev. 23:39)

Yeshua was circumcised on the *eighth day* of His birth, according to Jewish law which fell on the *eighth day* of the Feast of Tabernacles. **Yeshua's birth** was on **the first day** of **the Feast of Tabernacles**, the **fifteenth of Tishrei** (mid-September to mid-October).

> "*Speak unto the children of Israel saying, the fifteenth day of this seventh month* [Tishrei] *shall be the Feast of Tabernacles for seven days unto the Lord . . . Seven days ye shall offer an offering made by fire unto the Lord; on the* **eighth day** *shall be an holy convocation unto you . . .*

it is a solemn assembly; and ye shall do no servile work therein." (Lev. 23:34-36)

According to Luke 2:20, the shepherds in the fields returned immediately to their flocks after seeing the newly born Messiah. The very next verse (21), states: *"And when the eight days were accomplished for the circumcising of the child . . . ."*

I know that most people celebrate the birth of Yeshua at Christmas on the twenty-fifth day of December. That is OK (at least the world acknowledges His birth), but actually He wasn't physically born on December twenty-fifth, but rather in the fall, during the *Feast of Tabernacles* (fifteenth of Tishrei). The scriptures tell us the time of His birth. Isn't that an amazing **"Gem"**?

Speaking of the traditional Christmas season, I have included a poem, not about the Christmas tree, but another tree long ago. Could we reflect upon it, too, when we see a Christmas tree?

The Tree

Long ago, there was a special tree,
Cut to make a cross and placed at Golgotha,
No ornaments of silver and gold hung upon it,
No star adorned the top thereof;

A sign, "King of the Jews" was nailed there,
Scorners laughed and mocked His Holy Name,
No crown of gold and jewels did this King wear,
Only one of thorns to bring Him shame;

God's greatest Gift of Love hung there,

His blood stained that ol' tree,
Ran down until it touched the earth below,
Covered man's sin and set them free.
What an awesome, wondrous love;

God's Son sent from heaven to die for me,
The glory and grace of salvation fulfilled,
Good news of the gospel adorned that ol' cross,
The Light of it still outshines all Christmas trees!

As mentioned earlier, Yeshua **did** *first come* at *conception* in the womb (**not** His birth) on or about the *twenty-fifth* (25th) of December (month of Kislev) around the time of **Hanukkah** (Jewish holiday). However, Hanukkah doesn't celebrate the birth of Yeshua. Rather, Hanukkah commemorates the victories of Judas Maccabeus and the purification and rededication of the Jewish Temple.

Hanukkah is known as the "Feast of Dedication" or "Feast of Lights." Yeshua walked in the Temple in Jerusalem in Solomon's porch on that Day.

> *"And it was at Jerusalem the feast of dedication and it was winter. And Jesus walked in the temple in Solomon's porch. Then came the Jews round about him, and said unto him, How long doest thou make us doubt? If thou be the Christ, tell us plainly."* (John 10:22-24.
>
> Yeshua's reply: *".. I told you, and ye believed not: the works that I do in my Father's name, they bear witness of me."* (John 10:25)

Hanukkah is not connected in any way to the Christians' holiday of Christmas, but it is also a time of celebration for the

Jews. It is celebrated by lighting candles on the eight-branched Hanukkah Menorah (*Chanukiah*, Hebrew) and giving gifts.

The Temple in Jerusalem had been desecrated by an enemy of the Jews, Antiochus IV, in 164 B.C. He was a ruthless Greek ruler over Israel. He hated the Jews because they served the one true God of Israel. The Jews would not live by his pagan rules nor worship or bow down to his gods.

Antiochus IV became very angry at the Jews, so he and his army took the temple from the Jews. His armies killed thousands of Jews. They tortured children to death in the presence of their parents. He outlawed the Torah and the Sabbath and forced the Jews to work on the Sabbath. Antiochus stopped their animal sacrifices and slaughtered pigs on the altar in the temple. He then smeared the pigs' blood all over the Holy of Holies and the holy articles of the temple. He also polluted the Temple with images of Zeus, a pagan god and commanded everyone to worship them. Those who refused were killed.

Judas Maccabeus, a brave Jew nicknamed "Hammer," with his small army of Jewish warriors called the "Maccabees," led a revolt against the Greek forces. After about three years, they miraculously regained control of the temple. According to the Jews, it took eight days to cleanse the temple and rededicate it to the Lord.

According to Jewish tradition, it is said that the Jews only found enough oil to burn the menorah for one day in providing light. The Menorah provided the only light in the Temple. The small amount of oil was not enough to light the Temple for the time needed to clean up the desecration left by Antiochus IV. However, the oil that should have lasted for only one day burned miraculously for eight days. The menorah had supernaturally supplied enough light to complete the cleansing and rededication of the Temple.

The *eight-branched menorah* including a center shaft is called a *"chanukiah."* It is lit during Hanukkah in celebration of the small amount of olive oil that miraculously burned for eight days. There are four candles on each side of the center shaft. The center shaft is lit first, and is called the "Servant Branch" (representing Yeshua) from which the oil flows out to light the candles. "**Gem**"!

This Feast, *Hanukkah*, was a time of celebration and thanksgiving to God for deliverance from pagan oppression and for possession of the temple from Antiochus IV. Once again it was a holy temple in which they could pray, read the Torah, worship and bring their sacrifices. These observances had almost been wiped out by the pagans.

By the way, Antiochus died a horrible death. He was stricken with a fatal intestinal malady. He suffered a long torturous death as parasites ate away at his rotting body. It produced such a foul odor that his own men and caregivers couldn't stand to go near him! How fearful to fall under God's judgment for one who mistreats God's beloved people!

Yeshua was born to tabernacle (dwell) among us in the flesh on the Feast of Tabernacles. Yeshua will soon come again to tabernacle with us forever in the Heavenly Tabernacle in Jerusalem! **Gem!**

> *"And I saw a new heaven and a new earth...And I heard a great voice out of heaven saying, Behold, the tabernacle of God is with men, and he will dwell with*

them, and they shall be his people, and God himself shall be with them, and be their God." (Rev. 21:1,3)

Hallelujah!

CHAPTER 17

SEED OF KING DAVID

From the beginning of God's Word, the good news of the **"Seed"** is proclaimed by God Himself and His prophets. All of God's prophets prophesied of the Divine **"Seed"** from the lineage of King David, Israel's Messiah, the coming King to rule and reign over His everlasting Kingdom.

In this Chapter, let's look closer at King David, and God's prophecy to him of his Descendant, Yeshua, called the "Seed of David."

In relation to prophets, let's not forget King David Himself and all the compositions he wrote fitted to be sung of His Messiah. David was the penman of most of the Psalms, but not all. He is called the "Sweet Psalmist of Israel" (2 Sam. 23:1). Included below are some of the awesome prophecies of King David about His Messiah:

The hands and feet of Yeshua would be pierced:*". . . the assembly of the wicked have enclosed me: they pierced my hands and my feet."*(Psalm 22:16)

Yeshua's garments would be parted and lots cast for them: *"They part my garments among them, and cast lots upon my vesture."*(Psalm 22:18)

Many would be watching Yeshua during His crucifixion:*". . . They look and stare upon me."*(Psalm 22:17)

He prophesied that no bone of the Passover lamb would be broken (also prophesied in Exodus 12:46): *"He keepeth all His bones; not one of them is broken."*(Psalm 34:20)

The betrayal of Yeshua by Judas was foretold: *"Yea, mine own familiar friend, in whom I trusted, which did eat of my bread, hath lifted up His heel against me."* (Psalm 41:9)

In the first *verse* of Psalm 22, David prophesied the very words of Yeshua at the height of His suffering: *"My God, My God, why hast thou forsaken me?"* In the last verse of Psalm 22, David refers to the finished work of salvation, *". . . that He hath done this."* This last verse in Hebrew literally reads: *"For it is finished."*

In the following scriptures, Isaiah prophesied that the Messiah would come out of the root of Jesse (King David's father); that the Seed (also called a Branch) would be a Descendant of King David upon which the Holy Spirit (7 Spirits) would rest:

> *"And there shall come forth a Shoot out of the stock of Jesse [David's father] and a Branch out of his roots shall grow and bear fruit. And the Spirit of the Lord shall rest upon him... And the Spirit of the Lord shall rest upon Him, the Spirit of wisdom, understanding, the Spirit of counsel, and might, the Spirit of knowledge and of the fear of the Lord."* (Isaiah 11:1,2)

Isaiah also prophesied that the Root of Jesse would be an ensign to the people of Israel. Not only would He be an ensign to the Jewish people, but to the Gentiles who would seek Him and find His rest:

> *"And in that day there shall be a Root of Jesse, which shall stand for an ensign of the people; to it shall the Gentiles seek; and His rest shall be glorious."* (Isaiah 11:10) Amen!

When the angel appeared to Mary (*Miryam* in Hebrew) at Yeshua's conception, the angel Gabriel spoke in Davidic terms:

> *"He shall be great, and shall be called the Son of the Highest; and the Lord God shall give Him the throne of His father David. And He shall reign over the house of Jacob forever; and of His Kingdom there shall be no end."*(Luke 1:31)

In the book of Revelation, Yeshua proclaims Himself to be the "Root and Offspring of King David." Yeshua is seen fulfilling the prophecy of His Kingly role on the throne of His forefather King David.

> *"I Yeshua have sent my angel to testify unto you these things in the congregations. I am the root and the offspring of King David, and the bright and morning star."*(Rev. 22:16)

The Book of Revelation promises a blessing to those who read it and heed its message. The blessing is not only in the first chapter, but is also repeated in the last Chapter of Revelation. Yeshua at the same time also warns of His return.

> *"Blessed are the readers and hearers of the words of this prophecy, provided they obey the things in it. For the time is near!"*(Rev. 1:3)

> *"Behold I come quickly; blessed* is he that *keepeth the sayings of the prophecy of this book."*(Rev. 22:7)

The Book's main theme is the revelation of Yeshua. "Revelation" means "revealing" or "unveiling." Yeshua is the

"Lion of the tribe of Judah", the "Root of David" who is revealed fulfilling His Kingly role on the throne of His forefather King David. He is the King of Kings and Lord of Lords who comes in great power and glory to overthrow Satan and his Kingdom. He prevails over all who oppose Him.

> *" And one of the elders saith unto me [Apostle John], weep not; behold, the lion of the tribe of Judah, the root of David, hath prevailed to open the book . . . ."* (Rev.5:5)

> *"And He hath on His vesture and on His thigh a name written, King of Kings, and Lord of Lords."* (Rev. 19:16)

In Matthew, Chapter 1, in the genealogy of Yeshua, He is called the **"Son of David"**, the Son of Abraham.

In John 7:42, He is called the **"Seed of David"**: "…that Christ cometh of the seed of David, and out of the town of Bethlehem, where David was?"

Yeshua is seen holding the **"key of David"** in Revelation 3:7:

> *"And to the angel of the assembly in Philadelphia, write: These things saith he that is holy, he that is true, he that hath the key of David, he that openeth, and no man shutteth, and shutteth and no man openeth."*

What is the significance of Yeshua holding the "key of David"? What does it represent and what was Yeshua really revealing? What statement was He making in reference to the "key of David"? To find the answer, let's go back to the Old Testament where God made a declaration to King David during his reign. Let's look at the circumstances surrounding God's promise to King David.

King David had brought the Ark of the Covenant back to the City of David. The Ark had been kept safely at a Levite's house, the house of Obed-edom. It had been kept there for about three months after being retrieved from the Philistines. The Ark was most sacred to Israel and a token of God's presence with Israel and means of communing with God. *Spiritually*, the Ark is *figurative* of Yeshua, the Token of God's presence with us and our means to communicate with God! **"Gem"**!

The priests carried it upon their shoulders from Obed-edom's house into the royal City of David. King David had set up the tabernacle for the Ark while it was at Obed-edom's house. The tabernacle having been made ready, the priests moved towards the tabernacle to place it in the Holy of Holies. The people along the way shouted and rejoiced before the Lord as the Ark moved forward! King David was overwhelmed with joy and danced before the Lord with all of his might! The Ark was back in the possession of Israel!

> *"And David danced before the Lord with all of his might, clad in a linen ephod. So David and all the house of Israel brought up the Ark of the Lord with shouting and with the sound of the trumpet."* (2 Samuel 6:14,15)

Everyone was rejoicing and worshipping the Lord, except one! David's wife! She was furious at him! She saw his behavior as very unfitting for a King! King David had stripped off most of his Kingly attire and was dancing in the streets half-clothed, for goodness sakes! Of course, he still had on a robe, the ephod, which covered most of his body. His wife might also have been a little jealous of her handsome husband dancing in the streets before the other ladies! Smile, ladies!

It was at this time that David desired in his heart to build a beautiful temple (house of worship) for God in which to place the Ark of the Covenant. King David had built a beautiful place for himself and a beautiful city for the people. Yet, the precious Ark of God dwelt behind curtains in an old tabernacle (tent). David said to the prophet, Nathan:

> *"See now, I dwell in an house of cedar [fine house], but the Ark of God dwelleth within curtains [in the tent/tabernacle]."* (2 Samuel 7:2)

Even though God was pleased with the intentions of David's heart, it was not in God's plan for David to build the temple for God. In fact, instead, God promised David that one of the fruit of his body would build the temple. We know that Solomon, David's son, built the temple called "Solomon's Temple" that David had desired to build.

However, God made an even more astounding promise to King David (the Davidic Covenant). God declared (promised) to David that **He (God)** would build David a house through Another (the Messiah) from the fruit of his (David's) body! He would be that Fruit (Seed) of his body that God would establish upon the Davidic throne, and His Kingdom would be everlasting.

Through the prophet, Nathan, these words were sent to David:

> *"...and I will cause you to rest from all your enemies. Also the Lord declares to you that He will make for you a house; And when your days are fulfilled and you sleep*

with your fathers, I will set up after you your offspring who shall be born to you, and I will establish his Kingdom. He shall build a house for My name [and My presence." (2 Samuel 7:11,12).

In the New Testament, Paul speaks of the fulfillment of the covenant God made with King David of the Messiah:

"And when God had removed him [Saul], he raised up unto them David to be their King; to whom also he gave testimony, and said, I have found David the son of Jesse, a man after mine own heart, which shall fulfill all my will. Of this man's seed hath God according to His promise raised unto Israel a Savior, Jesus [Yeshua]." (Acts 13:32) Amazing prophecy by Nathan, God's prophet to King David!

David believed God, and he recorded it in Psalms 132:11. *"The Lord swore to David in truth; He will not turn back from it: one of the fruit of your body I will set upon your throne."*

That Offspring of King David, the Messiah, would build a house (temple) for David and rule over an everlasting Kingdom. We know it wasn't Solomon because his rule and earthly kingdom was temporary and has long ended.

Yeshua is still building that *spiritual* house (temple) in the Kingdom of God on earth as every born-again believer enters and become sons and daughters of God's kingdom. This *heavenly* Kingdom is everlasting, and is the *perfection* and *perpetuity* of David's *earthly* Kingdom! **"Gem"**!

> "Now, therefore you are no more strangers and foreigners, but fellow citizens with the saints [Jews], and of the household of God and are built upon the foundation of the Apostles and Prophets. Jesus, Christ Himself being the chief cornerstone in whom all the building fitly framed together grows into a holy temple in the Lord: in whom you also are built together [Jews and Gentiles] for a habitation of God through the Spirit. (Eph. 2:18-22) **Praise the Lord!**

Yeshua is seen holding the "key of David" in Revelation 3:7. He is revealing that He is that Descendant (fruit of David's body) promised to King David so many years before. Yeshua holds the key to the everlasting Kingdom of God through Whom the kingdom came. The *only Way* in is through Him. He opens the door or shuts the door into the Kingdom. Only the redeemed can enter and walk in it.

> "Jesus answered and said unto him [Nicodemus], verily, verily, I say unto thee; except a man be born again [anew from above, Spirit], he cannot see [experience] the Kingdom of God." (John 3:3)

> "Now, after that John was put in prison, Jesus came into Galilee, preaching the gospel of the Kingdom of God. And saying, the time is fulfilled, and the Kingdom of God is at hand; repent ye, and believe the gospel." (Mark 1:14,15)

Did the Kingdom of God come with a price? Yes, a great price! God, the Father, gave His only begotten Son Who loved us and gave His life that none should perish.

> "And from Jesus, who is the faithful witness, and the first begotten of the dead, and the Prince of the Kings of the earth. Unto Him that loved us, and washed us from our sins in His own blood. And hath made us Kings and priests unto God, His Father, to Him be glory and dominion forever and ever. Amen." (Rev. 1:5,6)

At the end of the Great Tribulation, Yeshua will return to set up the Millennial Kingdom on earth in Jerusalem after the binding of Satan. He will sit on the Davidic throne and rule and reign on earth in Jerusalem!

> "Then I saw an angel coming down from heaven, having the key to the bottomless pit and a great chain in his hand. He laid hold of the dragon, that serpent of old, who is the Devil and Satan, and bound him for a thousand years...But after these things he must be released for a little while." (Rev. 20:1-3)

> "And I saw the souls of those who had been beheaded for their witness to Jesus and for the word of God, and who had not worshipped the beast or his image, and had not received his mark...They lived and reigned with Christ for a thousand years..." (Rev. 20:4,5)

The above scripture describes a period of time on earth when the saints of God will rule and reign with King Yeshua! They will have resurrected bodies as was seen when Yeshua arose from the dead. He interacted with the disciples, and did not have a ghostly body. He ate with them and told Thomas to touch the nail prints in His hands and place his hand in His side. I believe this foreshadowed the life and body of the resurrected saints!

In Chapters 40-48, Ezekiel describes a glorious Temple where many peoples and nations will go to worship in the Holy City, New Jerusalem.

This seems to be a *literal* Temple because Ezekiel gives a very detailed description of the Temple. Could **it** be the *ultimate* Temple that God promised to David? Will it be Israel's *final Temple* where the Sh'chinah glory of God abides, never to depart again? Can't you see David dancing with all of his might again before the Throne of God there? **"Gem"!**

Who **is** this **"Seed of King David"**? He is the **"Seed of Woman"** who was promised in the Garden of Eden in Genesis and has fulfilled that promise! He is our Salvation, Redeemer and soon-coming King who will sit on the Davidic throne in New Jerusalem in the City of God! That latter Temple of God will be more glorious than one can imagine! Yeshua's kings and priests will serve Him and be blessed beyond measure! It will be joy unspeakable and full of glory! **Amen and Amen!**

> *"And it shall come to pass in the last days, that the mountain of the Lord's house shall be established in the top of the mountains, and shall be exalted above the hills; and all nations shall flow into it. And many people shall go and say, Come ye, and let us go up to the mountain of the Lord, to the house of the God of Jacob; and he will teach us of his ways, and we will walk in his paths; for out of Zion shall go forth the law, and the word of the Lord from Jerusalem."* (Isaiah 2:2,3)

The tree of life is seen accessible again in the new heaven and new earth in the Holy City.

> *"And I saw a new heaven and a new earth...And I John, saw the holy city, New Jerusalem."* (Rev. 21:1-2)

The scripture reveals something **extraordinary** about the literal tree that we didn't see in Genesis, the **fruit** of this tree! It had **twelve (12) different kinds of fruit** upon it, a different fruit bearing each month, and its **leaves** for the **healing** of the nations. **"Gem"**!

> *".... In the midst of the street of it, and on either side of the river, was there the tree of life, which bear twelve manner of fruits, and yielded her fruit every month; and the leaves of the tree were for the healing of the nations.* (Rev. 22:1)
>
> *"Blessed are those that keep his commandments that they may have right to the tree of life, and may enter in through the gates into the City."* (Rev. 22:14)

This journey in search of **"gems"** beginning in Genesis and ending in Revelation has revealed the true **Tree of Life**, **Yeshua HaMashiach** (Yeshua, The Messiah)! **"Priceless Gem"**!

> *"And this is the record that God hath given us **eternal life**, and this life is in His **Son**. He that hath the Son hath **life**, and he that hath not the Son, hath not life."* (I John 5:11,12)
>
> *"He which testifieth these things, saith, 'surely I come quickly [swiftly]'"...* (Rev. 22:20) **Shalom!**

CONCLUSION

In conclusion, the purpose of this Book has been to reveal God and His plan of redemption through Yeshua, the Central Figure and Priceless Gem in this book. This book has been written to reveal and uplift **Yeshua, the Messiah**, the only One through Whom eternal life is given. This author has also endeavored to reveal the many ways in which the Gospel of the Kingdom of God is proclaimed from Genesis to Revelation.

By the "signs of the time" that are unfolding before our eyes, surely His coming is soon. Keep watching events around Israel and Jerusalem, especially the Temple Mount!

We do not know the day or the hour of Yeshua's coming, but we do **know the season**. The Feasts of the Lord and the prophetic messages of God's prophets still have a word for us today.

If you do not know Yeshua (Jesus), I pray you will seriously consider inviting Him into your heart. Soon the shofar will sound. He will appear, and it will be too late. Yeshua bids you to *"come"*. You are loved, and He gave His life for you.

To Believers, the Holy Spirit has impressed upon my heart to conclude this book with two specific words: **WATCH** and **PRAY**!

*"So ye in like manner when ye shall see these things come to pass, know that it is nigh, even at the doors…Take ye heed, WATCH and PRAY; for ye know not when the time is…WATCH ye therefore; for ye know not when the master of the house cometh…lest coming suddenly, he find you sleeping. And what I say unto you, I say unto **all**, WATCH!* (Mark 13:27-37)

www.ingramcontent.com/pod-product-compliance
Lightning Source LLC
Chambersburg PA
CBHW061631040426
42446CB00010B/1361